CHARLES BOYER

CHARLES BOYER
The Reluctant Lover

❊❊❊❊❊❊❊❊❊❊❊❊❊

Larry Swindell

DOUBLEDAY & COMPANY, INC.

GARDEN CITY, NEW YORK

1983

PICTURE ACKNOWLEDGMENTS

In the insert of personal photographs, all are from the Museum of Modern Art Film Library in New York City, other than these exceptions:

The publicity photo of Pat Paterson as an American screen actress, and the photo of Boyer with Dick Powell and David Niven are used through the courtesy of the Fort Worth *Star-Telegram*.

The photo of Boyer with Mary Martin in *Kind Sir* on Broadway, and the photo of Boyer with playwright S. N. Behrman are from the Theatre Collection of the New York Public Library.

The photograph of Michael Boyer is from United Press International.

In the insert of motion picture stills, all representations are from the Museum of Modern Art Film Library in New York City, with the single exception of the Boyer portrait that completes the insert; it is from the Academy of Motion Picture Arts and Sciences Library, Beverly Hills, Calif.

Library of Congress Cataloging in Publication Data
Swindell, Larry.
Charles Boyer.
Includes index.
1. Boyer, Charles, 1899–1978. 2. Actors—United States—Biography. 3. Actors—France—Biography. I. Title.
PN2287.B67S9   1983   791.43′028′0924 [B]

ISBN: 0-385-17052-1
Library of Congress Catalog Card Number 81–43419

For Doris Eby,
who admired Charles Boyer in films
long before she became my mother-in-law

AUTHOR'S NOTE

Although I didn't know it then, the seed for this book was planted by John Cromwell when he visited me in Bucks County, Pennsylvania, in 1969. Besides entertaining me with his account of the *Algiers* filming, John presented a strong case for Charles Boyer as a great actor. My notes from that meeting were the substance of a newspaper tribute when Boyer died in 1978. That article became a blueprint for this biography, which is also served by those notes.

I am grateful to everyone who contributed information or insight to this biography, but especially to two Boyer directors who unconsciously were its catalysts. John Cromwell, a good friend, died during the progress of the manuscript. Anatole Litvak, whom I knew only slightly, died some years earlier; but I could recall Litvak's rating of Boyer as the screen's *best* actor, and his insistence that Boyer was underrated—particularly by American audiences who consistently took his splendid work too easily for granted. Having viewed again the main body of Boyer's screen work while preparing his biography, I must agree that Boyer is in the top class.

Special thanks are given here to several persons whose contributions would not otherwise be apparent: Mary Corliss, a valuable adviser beyond her function as mistress of the Museum of Modern Art's film still collection; Eleanore Tanin of the UCLA film archives; Rod Bladel of the New York Public Library's Theatre Collection; and various helpful folk at the Library of Congress and at the Margaret Herrick Library of the Academy of Motion Picture Arts and Sciences. Thanks, too, to Richard Altman, Carl Brandt, Charlotte and Morris

Green, Joan and Vince LaCorte, and Robbin Reynolds; and to my editor, Lisa Drew, and her assistants, Anne Hukill and Sarah Parsons.

Everyone in my family is a collaborator in ways beyond encouragement and mere patience. So I must also thank my daughters, Julie, Susan, and Wendy Carol; my sons, Tod and Mark; and my wife, Ellie, who always has some ideas of her own.

Fort Worth, Texas
September 13, 1982

I

In the international measure of fame, Charles Boyer was France's representative actor. As a star primarily of American motion pictures, he was the wishful approximation of what every Frenchman eternally should be. His screen image retained a permanent lacquer of continental sophistication, but he was a product of the rustic French heartland.

Boyer was born in a lovely part of France that only the French know—the pastoral Southwest, in Figeac, an ancient and beguiling provincial town in the department of Lot. This flower garden was once a part of the fabled province of Guyenne, but Figeac slept into the twentieth century on a heavy legacy of history and did not catch the modern tempo. Now the major thoroughfares pass it by. Few Americans or other world travelers know its sedate charm.

The gentle river Célé winds through the town that grew around a Benedictine abbey founded in the ninth century. Through the ages, most who were born in Figeac also died there. The sons of Figeac have not by custom sought worldly attainment; yet one of them conquered Paris, then Hollywood and the world.

Figeac was Charles Boyer's home for his first nineteen years. Later on, he would seldom make reference to his birthplace, and he never sentimentalized it. Perhaps he was embarrassed by his provincial heritage. Yet the years in Figeac may essentially have shaped him.

When Charles Boyer departed his home town, his personality already had the veneer of high seriousness that it would never lose. Pierre Blanchar, who knew Boyer even before his earliest fame, once observed that "the Charles who returns often to Paris from triumphs all over the world is the same Charles who once came to Paris from Figeac. His attitudes were fixed then, and they have never changed. Wealth and culture came to him, but did not make him a Parisian. There can never be any foolishness in him, and for that he holds Figeac responsible."

The citizens of Figeac, numbering about five thousand at the century's turn, were hard-working agrarians with no accommodation for nonsense. They were jealously proud of their identity as producers of the best pâté de foie gras in the world. Virtuous to the point of sanctimony, they relied on the Church to provide a discipline for their well-ordered lives. Charles's parents responded dutifully to that regimen, but in some ways they were atypical of the workaday populace, and not only in their prosperity.

Maurice Boyer was an enlightened man, if a highly self-educated one. It was Charles's belief that his father had once aspired to the legal profession. In Maurice Boyer's small but selective personal library, law books shared the shelves with the literary classics. Among the latter were volumes of Greek and Roman drama and a complete set of Shakespeare's plays; they would be a powerful early influence on his son.

Charles's mother played the harpsichord. Louise Boyer may also have fancied herself a singer. Her son would recall that "When I was a little boy, my mother seemed always to be singing arias from the grand operas, and I had the distinct impression that no one enjoyed hearing her."

Charles was an only child—a most unusual circumstance for that time and place. He was born during a siege of oppressive summer heat. The date of August 28 has not been challenged, but the year of his birth seems to have been disputed in certain reference books and mini-biographies. The year given in most sources is 1899, but other claims for 1897 suggest that Charles Boyer may have secretly deducted two years—a ruse of vanity that is characteristic of the acting profession. Yet birth records both in Figeac and in the nearby town of Cahors show the date of August 28, 1899, and carry a suggestion of premature delivery; it is noted that the baby weighed only 2.2 kilograms at birth—not quite five pounds. He was small for his age throughout his childhood.

That the Boyers of Figeac should have produced any child may have been a surprise in itself. They were a vaguely middle-aged couple, childless throughout the first eight years of their marriage. Mme. Boyer is recalled clearly by some elderly Figeac residents, and impressions of her have been passed down through recent generations. Maurice Boyer, however, is a shadowy figure, lost to memory, and recalled mainly by Charles Boyer's own depositions—which have been contradictory in themselves. By one account his father had been a determined bachelor until, at a relatively advanced age, he married Charles's mother. By another, Maurice Boyer was a widower for fully a decade before taking a second wife, his first bride having died after delivering a stillborn child. Whatever, Maurice arrived in Figeac in either 1886 or 1887, and seems to have come there from the neighboring town of Capdenac where he had failed as a grain merchant.

Soon after Maurice opened a bicycle shop in Figeac, he made the social acquaintance of Augustine Louise Durand, who had lived there most of her life. Although thirtyish, she was already regarded as a spinster by her neighbors, and she looked the part—thin, withered, and sharply grim-featured, with pointed nose and jutting chin. The man she married was short and paunchy, had the thick moustache then obligatory for any respectable Frenchman, and was completely bald. Rather incongruously, these were the parents of a boy who would become a matinée idol, and then a great lover in the international cinema.

When Maurice and Louise married, a substantial dowry may have been part of the arrangement; the Durands were people of comfortable means. Whether because of that, or for the enlistment of his new wife as bookkeeper, Maurice's business fortunes improved steadily from the time of their marriage. The Boyers occupied ample living quarters above the bicycle shop, and eventually their son was born there. But

Charles was still a toddler when the three Boyers moved into a more substantial house.

In 1900 Maurice acquired a more thriving business. He became a dealer in farming implements and equipment, and also revived his granary in Figeac. Within a few years he was also a coal merchant. Maurice sold the bicycle shop and invested his income in additional farm machinery, speculating successfully on a new and advanced harvesting machine. At no time was he a manufacturer, as some later studio-produced accounts would identify Charles Boyer's father; but as a merchant he employed a large staff of salesmen and other workers—all of whose names and vocational specialties Charles could specify before he was two years old.

His precociousness may have been a local legend. It certainly became that later, when publicists began to romanticize the Boyer childhood. There were accounts of little Charles being able to recite dramatically the story of the Crucifixion before he was three years old, or even before that. He said he never knew how that story got started; he had excellent memory for events and accomplishments of his childhood, but did not believe he had ever memorized or recited the story of the Crucifixion. However, there were some striking similar accomplishments.

He said his mother taught him to read, although his mother insisted that Charles really taught himself—with astonishing early curiosity about letters and their sounds, and the formation of words. He was a facile reader before he began formal schooling. While his classmates struggled with the alphabet, Charles was discovering the works of Shakespeare. And he was otherwise "different"—an introverted child who was indifferent to childhood pastimes and was particularly disinterested in athletic games.

From a distanced perspective, the grown and established actor would insist that he had never been shy: "I was sociable. I did not dislike other children, but I had more to say and do with adults. I was a very old man with quite a strong physical resemblance to a little boy, with whom other children had difficulty in forming friendships."

His association with other children was hardly encouraged

by his mother, who was intolerant of all the frivolities of childhood. Prior to adolescence Charles had no close ties other than familial ones; and soon he had only one parent, and was more strongly under the influence of the mother to whom his attachment had always been greater. Their devoted companionship was very nearly exclusive, even before Maurice Boyer's death in 1909, before Charles marked his tenth birthday.

Although his father had been a consumptive, his death was sudden and unexpected, apparently following a stroke. One day Maurice Boyer was absorbed in his business, and was known to have been arguing politics in a Figeac café; and the next day he was a corpse, to whom young Charles did not know how to respond.

They had not had a close relationship. Father and son were friendly but distant, although Maurice boasted of his son's mental agility. Charles's most vivid memory of his father was of the elder Boyer placing the boy atop a counter in his own or someone else's shop, and beaming while Charles recited some very long poems and dramatic speeches. Maurice may have perceived in his son the lawyer he had himself wished to be. Charles was delighted: his father had introduced him to that most powerful agency, the audience. He believed that the idea of becoming an actor first came to him when he was reciting a poem by François Villon in his father's shop, and first sensed the approving wonder of the throng.

Louise Boyer had scolded her husband whenever he showed off Charles in this manner. But she probably registered automatic disapproval of everything Maurice did, underscoring her belief that she had married beneath herself. She also had insisted that Maurice owed his belated success in business to her own administrative ability—certainly to her penchant for frugality and hard bargaining. Charles later reasoned that while his parents seldom showed hostility toward each other, they probably had a loveless relationship, a marriage of convenience. Although shocked by the suddenness of her husband's demise, Louise was not overcome by grief. She consoled Charles with assurance that they would do very well by themselves. There was a clear suggestion that their life thenceforth would be even better, and she promised to take him to Paris.

She wished to provide her son with a life of privilege. Not long after Maurice Boyer's death, Louise sold the business that he had willed to her. She probably realized a splendid profit, to supplement a handsome inheritance income. After an appropriate period of mourning, she began to dress in the finery expected of one who now wished to be addressed as Madame. Accordingly, she concentrated on raising her son as a young gentleman of leisure. At age eleven, Charles began violin lessons, which would continue throughout his residence in Figeac; and he said that playing the violin was the hardest labor he performed in all that time.

*   *   *

He was also eleven when he was twice powerfully smitten, first by the movies and then by his first exposure to the professional theater.

By 1911 Figeac had its first cinema, and Charles was an eager patron. Photoplays had not yet attained feature length, and the programs consisted mainly of short comedies that captivated Charles without exception. But he could distinguish between an ordinary performer and a gifted one, and very quickly he settled on Max Linder as his favorite. Mme. Boyer did not entirely approve of the cinema and did not allow Charles to attend as often as he wished; but she also liked the Linder comedies, and accompanied him whenever one was on the program.

For most patrons, Max Linder was someone to be laughed at, but for Charles he was an actor and a mime whose techniques were worthy of study. And then he discovered Lucien Guitry.

Although his mother did not take Charles to Paris immediately, they began to make journeys by rail to closer cities, where they would patronize the smart shops and take rooms in hotels more opulent than those in Figeac. Charles Boyer believed he was still eleven when, on a trip to Toulouse, he saw his first play.

The drama was Henry Bernstein's *Samson*, and the title role was enacted by Lucien Guitry, who had already played it to great success in Paris. Guitry immediately became the ideal and example for Boyer the actor, and would never lose that status. *Samson* was even more remarkably a harbinger of things to come, for playwright-director Henry Bernstein would be perhaps the most vital single influence on Boyer's formative phase as an actor.

When Charles took his first communion in 1911, it prompted someone's observation that the meditative boy was almost certain to become a priest. Charles responded, "No, I will be an actor, like Lucien Guitry." It was a shocking pronouncement. Acting surely rated as a disreputable profession to the people of Figeac, whose opinions were based mainly on the seedy itinerant companies that sometimes performed in Figeac's opera house. Mme. Boyer assured her friends that Charles had only a passing infatuation with the theater. She was confident that he would honor them all by emerging eventually as a doctor or lawyer, if not a priest.

Charles, though, had succumbed to the special magic of the theater. He resolved to be not only an actor but a dramatist, a director, a stage designer. Of course, he needed a stage to design; and his mother provided one—the granary in the barn that was no longer in use. The granary had an elevated platform that could be used as a stage. So Charles devised a streamlined version of *Macbeth* with himself in the title role, and invited his schoolmates to participate in a play that could be witnessed by their parents. Several boys responded, but there were no willing actresses, so Charles gave the title role to another boy and cast himself as Lady Macbeth. His mother indulged his every whim, providing material for elaborate costumes, then paying a seamstress to produce them.

The production was politely applauded by adults who paid admission voluntarily. Euphoric over his triumph, Charles was seized by the ambition to stage *all* of the Shakespeare plays, until his fellow actors soon lost interest. There were some other offerings, including Charles's own version of *Samson*, based on his memory of the play he had seen. But with the defection of his actors, he also lost his audience, suggesting that a budding actor-manager career was at its end. No matter, he would act anyway. Charles continued to memorize the great speeches attached to the foremost classical roles. Alone on the granary stage, he would recite Hamlet's soliloquies as he imagined Lucien Guitry might deliver them.

Many years later Boyer would insist that his all-consuming youthful interest in Guitry was never frivolous or without solid foundation: "Young I may have been, but I recognized a grandeur in Lucien Guitry that I did not then realize had been acknowledged by the most discerning critics. Soon I was reading everything about Guitry that I could find."

He could find a lot. It was a great age of French theater, adorned by an abundance of scholarly dramatic journals and others more nearly constituted as fan magazines. Charles read them all. He learned the identities of all the leading players, of whom none could challenge Lucien Guitry for Charles's fascination—not even Sacha Guitry, son of Lucien, himself already established as both actor and playwright. When Mme. Boyer took her son to Paris for the first time in 1913, they saw Sacha Guitry on stage and also saw the great Harry Baur portray Shylock. Charles's regret was that Lucien Guitry was again on tour, not to be found on the Paris boards.

Remembering his first visit to Paris much later, Boyer would have vivid recall only of the plays he saw there, "and the actors, especially those of the Comédie-Française." His mother may have been impressed by the shops and restaurants, perhaps by the museums; but none of them had real meaning for Charles. He dreamed now of being an actor in Paris, where inferior actors would not be tolerated.

Mme. Boyer may have wondered if the trip to Paris had been such a good idea. She could no longer dismiss Charles's acting ambitions as a childish notion he would outgrow. Charles unmistakably possessed the high intelligence required for the well-paying professions, and she insinuated more pointedly that he should plan a career in medicine. They had no income beyond her nest egg, and Mme. Boyer probably counted on Charles as the financial provider for her old age. Now she conspired to have his teachers guide Charles into an honorable endeavor—if not medicine, then anything other than acting, to which she was now more resolutely opposed.

Of his adolescent ambition, Boyer said that "My instructors at the lyceum of Figeac were not alarmed, but they were curious. To them I was not the sort of boy who would consider acting as a life's work. I was withdrawn; I had few friends. I suppose I was moody—not unhappy, but of so serious a nature that I seldom smiled. So in other eyes I must have been the embodiment of gloom itself. Certainly I was not the outgoing kind, nor the exhibitionist one expects an actor to be."

He had always been an exemplary student without great effort. Now he was at the head of the class—a boy in his early teens, responding to a classroom assignment by writing brilliantly about the drama. He prepared and then delivered orally a paper on Molière that brought him first prize in a competition enlisting students throughout the department of Lot. It was also an early indication—to his teachers and classmates, and possibly to his mother as well—that his interest in the theater had an intellectual basis.

Only a few years later, he would compose a keen analysis of the art of acting, using Lucien Guitry as his subject—but at the Sorbonne, for a class in philosophy.

* * *

The ugly duckling discovered that it was a swan after all. At about age fourteen, Charles Boyer suddenly was transformed from an ordinary-looking, undersized child into an exceptionally handsome young man. Now almost robust, he was an early grower. He shot past most others his own age, although finally he was disappointed in his failure to attain good height.

If young girls in Figeac began to take notice of him, he remained indifferent, or pretended to; he said that girls and then women were an eternal mystery to him, and believed that the mystery had little or nothing to do with sex. He never knew what to say to them.

If he had known what to say to boys his own age, he kept the knowledge and said very little. He was a loner by choice, and difficult to approach. He did not join the group activities of other youths, considering them frivolous. Reading was his

favorite pastime, especially stimulated by his growing interest
in history. The few real friendships he formed were with boys
of similar cerebral bent who could share his interests without
imposing theirs on him.

An older youth named Yves Garand had a fascination for
grand opera similar to Charles's for the theater. They had
shared interests, and Charles acquired such a fascination for
music as playing the violin had never given him. Yves Garand
also had an automobile—one of the first in Figeac—and drove
both Charles and Mme. Boyer to Toulouse for a performance
of *Lohengrin,* the first opera Charles attended other than the
modest ones occasionally staged in Figeac.

If Yves Garand also gave Charles instruction in earnest cultural snobbery, Philippe Gambon could exercise a more hu-
manizing influence. Charles had known Philippe Gambon
from a distance, and without affection, since earliest childhood. They were the same age, but Philippe had always been
huskier than Charles and was a contrast to him in other ways
—gregarious and irrepressibly merry. Philippe was also an accomplished performer on the soccer field, such as Charles
wasn't and didn't care to be. Yet they developed a strong
friendship around shared intellectual pursuits, each seeming to
fill a need in the other. Philippe Gambon had only an elemen-
tary acquaintance with literature and the arts but was curious, and Charles gave instruction. Philippe, however, also
began to instill in Charles a political conscience. He held
strong opinions about the moral responsibility of the legal
profession, to which he aspired.

Mme. Boyer encouraged this adolescent friendship, perhaps
believing that his friend might influence Charles to study law
where others had failed. Such influence may well have been
exercised, for Charles did begin to talk about law as a possible vocational direction. He told his examiners at the lyceum
of Figeac that he intended to study law following his graduation in 1916. He may have considered it merely a more satisfactory ambition, for the academic record, than acting. But
what he said hardly mattered to anyone: France had become
embroiled in the Great War, and the very survival of humanity had become a matter of doubt.

Charles Boyer would recall that he and Philippe Gambon were together at the Figeac railroad station in August of 1914, absorbing the first newspaper accounts of France going to war against Germany and Austria-Hungary.

"Most of the boys we both knew were excited, and some were deliriously happy, such as Yves Garand who enlisted right away and went off to war. It was all an adventure to everyone, except to Philippe and myself. We decided that among boys of our age, we were the only pacifists in all of France. Perhaps we had better knowledge of history than they did. We knew that war is terrible and we were very sad, even though we did not expect to be involved. I was just turning fifteen, and everyone seemed to think the war would be over in just a few weeks."

Weeks churned into months and then years, but the war remained remote. The battle had become interminably stalemated in Belgium and northern France—the bleak Western Front. Only in 1916 did the horror of war become visible for the people of Figeac. A hospital was set up near the town for the treatment and recuperation of Allied soldiers wounded at the front. Charles became a volunteer orderly at the hospital —working without pay but working, at least, for the first time in his life. He and Philippe Gambon sometimes took hospital duty together. They became accustomed to the sufferings of other persons, and steeled themselves against being overcome by the soldiers' ordeals of pain. Charles sought to cheer the ailing soldiers who were mostly far away from their homes, but usually to no avail—he simply wasn't the cheerful sort.

He also wasn't happy about the shape of his life. Upon his graduation from the lyceum, he resolved the conflict with his mother on the matter of his future—or appeared to resolve it, by means of a compromise.

Their only point of agreement had been that he should continue his education—unlike most youths of his own approximate age, who were taking apprentice positions in the working life of Figeac, or were enlisting in the Army. Mme. Boyer, still prodding Charles toward some honorable profession and prepared to finance his educational pursuit of one, would have enrolled him at a nearby university, preferring Toulouse or Cahors. Charles, though, had begun to think only of Paris, and his specific goal was the conservatory there—the Conservatoire National Supérieur de Musique et de Déclamation, to which, however, he could hardly expect to gain admittance. It was not a training school in the performing arts, but an advanced professional program for artists who already had gained some establishment. Mme. Boyer was opposed to any thought of advanced education in Paris, for a logical reason: trench warfare was being waged nearby both north and west, and Paris was a beleaguered city, always on the alert for a German attack. Finally mother and son agreed on the Collège Campollion near Figeac, which Philippe Gambon also planned to enter.

Acting had lost none of its appeal for him, but Charles was himself yielding to practical considerations, certain that he could not undertake an acting career without his mother's financial support. By his own admission he had become a young dilettante, more favorably disposed to living comfortably than to struggling for his own causes. But a doctor? Never! If he needed assurance that he was not constituted for the medical profession, the experience at the army hospital provided it. Furthermore, his interest in law had been lukewarm at best, and was waning. For a brief time, though, he convinced himself that he wished to become a teacher, ideally a university professor of history or philosophy.

That was vaguely his plan upon entering the Collège Campollion—where, however, he was very nearly an academic failure for the first time. Despite his apparent ability to master any subject, he increasingly neglected his studies and his attendance was spotty. Time that might have been given to his studies was spent, instead, reading plays, or reading essays about the drama. He was also distracted by occasional opportunities to perform.

Charles acted in a college production of a tragedy by Racine; and in a civic pageant on Bastille Day, he portrayed for the first time one of his personal heroes of history, Georges-Jacques Danton. Such adventure at the primitive levels of theater rekindled Charles's desire to act professionally, while convincing others that he had a flair for it. Early in 1917, that flair gained a wider recognition.

Resuming his volunteer assistance at the army hospital after a layoff, Charles immediately sensed a deterioration of the soldiers' morale. After nearly three years of destructive but inconclusive fighting, the European war was grinding down its participants. Battle statistics were ever more grim. Among those killed in the battle of the Somme was Charles's opera-loving friend, Yves Garand. Some of the soldiers recuperated in the hospital and rejoined their comrades at the front, only to come back to Figeac with new wounds and a more acute bitterness. As the casualties kept on arriving, each wave revealed more clearly the war-weary disillusionment. Soldiers and civilians alike began to fear that the war might go on forever, until no one was left to fight.

In February of 1917 the United States broke off diplomatic relations with Germany, giving rise in France to a hope that America would soon join the Allied cause and bring about a quick and victorious end to the Great War. When that didn't happen immediately, morale appeared to sag even lower. The convalescing soldiers needed to be entertained, and finally Charles set himself up as their entertainer.

Arriving at the hospital for his chores as an orderly, Charles observed a group of nurses practicing a comical song about the Kaiser. They had written the number themselves, and intended to sing it for the soldiers. Charles knew that the number was witless, and had an inspiration. With the nurses as his confederates, he presented himself to the hospital's only doctor, asking permission to perform songs and skits for the troops. With permission granted, he began devising revue sketches, borrowing most of his material from plays both comical and serious.

For performers to complement the willing nurses, he engaged some Figeac citizens of his acquaintance, and even some of the healthier soldiers. Philippe Gambon was a willing performer, but Charles gave himself the choice roles. He was no singer or dancer, but did a little of both in the hospital shows, and also played his violin.

The hospital shows may have been humdrum affairs, but "they were the most important thing that had happened to me to that point"; and for Charles Boyer they were the early proof of a gift that must have come from God. When he became a performer before an audience, he was somehow transformed. All the inhibitions that made him a withdrawn figure in the routine of daily life seemed to vanish. Performance enabled him to become a person very different from himself, and indeed different from anyone. He was also an instant roaring success. The soldiers cheered him; they couldn't get enough of *le petit Charles*.

Now he sensed his growing indebtedness to the cinema. More popular with the soldiers than his capsule adaptations of plays were the skits Charles constructed from the stored memories of film comedies he'd seen—not only those of Max Linder, but also the farcical pantomimes of Charlie Chaplin, for whom Linder had been a primary stylistic influence. Chaplin's popularity had come to outstrip Linder's, even in France, and Chaplin imitations already were commonplace throughout the world. Yet the Boyer version may have been better than most, and his audiences thought it was.

Charles also staged brisk melodramas based on some Pearl White serials he had enjoyed, adding some original dialogue. But however successful the hospital shows may have been, they only persuaded the triple-threat teenager that he had no real desire to be any kind of writer for the theater, or even a director. There was no enjoyment in writing, and there was only frustration in working with other performers, who could not be taught to do the things he could do instinctively. If he was to have any kind of theatrical career, it would have to be as an actor.

One of his last hospital shows was certainly the most fulfilling, and the most memorable. He was at the hospital about to offer a program of farcical skits when the tumultuous news circulated that the United States had made a formal declaration of war against Germany. Now there was jubilation; and with morale soaring, Charles considered that an entire program of low comedy was not appropriate. There should also be something patriotically inspiring to honor the

occasion. So after an opening song-and-dance skit that he performed with casual soldiers, Charles raised his arms to quiet
the audience, and from memory gave his own rendering of
some of Danton's impassioned oratory. The soldiers were
transfixed in silent attention, after which they were boister-
ously inspired. Of course they sang "La Marseillaise," and of
course Charles sang with them, in a moment to be savored
and not forgotten.

*   *   *

In the summer of 1918, while France anticipated a victorious resolution of the Great War, Charles was a troubled
youth, aware of his mother's increasing emotional dependence
on him, sensing both his need to get away from home and his
ineffectuality for accomplishing that need. His deliverance
was unexpected, and could not have been planned any better.

A stranger knocked on the door of the Boyer home and
asked Charles, who answered, if he were any kind of actor.
The startled young man said yes, he believed he was an actor,
and certainly hoped to become one. The stranger identified
himself as a member of a Paris-based motion picture company
that was doing some location shooting in various parts of Lot.
An actor was needed to play a certain role, and someone in
Figeac had provided the information that young Charles
Boyer was the ablest actor in town, if not the only one.

The prospect delighted Charles, who rode with the man in
a little truck, a distance of several kilometers to the shooting
site. Then he did not get the part: the director appraised him
with the quick judgment that "It is impossible, he is much too
young." Another actor was found to play the part, although
Charles did appear in a group scene for which he received no
pay—a most obscure screen debut, in a feature film entitled
Travail. He lingered on the scene of the filming, on the banks
of the river Célé, and struck up a friendship with Raphael
Duflos, the picture's leading actor. In a calculated move,
Charles invited the actor to dine in the Boyer home; and in
only a few hours Raphael Duflos accomplished what Charles
had been unable to in nineteen years. He persuaded Mme.
Boyer that her son should go to Paris and become an actor.

Mme. Boyer was properly charmed by Duflos, who was an established actor on the Parisian stage as well as in motion pictures. Duflos believed that Charles Boyer also met the qualifications for both media: he was agreeably handsome for the silent drama, but possessed a voice that deserved to be heard from a stage. It was really the silken voice that most impressed Raphael Duflos. He reasoned that such a voice deserved the best possible training, and assured Mme. Boyer that the Paris conservatory provided that.

Yet Duflos also doubted that Charles was suitably prepared for the exacting artistic demands of the conservatory. First he should soak up the life of Paris, and make thorough acquaintance with the theater, the opera, and the other vital components of the city's culture. Mme. Boyer was reluctant for Charles to abandon his education for an acting career that might not materialize; whereupon Raphael Duflos said, "Then why not send the boy to the Sorbonne?"

The idea of Charles becoming a student at the Sorbonne appealed irresistibly to his mother's pride and vanity. It was decided very quickly over after-dinner brandy: Charles would continue his studies at the Collège Campollion until the end of the war, which now seemed imminent; then he would go to Paris and complete his education at the Sorbonne. After that, if he remained convinced that the theater was his destiny, he could pursue such a career and enter the Conservatoire National Supérieur de Musique et de Déclamation if it accepted him.

With November came the end of fighting and the Armistice. Charles stayed in Figeac through the Christmas holiday, then departed by train for Paris just before 1918 passed into history. And history was his intended field of study at the Sorbonne—although, following his enrollment, he would choose instead a curriculum in philosophy.

He packed one large suitcase with every article of clothing he deemed worthy of Paris; he would send for his precious books after he got settled. There was no sadness in any of his good-byes, not even to Philippe Gambon, for he did not expect to be gone from Figeac so very long. Yet thirty years would pass before he paid his only return visit to his birth-place and early home.

His mother accompanied him to the railroad station in a horse-drawn taxi on the last day of the year. Charles gave her a farewell kiss in the carriage, and Mme. Boyer returned home while he awaited the train's arrival, which was hours late. A gentle snow began to fall, and during the rail journey northward the snow whirled with blizzard fury. The city of Paris had a new white coverlet when Charles Boyer arrived there to begin a new year and a new life.

As matters developed, Raphael Duflos proved to be the precise catalyst for that new life. They were to meet often in Paris; and although Duflos and his young protégé were destined never to act together on stage or screen, Raphael Duflos was one of those who were always proud to claim title as "discoverer" of Charles Boyer.

※   ※   ※

It was also a new Paris, reveling in peace after the marathon conflict that had drained Europe of so much young manhood. Paris is festive by nature, but Charles Boyer believed it was never so exuberant as in those first months after the Great War. American soldiers were still in abundance, and luxuriating in the pampered attentions of the grateful Parisians while awaiting redeployment to the United States. They seemed right at home in Paris, where Charles only had the uneasy feeling of an outsider, hoping that his insecurity was not obvious.

He felt surrounded by Americans during his first visit to the Folies-Bergère, where the headliner was Maurice Chevalier, himself just returned from the war. Chevalier had learned the rudiments of English from a British soldier while both were prisoners of the Germans; and now he was playing broadly to the doughboys, asking them musically in English, "How you gonna keep 'em down on the farm, after they've seen Paree?"

Boyer had known no one in Paris other than Raphael Duflos, whose address he had clutched during his train ride to Paris. Duflos took his young friend to dinner in an expensive restaurant off the Champs-Élysées; and Charles Boyer would reflect that "My first meal in Paris was the only good one I had for nearly a year." Duflos found an inexpensive room for Charles near the Sorbonne, in the Latin Quarter. Afterward they saw one another only fitfully. Then Charles took up the study of philosophy, of which pursuit very little specific knowledge exists.

Persons who became his friends not long afterward, such as Joseph Kessel and André Benim, would in later years express doubt that Boyer had really attended the Sorbonne. He undoubtedly did, although he did not take "a degree in philosophy" as is stated in many sources, and which Boyer both confirmed and denied in various interviews. He obtained no degree, if records at the Sorbonne are reliable, but there is proof of his enrollment in 1919. He was quoted as having been at the Sorbonne "only a few months" and "almost two years," and was probably there less than a full year, but very nearly that. Yet he seems to have had no memorable personal associations there, and people claiming to have known Charles Boyer at the Sorbonne have never materialized. His departure from the Sorbonne was probably quite sudden, and can logically be related to the fabled stroke of good fortune that made him a professional actor.

Before that occurred, he quickly made satisfactory social adjustment to his new environment. In Figeac he had few friends or close acquaintances, but in Paris he collected them quickly and in plentiful number—if not at the Sorbonne, then in the theater district. He made application to the conservatory, on which no action was immediately taken; but he also made acquaintance with several of the conservatory's younger actors, among them Philippe Heriat, who would be perhaps Boyer's closest friend during his early years in Paris. To save on expenses, Boyer accepted an invitation to move into an apartment that Heriat had been sharing with Pierre Brasseur, an experienced professional actor although still in his teens. Brasseur was going out on tour, and Boyer was pleased to become Heriat's new roommate, both for economy and companionship. Through Heriat and Brasseur, he met a host of would-be actors and dramatists, whose open-end conversations in the little cafés were festivals of ideas. They dreamed of rebuilding, with their art, a war-torn world.

Throughout 1919 Boyer connived to meet theater managers, playwrights—anyone who might be able to help him get started professionally as an actor. He obtained a few auditions but no employment, and had one particular disappointment. While attending a performance of the Comédie-Française, he recognized the name of one of the actors—Victor Francen—as a special friend of Raphael Duflos. Francen, a mature Belgian soon to achieve considerable fame in French films, received the young Boyer cordially in his dressing room, and was impressed by his gracefulness and sincerity. He arranged for Boyer to be auditioned by the Comédie-Française, and even acted a scene with him before the jury. Boyer was rejected, though—and rather curtly, he believed—on the grounds of his obvious inexperience. Later he learned that his audition had displeased Pierre Fresnay, a handsome young leading actor with the Comédie-Française, who may have recognized a potential rival. In years to come, though, Fresnay and Boyer formed a solid friendship based on mutual professional respect.

Boyer was never emotionally constituted for defeat. Rejection by the Comédie-Française plunged him into deep gloom, causing him to believe that he hated Paris and hated acting. He considered returning to Figeac—which, however, he believed he hated even more. So he got drunk instead. While his roommate visited his family, Boyer spent the 1919 Christmas holiday alone in the apartment, drinking all of the wine. It was mostly cheap burgundy, and having survived the binge, he never drank burgundy again.

During those months of his presumed study at the Sorbonne, Boyer was "desperately poor" by his own account, eating only irregularly; yet he seems to have had unlimited funds for attending the theater. He consumed the Paris theatrical scene in great swallows. When he was impressed by a powerful feat of acting, he would return to study the performance again and again. It intrigued him that such titanic actors as André Lefaur and Harry Baur seemed never to give the same performance twice; and he helped develop the legend that he saw ten successive performances of a *Samson* revival that again starred his foremost idol, Lucien Guitry.

There are several versions of Boyer's eventual meeting with Lucien Guitry. They differ slightly in their particulars, but all of them were probably originated by Boyer himself. In the account he gave Digby Diehl more than half a century later, Guitry had been made aware that a young man was watching his performances night after night, and inquired who he was. Boyer was invited to visit with the great man in his dressing room; and Guitry, who was then past sixty, "told me a lot of things which gave me a pattern for my last years of study. Although today I have a different style of speech, I still handle lines much the way Guitry used to."

Lucien Guitry impressed upon Charles Boyer that speech had to be unexpected: "The audience is always asleep, dozing because all plays sound alike, really, and you must come forward with such a striking reading that they must be jarred. You have no right, if you are an actor, to say 'good night' twice the same way."

Boyer believed that from the moment of receiving that advice, he never duplicated one of his stage accounts exactly, or even a film scene regardless of the number of "takes." Lucien Guitry's counsel must have been valuable, for it is believed that Charles Boyer never failed another audition. He was about to break through as an actor, and the manner of his emergence is a part of French theatrical folklore.

In the first days of 1920, while the distraught Boyer was recovering from his first monstrous hangover, a once-popular play called *Les Jardins de Murcie* was being readied for a professional revival, under auspices of the conservatory. On the eve of its official opening, the leading man collapsed onstage during the final rehearsal. Stricken by some acute malady, he was sent home to bed with a high fever, and the attending physician said he could not return to the stage for a matter of weeks. The actor had no understudy, and no one known to be familiar with the role could be located in Paris. Philippe Heriat, arriving at the conservatory the next morning, heard about the calamity which would necessitate canceling the engagement at a considerable loss of money.

Heriat asked to see Firmin Gemier, the producer. Besides being one of the leading impresarios of the day, Gemier was the director of *Les Jardins de Murcie*. Heriat excitedly told Gemier about his talented roommate, who had an amazing ability to memorize very quickly, and who *was* an actor. Gemier was skeptical but must have reasoned that he had nothing more to lose; he wanted to meet the unaccountably gifted young man at once.

Roused from morning sleep, Charles Boyer saw Philippe Heriat and another man whom he didn't recognize, but who was asking him an extraordinary question: Could he, in only twelve hours, learn the lines for a leading part in a play? And could he then give a performance that would not bring disgrace upon the Conservatoire? Upon sensing the challenge, Boyer shared Firmin Gemier's panic, but was not going to let such an opportunity elude him. He muttered, "Yes, of course I can learn the lines."

Boyer was taken to the theater, where he met some of the actors in *Les Jardins de Murcie*—the ones who had answered a hurry-up summons from Gemier. Gemier explained that the performance was not to be canceled after all. He could decide to cancel it at any moment before curtain time, if Charles Boyer had not made sufficient progress in memorizing the dialogue. But meanwhile, a tailor was summoned to shorten the other actor's trousers that Boyer would now wear. Gemier decided that he would place his fate not in the hands of the gods, but in the trust of a twenty-year-old who had never acted on a Paris stage, but who was now insisting upon absolute privacy for memorizing his role.

Boyer was placed in the solitary confinement of a dressing room, and was given the director's copy of the playscript with the scribbled-in stage directions that he promised also to memorize. It was now likely that he would go onstage without benefit of rehearsal with the other actors. He was left entirely alone; but after the passage of several hours, Firmin Gemier intruded with a considerate suggestion. It had occurred to Gemier that two of the character's very long speeches could be cut without a serious loss of literacy, and he instructed Boyer to eliminate them. Boyer was clearly annoyed. The young actor said "I cannot now eliminate a single word. I have memorized the *entire play*, and to begin cutting it would only confuse me."

He really had no confidence whatever. When Gemier confronted his theater audience a few minutes before curtain time, Boyer was applying his stage makeup while Philippe Heriat fed him his lines. Gemier was explaining the circumstances of the late casting change, asking the audience to be understanding; and Boyer, getting into his first costume, was devastated by the realization that he had not even met the leading lady who would share the opening scene with him. She had not been present at the director's hastily called meeting hours earlier. He did not even know what she looked like; yet moments later, they were together onstage before an audience.

Gemier would have been delighted with a performance that approached bare adequacy, but Boyer was *good*. Or the sympathetic audience was in a mood to think so. He believed he was dreadful, reciting his dialogue accurately but not capturing the meaning of the words. Yet he met the pressure as a seasoned veteran would. When another actor forgot his own lines, Boyer improvised a speech that got the sense of their exchange and kept the play moving. And he kept himself moving. If memory of Gemier's stage directions failed him, the movement came instinctively.

Boyer believed soon afterward that nervousness probably had given his dialogue a valuable edge of tension. Gemier supposed that in Boyer's subsequent renditions of the role, a confidence settled in that made the performance less exciting. But there was excitement enough in that first performance. Before the curtain had fallen on the final act, the audience was wild with cheering—not for the play whose merits were irrelevant under the circumstances of the performance, but for the actor. The audience, assured in the earliest moments of Boyer's ability, may then have perceived something that had not initially occurred to the panicky Gemier: the new actor had a somber handsomeness that suggested no other well-known personality.

That Boyer became an overnight celebrity was no exaggeration. He was a wonderful prize found in a grab bag. The newspapers sought him, and his first interviews defined a grimly handsome, almost sinister youth who spoke with a provincial accent if he spoke at all. They may not have understood that he was in a sustained state of shock.

There was a second performance, and a third . . . and *Les Jardins de Murcie* settled in for a run, its box office building a momentum on the topicality of the leading man. Boyer got the feel of the play beyond the rote memory of his lines, and rated it a mediocre theater piece. He did establish a playing rapport with the other actors, and soon was approaching his own idea of a good performance. Before he had attained it, however, he was watching the play from the wings.

Later it was easily forgotten that the original actor resumed his role, causing a box-office sag and a shorter engagement than would have been managed with Boyer retained in the part. No matter; Boyer's initial fame was established, and his long tenure as an eminently employable actor was only beginning. He would soon be acquainted with almost everyone of consequence in the Paris theater, among whom there were many eager to champion him. One of those was Firmin Gemier, who still felt eternally in debt to Boyer after having made every reasonable accommodation for the actor who had saved his production.

Gemier arranged that Boyer would receive the substantial salary that a leading actor might expect. Then he asked if there were anything else he might possibly do for Charles Boyer.

There was. Managing an uncharacteristic smile, Boyer said "Please, Monsieur Gemier . . . since I have not disgraced it, can I now perhaps be enrolled in the Conservatoire?"

2

His two years at the Paris conservatory were stimulating ones for Charles Boyer. It was a time of intellectual ferment for him, while increasing recognition of his dramatic ability also gratified his ego. Zealously he pursued a rather elevated study of theatrical art, but at the same time he was earning money more or less regularly as an actor for both stage and screen.

On his twenty-first birthday he declared his financial independence, informing his mother in a letter that he would accept no further assistance from her. He found other part-time employment when he was "between engagements" as an actor, sometimes playing violin in Parisian nightspots, and even briefly serving the Sûreté as a detective. How he came by such employment must remain a mystery, but Boyer often boasted that he had once been an efficient detective, and that the experience initiated an interest in criminology that he would retain.

He continued to form close personal associations, some of which would be nurtured into lifetime friendships. There was some conscious selectivity on his part, indicating Boyer's early mastery of theatrical politics. He tended to cultivate friendship with persons of professional eminence, or with others so obviously gifted that fame could not be denied them very long. He possessed remarkable antennae for finding unknown and unestablished persons who, however, would someday be as famous as he, or almost. He seems to have known everyone of major accomplishment in French theater and films before they made their names.

He gravitated to persons of serious disposition, similar to himself. What Boyer himself lacked in gaiety in those years was compensated by his admirable high-mindedness. Colleagues at the conservatory found Charles to be always absorbed in thought, a remarkably intense young man. His presence stifled the promise of laughter, but his conversation was invigorating, and informed by the nervous energy that made him an interesting performer on stage.

Pierre Blanchar was of a demeanor perhaps even sterner than Boyer's. At the conservatory they became close friends and also rivals. Boyer probably felt the rivalry more acutely, for Pierre Blanchar was the consensus choice as the conservatory's finest actor. Boyer was rated highly, though, as indeed was Philippe Heriat; and for a while they were an inseparable trio—Boyer, Heriat, and their surrogate father who was Pierre Blanchar.

The Algerian-born Blanchar was rather more mature than most of the actors who had student status at the conservatory, and was Boyer's elder by seven years. He had his own strong ideas about the craft and substance of acting. He was much less impressed by Lucien Guitry than Boyer was, assigning Guitry to that school of acting for whom technique is everything. Blanchar agreed with Boyer that emotional truth was the divine quest of the serious actor, but his own example was the younger Louis Jouvet, with whom he was acquainted. Jouvet's own company was then enjoying a long engagement in New York, performing the French dramatic classics in repertory. But shortly after Jouvet's return to France in 1921, Blanchar introduced him to Boyer and Heriat in the Théâtre des Champs-Élysées, where Jouvet was the new director.

The four of them dined together, after which Jouvet captivated his guests by evaluating the various new approaches to acting, with special emphasis on Constantin Stanislavsky's innovative approach for his Moscow Art Theater. The conservatory endorsed Stanislavsky's philosophy but not his approach, or "method"; but Jouvet persuaded them that Stanislavsky had to be right—that the florid nature of acting had to be purged as false, and that the art of acting was largely a matter of stripping away falseness. Louis Jouvet believed that silent motion pictures were threatening ruin for that art, with their overblown physical performances. He'd made a film or two but intended never to make another. By that time Boyer and Heriat had already made their first screen appearances, and Blanchar had registered a considerable hit in his movie debut in *Papa Bon Coeur*.

Boyer already understood the modern actor's dilemma. He wished to act on the stage, and there was a fair demand for his services. But the movies also were calling, and they paid better money.

*   *   *

To most persons in America and perhaps in every other country, the story of motion pictures is essentially the story of Hollywood. This is not fair to the French. Although the twentieth century's popular new art form has been dominated by American product in every vibrant era, France has usually placed a respectable second. A good case can also be made that the French have more often led the artistic vanguard. They were leaders in technology during the theatrical film's prehistory, so indebted to such legendary French figures as Louis Lumière, George Méliès, Léon Gaumont, and Charles Pathé.

In one respect the French film enterprise bore a remarkable resemblance to its American counterpart. As the story film developed to suggest an innovative form of theater, the newer medium rose as a competitor to the traditional stage presentation. Each began to covet the other's talent. But in France as in America, and wherever film commerce coexisted with an established theater, the economic advantage was easily held by motion pictures. This posed a dilemma for the more polished or attractive actors, whose preference was unmistakably for the stage (especially during that period when the movies had not yet acquired a voice), but who were tempted by the wider fame possible through film appearances, and certainly by the money. Although some actors worked exclusively on the stage or in films, most professional thoroughbreds gave themselves to both. Finally, though, there was a primary identity: there were stage players who also appeared in films, and there were screen actors who were glimpsed occasionally on a stage.

Charles Boyer was a dedicated stage actor who began to appear in theatrical films early in his career, because the movies wanted him and he could not easily refuse the money they offered. His film appearances in the twenties were scattered and of little significance, but they had some effect of defining him as a "popular" player rather than one of serious commitment. Boyer *was* committed, and he was nothing if not serious; but his development in the twenties did not follow his plan. While giving most of his professional energy to the theater, he suggested not the virtuoso he might have been, but the matinée idol whose limitations were prescribed, if they did not otherwise exist.

Boyer did not have a snobbish disposition toward the movies. He was fascinated by the medium, if in no way that touched on his own ambition. He believed the movies had little to do with what he believed to be real acting; but, harboring a standard vanity quotient, he was especially eager to see himself on a screen, photographed in motion—to see how he *appeared*.

Soon confronted by the actual evidence, he claimed to be appalled. He decided that his career as a motion picture actor was over almost as soon as it had begun, and he may have believed that.

After the experience of *Les Jardins de Murcie*, Boyer was employed steadily by Firmin Gemier in stage offerings both old and new—a revival of Victor Hugo's *Hernani;* a new play called *La Dolores* that was a failure; and the more successful *La Grande Pastorale* that gave him a leading role of virtuoso dimension. His performance in *La Grande Pastorale* was witnessed by Marcel L'Herbier, a young avant-garde director for the screen. L'Herbier offered Boyer a small role in *L'Homme du Large,* and Boyer accepted. The picture was shot in Paris in the autumn of 1920 and released soon afterward. It helped establish L'Herbier as a leading impressionist director, and favorable attention was given to Boyer in the reviews. The dissatisfaction was his own, and he vowed never to make another film. He repeated that vow to Louis Jouvet; and then, within only a matter of days, there was a new movie offer he believed he couldn't or shouldn't refuse.

Honoré de Balzac was one of Boyer's literary heroes, and Jacques de Baroncelli was a screen director whose literary adaptations Boyer had particularly admired. Baroncelli tempted Boyer with the role of Rastignac in his production of Balzac's *Le Père Goriot*. Boyer accepted the offer, having been encouraged to do so by Pierre Blanchar and most others at the conservatory. He reported for shooting, only to be told that he would have to sign a contract with Baroncelli's company. For at least a year he would be bound to a motion picture company whose projects would not generally be as prestigious as *Le Père Goriot*, and might not be directed by Baroncelli. He would have no authority for selecting his roles, and would not be at liberty to appear in stage productions. Certainly the money was tempting; but considering everything, Boyer told Baroncelli to get himself another Rastignac.

Louis Jouvet applauded Boyer's show of independence; and Boyer suspected that Jouvet was influential toward having a good stage offer come his way almost immediately. The property was *La Bataille* by Claude Farrère, and it was destined to be one of Paris's big dramatic successes of the twenties—a play about a Japanese war lord. Boyer was given a subordinate role, although he subsequently would enact the naval commander both in a later stage production and on film.

The succession of stage appearances from *Les Jardins de Murcie* to *La Grande Pastorale* had made him a familiar figure to playgoers in Paris in barely more than a year. Now his depiction of a young Oriental in *La Bataille* established him as one of the more promising young actors of the French stage, a *jeune premier*. He was now also apparently desirable. After *La Bataille* settled in for its long run, it became customary that a group of young Parisiennes would cluster outside the stage door at the Théâtre Antcine to get a glimpse of

M. Boyer and perhaps obtain his autograph. There had to come a time when the women would discover Charles Boyer.

* * *

He left the Conservatoire National Supérieur de Musique et de Déclamation, an accredited graduate, during the run of *La Bataille*. He took a private apartment that was surely more elegant than the one he had shared with Philippe Heriat, and he proceeded to become something of a dandy. That he also took a mistress was hinted but not easily confirmed; he was characteristically secretive about his private affairs. Never one to talk about his amorous activity, Boyer was paid high compliment by friends who respected him and his wishes. They chose not to discuss what they knew little or nothing about, since Boyer knowingly drew a curtain over part of his life.

In his own projected memoirs, Pierre Brasseur did say it was probably true that Boyer, as he claimed, was still an innocent upon arriving in Paris in 1919—all those nurses at the hospital notwithstanding. Charles left no sweetheart in Figeac, and did not find one soon in Paris. Brasseur confirmed that Boyer remained distinctly uncomfortable in the presence of women throughout his tenure at the conservatory, and consciously avoided them. Within a few years most of Boyer's intimate friends—Heriat, Blanchar, Brasseur—were married; but Boyer seemed terrified of the prospect of marriage, if not of sexual activity.

When he became a ladies' man in the early twenties, the ladies weren't actresses. This was no longer the Paris of La Belle Époque, but not even the Great War had obliterated the salon. At least until economic depression gripped France in the mid-twenties, the *cocotte* maintained her place in Parisian society. Boyer must have known a few of them, for he became a regular visitor in the city's most elegant salons. No doubt they pampered him, for he was becoming the matinée idol *par excellence*.

After *La Bataille* came *L'Insoumise*, rather less successful but affording Boyer his first starring role in the theater, still in 1922. His salary escalated during subsequent stage appearances—in *Charly* and *L'Homme Enchaîné*, both in 1923, and in *Le Voyageur* the next year. They were plays of limited merit but all attained some degree of popular success—an indication that Boyer was becoming a draw, someone who could attract an audience in no matter what role or play.

In those days he was regarded as a holdout against motion pictures, and he may have rejected offers that were more lucrative. Yet Boyer was merely being selective. He accepted movie projects if they appealed to him. After playing another small screen role in *Chantelouve*, he essayed his first movie lead in *L'Esclave* in 1923. If it wasn't much as a picture, it did make Boyer's name known throughout France.

Boyer often found movie work a frustrating gamble. Pierre Blanchar quickly had become an important star, which clearly had an effect of qualifying him for the more desirable stage roles as well. Boyer probably counted on a success in films that similarly would advance his standing on the stage; yet if movie work brought him to a wider audience, it did not do much for his dramatic reputation. Boyer once noted that "In those days I really did not photograph well, besides which, even on the stage my best attribute was my voice, or so they said."

Film work offered him no stimulation beyond financial reward, and he was increasingly vexed that his popular success was not expanding his artistic dimension in either medium.

So when the great Henry Bernstein accosted him, Boyer was vulnerable.

*   *   *

Henry Bernstein is a fading figure in world theater, even though he was the dominant figure in the French theater for three decades. Although Bernstein had an incredibly long career, he did not prove to be a dramatist of lasting influence. Today, some of his plays are occasionally revived in France at the provincial level but are not performed elsewhere.

But he was a spectacular man. A Frenchman of Polish-Jewish ancestry, Henry Bernstein was born in Paris in 1876 and his first play was produced there in 1900. Altogether he wrote nearly thirty plays in a career that spanned more than half a century. His last play was produced in Paris at his own theater, the Ambassadeurs, in 1952—the year before his death at age seventy-six. Fourteen of his plays were produced on Broadway, and that is believed still to be the record for a foreign-language playwright in America.

Most of Bernstein's plays were great popular successes in his and their day. Yet now he is best known to Americans as a great French patriot. He fled to the United States just before Paris fell to the Nazis in 1940, and was perhaps the most articulate spokesman opposing the Vichy regime of Marshal Philippe Pétain and Pierre Laval. But in theatrical circles, even Bernstein's fervent anti-Nazism was overshadowed by his reputation as the foremost duelist in his profession. Bernstein's flamboyant career was punctuated by nine duels, in most of which he was the challenger bent on defending his honor. His most famous duel probably occurred in 1938 when, with a sword, he "pinked" the arm of Édouard Bourdet, producer for the Comédie-Française—thereby redeeming the honor that had been smeared by Bourdet's tardiness in staging a revival of *Judith,* one of Bernstein's biblical dramas.

Samson was another such; and the production that had made Lucien Guitry such a hero to the young Charles Boyer had also established Henry Bernstein as a larger-than-life figure. Bernstein was in his heyday in 1924, and to Boyer at that time there was no other theatrical figure so majestic or intimidating.

They first met in 1922, when *Judith* had its initial production, directed by Bernstein himself in the Gymnase, which he had acquired for his own theater. In that period Boyer was taking every opportunity to meet the persons of real consequence in the theater. He called on Bernstein to congratulate him for having attained another major success, after which Bernstein repaid the compliment by visiting Boyer in his dressing room following his first performance as *L'Homme Enchaîné.*

They met again when *Le Voyageur* was completing its engagement in August 1924. Boyer's fellow actors turned the occasion into a surprise twenty-fifth birthday party for the star. All of Boyer's friends were there—the movie star Blanchar; Heriat, who was making his own good headway on the Paris boards; Marcel Dalio, whom Boyer had met through Heriat; newer friends such as Jacques Feyder and his wife, Françoise Rosay; older friends such as Victor Francen and even Raphael Duflos; and some eminent figures in unexpected attendance, such as Henry Bernstein. There was revelry all around when Bernstein offered a toast to "the crown prince of the French theater."

Since Bernstein considered himself the king, he was subtly proposing a father-son relationship. His idea was that Boyer would bloom under his management, intimating that he sought an exclusive contract. Furthermore, he had conceived a leading role in a new play with Boyer expressly in mind. Boyer protested firmly, viewing a contract as an enslavement for an actor, whether the profferor was a movie company or the most fashionable playwright in France. Yet he would not ignore the opportunity of a prestigious theatrical association that promised deliverance from the mediocrity of his customary participation. No contract was signed. Boyer retained his freedom to appear in other people's plays, as he often would; but Bernstein gained artistic dominance over him for half a dozen years, writing one role after another especially for Boyer.

Bernstein always directed his own plays, and was something of a martinet. Boyer said he "suffered under" Bernstein, reflecting on an experience of some exhilaration and much anguish. His tenure as Bernstein's star actor was unsettling for Boyer, who must have heard the gossip about Bernstein's having fallen in love with him.

Henry Bernstein was robustly heterosexual, and had a solid reputation as a ladies' man before he entered into a long marriage. Yet he became unreasonably possessive of Boyer while the actor was under his management. Bernstein's actresses incited his wrath when they proceeded, almost inevitably, to fall in love with his new actor. Bernstein guarded Boyer jealously, and once dismissed a young actress from his company because she was "distracting" Boyer from his attentions to a Bernstein drama. Then, when Boyer became infatuated with one of the company's veteran actresses, Bernstein as director appeared to persecute Boyer diabolically, until the affair had run its course.

There were compensations for Boyer. Bernstein made him one of the highest-paid actors on France's legitimate stage; and even without a binding contract, the association with Bernstein gave him extraordinary job security. Boyer barely understood the ordinary actor's frequent plight of being out of work. He was always working, or always had the opportunity. There was a period of ten years in which not a night passed without one of Henry Bernstein's plays being performed in Paris, and at one time as many as eighty performances of Bernstein plays were going on in Europe. Boyer could work for Bernstein in Paris or elsewhere, on the summer tours; and eventually he appeared in Bernstein plays in nine countries.

His first venture for Bernstein was *La Galerie des Glaces*, which opened at the Gymnase on October 22, 1924, and ran five months, a long engagement for that era. Boyer was favorably received both by the press and his audience, but was not convinced that he had given the best account of himself. In preparing *La Galerie des Glaces* he and the playwright were continually at odds over how Boyer's part should be played—an argument over dynamics that would be sustained in most of their subsequent collaborations. The mercurial Bernstein would prod Boyer toward a more demonstrative style, where Boyer strove to underplay. Furthermore, Boyer was increasingly distressed that Bernstein shaped only traditional leading-man roles for him to play. He believed that he would do best as a young character actor, but Bernstein fixed his roles in the romantic and melodramatic conventions, until Boyer was often at sea grasping for what he considered real characterization.

After *La Galerie des Glaces* closed, Boyer accepted a film role offered by Jean Manoussi, whom he had known at the conservatory. The project was *Le Grillon du Foyer* and Philippe Heriat also was in it. That the picture did not make an impression only deepened Boyer's mistrust of the medium. He was also disappointed that he failed to make the cast of *Madame Sans-Gêne*. It was a rare thing for that era—an

American film shooting in Paris, and being produced lavishly with Gloria Swanson in the title role.

In France as elsewhere, American motion pictures rated as a class above any other, and certainly Gloria Swanson was one of the more glittery stars in the firmament. Every other role was being cast locally, and Pierre Brasseur had landed a part. Boyer also knew the director, Léonce Perret, who proposed him for a primary supporting role—until Miss Swanson intervened. Her assessment was that Boyer was too tall for her, so a shorter actor was chosen. Years later he could savor the irony that he had once been too tall for a leading lady— particularly when he was made to stand on a box to embrace Ingrid Bergman for the movie cameras. Gloria Swanson, though, was indeed a tiny thing, barely managing five feet, while Boyer in his smartest upright posture scaled five-nine at best. Many years later Gloria Swanson was astonished to learn that she'd once met a very young Charles Boyer in Paris: "He certainly never told me!"

❊   ❊   ❊

There was no busier actor in Paris. New playscripts piled up in his apartment, and his willingness to appear in one could guarantee its production. When he wasn't working for Henry Bernstein, he was favoring other dramatists who then rated highly and are now forgotten. He was in two plays by Charles Mère—*Le Plaisir* and *Le Lit Nuptial*—and both were hits. So was *Le Rubicon,* written by the same Édouard Bourdet with whom Henry Bernstein would later duel.

Mainly, though, he was in Bernstein's employ. In the spring of 1926 he undertook the title role in *Félix,* which had been written especially for him. It did not attain the success that most Bernstein plays enjoyed, and was withdrawn after a few weeks. Then Bernstein revived one of his best-known plays, *Le Secret,* and with Boyer in the leading role it repeated its big hit of a decade earlier. But Boyer frankly did not like it, and believed that both *Le Secret* and *Félix* were artificially melodramatic, besides offering him uninteresting stereotyped roles. He let his feelings be known to Bernstein, and they had an ever more uneasy relationship, even if they never drew dueling swords.

Whether or not Bernstein was making an earnest effort toward accommodation, in *Le Venin* he gave Boyer a role of intellectual substance. It played a substantial engagement in the middle months of 1927, and was regarded as a lively theater piece. At the time of Bernstein's death, Boyer reflected that "Henry may not have been the great playwright that everyone supposed, but he was a better director than we realized. I do not mean that he was a good director of actors, but in shaping the entire stage. A Bernstein stage had vitality. It crackled. Henry believed that jittery actors were desirable over placid ones, and he always managed to make his actors jittery."

Since he was now in such demand for both stage and screen projects, Boyer decided it was time to have an agent. He had become acquainted with the refined and courtly André Benim, who was his own age. Benim possessed the urbanity and natural sophistication that Boyer believed was lacking in himself. He chose Benim as his agent for that reason, and perhaps because Benim seemed to have friendly acquaintance with all the leading figures in the French performing arts. Benim was productive, not only in negotiating increasingly lucrative contracts for Boyer, but in delivering him many important new friends. Through Benim, Boyer met Maurice Chevalier and Mistinguette, Madeleine Guitty and Sacha Guitry. It was also through Benim that he met the novelist Joseph Kessel, who would be a lifetime friend. Kessel provided the intellectual stimulation that a part of Boyer always craved, while Chevalier became a friend of another sort, capable of inducing frivolity in Charles where others had failed. If Boyer didn't already *know everybody*, André Benim filled in the gaps.

There were more leading roles in new plays—*Le Bien Aimé; La Marche au Destin*—and there was a film appearance of some prestige. André Benim encouraged Boyer to be more receptive to overtures from the moviemakers, but appearing in *Le Capitaine Fracassé* was probably Boyer's own idea. The director was the sensational young Alberto Caval-

canti, near the beginning of a remarkable forty-year international career. Even more appealing to Boyer was the prospect
of working with Pierre Blanchar, who had the title role. Boyer
was accorded costar status, and rated *Le Capitaine Fracassé*
a satisfying experience all around. He was in good position to
advance in the hierarchy of filmdom, but for his absolute refusal to sign a contract with Gaumont or any other studio that
might "build" him.

He later regretted that in the aftermath of *Le Capitaine
Fracassé*, he refused an offer to work with Jean Renoir in *La
Petite Marchande d'Alumettes*, whose title role ("The Little
Match Girl") was played by Renoir's then wife, Catherine
Hessling. Boyer long believed that the red-haired Hessling,
who had been Auguste Renoir's last model, was the most
beautiful woman he had ever seen. He had agreed to make
the film, but excused himself when he had opportunity to
make an extended international tour, performing several of
Henry Bernstein's plays in repertory.

The troupe followed a circuitous route from Belgium to
Egypt and Syria, then on to Turkey and back to France by
way of Romania. Boyer had not previously traveled outside of
France, and expected to do a lot of sightseeing. But the sights
that captivated him proved to be the casinos that flanked almost every performance scene.

Gambling had already become a favorite pastime for him.
Boyer once told Ed Sullivan: "In France I had a good salary,
as stage salaries go, but I would lose it all at roulette and
chemin de fer. I lived well enough but I couldn't get ahead. I
looked forward to the foreign tour as a means of building my
income, but it was the opposite. Everywhere we went there
were casinos and I could not resist them. Every time was
going to be the last time, I would say. When I finally returned
to Paris I was completely broke. Worse than that, I was in
debt, having borrowed money from other cast members and
then losing it all."

To recover capital he made another film, *La Ronde Infer-
nale,* and registered a personal hit. As a follow-up film to *Le
Capitaine Fracassé,* it placed Boyer near the front rank of
French film players. Now the handsome film offers started

coming his way. Once more, though, he was seduced by
Henry Bernstein, who had conceived the central role in *Melo*
in Boyer's image. Although not enamored of the play, Boyer
saw the ingredients of a popular success, and accepted the
role in the interest of a long run.

Following its opening at the Gymnase on March 11, 1929,
Melo indeed became the box-office sensation of the age. It
was an effective potboiler, and Boyer gave an able and colorful performance that did not tax his resources. Film rights
were sold, and Boyer expected to appear also in the screen
version.

Melo finally ran more than a year, but Boyer was enlisted
only during its early months. He did some more long-distance
traveling, this time to Hollywood.

The movies had learned to talk.

3

The movies started talking in earnest late in 1927 when Al Jolson was *The Jazz Singer*. Actually the medium had for many years known that it could talk—ever since Léon Gaumont successfully demonstrated talking pictures at a Paris exposition early in the twentieth century. But to the captains of motion picture industry in Europe as well as Hollywood, talking pictures could only be an expensive bother. Silent features were expected to endure because the customer was satisfied with them. Even when the brothers Warner began producing fully talking pictures, there was no great excitement in France. But every national film enterprise eventually followed America's lead in those days; and in the spring of 1929 Hollywood abandoned silent film production altogether, correctly expecting the world to follow suit.

The transition was slower, calmer, and more orderly in France and Germany, the leading filmmaking countries after the United States. There was less evidence of panic; and because conversion was not rushed before the primitive recording equipment could be refined, fewer careers got ruined in Europe. In France particularly, the advent of talking pictures was a cause for rejoicing. Sacha Guitry, for example, welcomed an opportunity to transfer his own fanciful plays to the screen with dialogue intact. Eventually even Louis Jouvet became a regular player in French talking films. Boyer, with an acknowledged fine voice, had new enthusiasm for the medium, and expected to make his bow as an actor for the talking screen with the *Melo* film.

Instead, he went to Hollywood.

One of the things that had delayed the talkie takeover in America was the matter of how pictures with sound should be prepared for foreign distribution. Silence had been the international language of the movies; it had been simple enough to provide title cards in other languages for foreign distribution—from America to Europe primarily, but also from Europe to America. A tentative resolution was to shoot several versions of the same story film more or less simultaneously, in different languages. Such procedure did not become a common studio practice after all, and the experiment was abandoned altogether within two years. But for a while it created new opportunities for French and German actors particularly, because revenue from those countries was vital to Hollywood commerce. There was a shortage in Hollywood of actors who could speak foreign languages, so many European actors now were packing up and going to Hollywood, speculating on another gold rush. Others were receiving specific invitations, and Charles Boyer was one of them.

Early during the run of *Melo,* Boyer received a visitor from Hollywood who spoke excellent French—Paul Bern, an emissary for Metro-Goldwyn-Mayer's young production chief, Irving Thalberg. Boyer was invited to come to Hollywood to make the French talking versions of some ambitious M-G-M projects. Bern's intimation was that Boyer could begin as Greta Garbo's leading man in *The Kiss,* then foreseen as her talkie debut, the expectation being that the multilingual Garbo would speak her own French. Boyer accepted the proposition because the salary—four hundred dollars a week —seemed enormous to him; and because many of his friends would be there, having accepted similar offers. Maurice Chevalier had already gone.

Boyer was not comfortable about this latest development, however. He dreaded going to a country where the language was utterly foreign to him. He could converse in German, Italian, Spanish, and Portuguese but knew absolutely no English and had consciously avoided learning it. Most Parisians had at least a rudimentary acquaintance with English, and Boyer's ignorance of the language betrayed his provincial origin. Still, he liked Paul Bern, who in any event was not urging a term contract upon him. If Charles didn't like Hollywood, he wouldn't have to stay.

So Boyer crossed the Atlantic for the first time; there would soon be so many voyages that he would lose count. By coincidence, two of his sailing companions were already his very good friends—Jacques Feyder, an established director into whose intimate circle Boyer had insinuated himself, and Françoise Rosay, Feyder's wife. A greater coincidence was that Feyder was going to Hollywood to direct Greta Garbo in *The Kiss*. He was delighted to learn that Boyer would be in the picture—something Paul Bern had not told him.

Françoise Rosay hoped to do some French versions for M-G-M or Paramount or both; they were the Hollywood studios with ambitious plans for multilanguage versions. Boyer adored Françoise, as most men did. She was a "man's woman" —warm, easy, companionable, and supremely intelligent, besides being a fine actress. Boyer once said "I had vowed never to marry, but I would have married Françoise in a moment if she hadn't already been taken." She was older than Charles by several years, and indeed had a maternal attitude toward him. So she became his Hollywood mother, and also his co-star.

Charles Boyer did not appear with Garbo in *The Kiss* because no French or any other talking version was made of it. Irving Thalberg's judgment was that the divine Swede was not yet sufficiently practiced in English to be subjected to a talkie, so Feyder directed the only version of *The Kiss* as an entirely silent picture—the last one filmed in Hollywood, other than some caprices of Charlie Chaplin. So Boyer was assigned instead to *Le Procès du Mary Dugan*, a courtroom drama and essentially a photographed stage play. *The Trial of Mary Dugan* had been filmed some months earlier, and was still playing in American theaters when the French version was made. It was a prodigious hit in America, launching the illustrious talkie career of Thalberg's wife, Norma Shearer; so Thalberg had the sets dusted off in expectation of a similar success in France. The French version was filmed quickly and efficiently, and Boyer found it an odd experience, rather like acting onstage without an audience. It was an enjoyable occasion, though, because Mary Dugan was none other than Françoise Rosay.

His first stay in Hollywood was only for a few weeks—days given to shooting, evenings spent mostly in the company of the Feyders. He had opportunity to watch Jacques Feyder direct *The Kiss,* and he met Greta Garbo. He also met Irving Thalberg briefly, with Paul Bern acting as their interpreter.

Before *Le Procès du Mary Dugan* had completed filming, Boyer had received an offer to go to Germany, again to act in French-language versions, this time for Germany's prodigious UFA company. The money was no better than what M-G-M offered, if as good; but there was no indication that M-G-M would retain him, and since he was not really content in Hollywood he decided to take the UFA offer as a means of getting back to Europe at someone else's expense. He was glad to have made the trip to Hollywood, to see what it was like, but he did not expect to be back.

He traveled by rail to New York, and before sailing for Bremerhaven he visited with Chevalier, who was filming *The Love Parade* at a Paramount studio on Long Island. Boyer met its director, the great Ernst Lubitsch; and he found it all very exciting—a motion picture that was talking (and singing) but not lazily imitating the methods of the stage. And Chevalier was blooming: he adored America and its people, but more especially he adored *all thees mon-ee.* He said, "Really, Charles, you must begin to speak a little English."

❋   ❋   ❋

The German project was called *Brand in der Oper,* but in French, as *La Barcarolle d'Amour,* it was technically the first talking picture to be exhibited in France—early in 1930, beating the first wave of native French talkies only by a matter of days. It was a considerable *succès d'estime* that was almost meaningless for Boyer, who was already into his second Hollywood adventure before it had been shown, and was typically morose over what had developed.

Impressed by the filmmaking discipline of the UFA studio in Berlin, Boyer had signed a contract to make two additional films there following *Barcarolle d'Amour*. Then M-G-M bought up his UFA contract, so anxious was Irving Thalberg to get Boyer back to Hollywood. When Thalberg screened *Le Procès du Mary Dugan*, he was regaled by every aspect of the Boyer screen persona—especially the voice, but also the face and by what he beheld as unmistakable star presence. Boyer was not excited by the prospect of returning to Hollywood, until he learned his salary was to be a thousand dollars a week.

Irving Thalberg took personal charge of Boyer, with the aim of developing him into an M-G-M star. He encouraged him to accelerate his study of English, even offering to provide a tutor. Boyer preferred to learn the language on his own, but he intended to be cooperative; he really liked Thalberg, who impressed him as an intelligent fellow truly interested in making fine motion pictures.

Boyer's new M-G-M assignment was the French version of *The Big House,* but Thalberg's long-range plan was to begin building Boyer for American audiences in the American editions as soon as he had some proficiency in English. Indeed, Thalberg had decided to discontinue the practice of duplicate versions, which had proved impractical. Dubbing of American films into foreign languages, which had been introduced by the Swedes, was becoming the preferred practice, and it was certainly more practical. *The Big House* was one of the last Hollywood projects to get the multilingual treatment, and they were shot more or less simultaneously, in studio sets and an actual prison, in four versions—English, French, German, and Spanish. Bedlam prevailed on the shooting sets, but somehow a good picture got made. Paul Fejos, a talented and sensitive Hungarian, directed both the French and German editions. *The Big House* was a major hit in America, but hardly more so than the French edition entitled *Revolte dans la Prison.* Boyer, enacting the inmate protagonist that Chester Morris played in the American original, gave a strong, somber portrayal that eventually earned considerable applause in France.

He began to enjoy himself in the filmland. There was a lively French colony in Hollywood, consisting mainly of actors employed for the French versions, most of them soon to be seeking work elsewhere. Boyer had a little romance with Sandra Ravel, an actress in the French paraphrase of *Slightly Scarlet,* a Paramount melodrama. His new friends included such well-assimilated French folk as Adolphe Menjou, Claudette Colbert, and the veteran director Louis Gasnier. He enjoyed an extended stay as Maurice Chevalier's house guest in a mansion with a swimming pool. He was also making good money, but was beginning to fret because he wasn't earning it.

After *The Big House* there was nothing. Thalberg asked him to be patient, but patience was not an aspect of the Boyer character; and he only rarely saw Thalberg, the only person in Hollywood who seemed interested in him. Finally he was assigned his first English-speaking role, in *Daybreak* from the Arthur Schnitzler play. It was only a small part in support of Ramon Novarro, but it figured to be an important picture, and Feyder was the director. Boyer was gratified to learn that most of the actors cast had foreign accents. He reported for work and even got measured for a costume, then learned that there were script difficulties and his part had been written out. So there was more prolonged waiting, and it began to grind him down. Boyer believed that it was this idleness in 1931 that turned him into a four-packs-a-day chain smoker. When he could stand it no longer, he pleaded with Thalberg to be released from his contract. Thalberg asked him to be patient a while longer, and soon they'd have something.

But it was Françoise Rosay who rescued Boyer from his prolonged inactivity. After *Mary Dugan,* she had made several other of Hollywood's "foreign" editions, including one with Chevalier. But foreign-language versions had been abandoned, and Françoise was now looking for work in the regular studio product. At Paramount she landed a second lead in *The Magnificent Lie,* a Ruth Chatterton vehicle that was set partly in France but was shot entirely on the Hollywood sound stages. When she learned that a minor role requiring a

French actor remained uncast, Françoise made a strong recommendation for Boyer and urged him to put in a bid.

For an American debut, it was anything but historic. Boyer in the unsympathetic role of an actor–con man, participated in a cruel deception of the leading man—Ralph Bellamy, in his own inauspicious debut. At least Boyer was supposed to be charming in a sinister way. He missed that quality, although his English was coherent. He disliked the role and was resentful that the director—the Viennese Berthold Viertel, who was "bertlevertle" to the Hollywood folk—paid no attention to characterization. Boyer was not surprised when *The Magnificent Lie* flopped, setting Ruth Chatterton's career on a downward trajectory. It also proved to be Françoise Rosay's last American picture for twenty years.

At his own urging, Boyer was taken off salary by M-G-M, which set him free to return to Europe. There he sensed that his status had diminished during, and because of, his American hiatus. His strategy was to throw himself into work with the zeal of someone starting from bottom. Commuting between Paris and Berlin, he was certainly busy. The UFA studio, still making French duplicates of German originals, put Boyer in three—*Tumultes; F.P. 1 Ne Répond Plus;* and *Moi et L'Impératrice*. The latter, charmingly retitled from *Ich und die Kaiserin,* also had an English version, and Boyer's primitive English was good enough to get him also in that one—called *The Only Girl* in Britain, again with Lilian Harvey who was in the German original.

Sandwiched between these kaiser rolls were meaty French plays—*La Nocce* and *L'Homme à l'Hispano*. There were French film offers which Boyer rejected as inferior, and he was bitter that the Hollywood exile had deprived him of the *Melo* film . . . which Pierre Blanchar played to some acclaim. This was a stormy time for Boyer. The actor who at thirty seemed poised on the threshold of greatness had a failure complex at thirty-two. He loathed Hollywood but desired revenge, needing success in American films because it was so hard for him to accept or admit defeat.

In times of such desperation, one is tempted to do desperate things—like get married. Boyer might have married Alice

Field at about this time, had she welcomed the prospect. In earlier years they had conducted a fitful romance; now they were together constantly. Alice Field, of British origin but an assimilated Frenchwoman, was a pretty and clever young actress. She had been with Pierre Blanchar on both stage and screen, and it was through Blanchar that she met Charles Boyer. Later they acted together at the Gymnase, and Boyer came to appreciate her intelligence. Alice Field was politically alert, well-informed on world affairs, a serious reader; she was also a devotée of the musical arts. Boyer had always been responsive to symphonies, operas, and ballets, but Alice Field gave him the benefit of her greater expertise.

Their somewhat cerebral romance was often tense and argumentative. Alice exercised a sarcastic wit at Boyer's expense, and to his frequent irritation. Their relationship survived the bumps because neither felt a pressure to get married. Boyer had resolved early in his career never to marry. He believed that marriage was a sharing arrangement but that acting was by necessity a selfish profession. Half joking, he said actors shouldn't be allowed to marry. Alice Field agreed, saying that if she should marry it wouldn't be with an actor. Pierre Blanchar, though, believed that Boyer did earnestly propose marriage, and that Alice rejected him.

Would he otherwise have made yet another trip to Hollywood?

❊   ❊   ❊

He went back, answering a summons from Paramount that was instigated by Claudette Colbert. She was Clive Brook's costar in *The Man from Yesterday*, and Boyer would complete the fictional romantic triangle. For Claudette to persuade Boyer to return may have been more difficult than persuading Paramount to import him, but she managed on both counts.

Boyer hoped that no one at Paramount would recall his participation in *The Magnificent Lie*. That picture had become a special humiliation for him, especially after it was exhibited in France with another actor dubbing Boyer's small role in French. *The Magnificent Lie* had been shot fully a year earlier, and in that era of mass production—Paramount then was making sixty pictures a year—the routine pictures could be quickly forgotten. Indeed, it seemed that everyone had forgotten both that picture and Charles Boyer—except Berthold Viertel, who was to direct *The Man from Yesterday*. It was unfortunate for Boyer that at a time when Lubitsch, Sternberg, Mamoulian, and DeMille were all directing for Paramount, he should draw the lackluster Viertel for both his early assignments there. *The Man from Yesterday* was the last and possibly even the best of Viertel's handful of American films. Still, it wasn't very good.

Boyer had figured that it would be. Claudette Colbert was a rising Paramount player and Clive Brook an established leading man there—and currently displayed opposite Dietrich in Sternberg's sensational *Shanghai Express*. *The Man from Yesterday*, though, was formula junk. What lured Boyer back to Hollywood was a variation on the old Enoch Arden story of the husband coming home years after being presumed dead. Brook was the shell-shocked soldier and Colbert the "widow" who dallied with French doctor Boyer while believing her husband dead.

Half a century after its production, Boyer's sensitive performance could be assessed as the picture's only striking feature, particularly in the scene in which he advises Colbert to return to her husband. Yet the picture caused no stir at the time of its release, and was forgotten as easily as was *The Magnificent Lie*. When it later was shown in France with a dubbed soundtrack, Boyer spoke his own French, but it still resembled a come-down for him. At his own urging, another Hollywood picture he made at about the same time was not exhibited in France.

Boyer was in good spirits during his third visit to Hollywood, again the guest of Chevalier who was also filming at Paramount. He had a lively social life, not only with Chevalier's circle. He managed to get invited to a party at Marion Davies's Santa Monica beach house, and through Paul Bern met most of the M-G-M crowd. The cosmopolitan Bern, an M-G-M associate producer and one of Thalberg's more trusted lieutenants, had begun squiring the platinum blonde Jean Harlow, who was becoming a valuable studio property.

Joan Crawford and Clark Gable were there, as were Irving Thalberg and a pregnant Norma Shearer. That Boyer was conversing easily in English delighted Thalberg, who insisted he had never lost interest in Boyer and still believed they should get something going.

They got something going at the beach party, and Boyer later suspected that his friend Paul Bern had engineered the whole thing. A picture called *Red-Headed Woman* with a smart Anita Loos script had been bought for Joan Crawford but now was being fashioned as Jean Harlow's first M-G-M starring vehicle. Thalberg's inspiration was that Boyer should play the small but strategic role of Harlow's chauffeur. Although Boyer had only commenced shooting *The Man from Yesterday*, M-G-M could "work around" him until he was available. And money talked: Thalberg's interpretation was that Boyer was still on leave of absence from an M-G-M contract, and his salary could be restored at a thousand a week—considerably more than Paramount was paying him.

Boyer would recall that "I liked all of the people involved, but the reason I agreed to play the chauffeur was simply that it was an M-G-M picture. In France and everywhere else, M-G-M pictures seemed more important than those of any other company. I intended to do well in the Harlow picture, and then get larger roles at M-G-M. And perhaps more money. There was some talk of putting me in a picture opposite Helen Hayes. When Irving promised that *Red-Headed Woman* would not be shown in France, I said 'Yes, I'll do it.'"

With the passing of years *Red-Headed Woman* would become an embarrassment to Boyer similar to *The Magnificent Lie*, but it wasn't that in the summer of 1932. Released almost simultaneously with *The Man from Yesterday*, it gave Boyer the hint of an identity with American audiences. It was also a hit. *Red-Headed Woman* sealed the Harlow stardom; and in a manner of speaking, Charles Boyer got the girl. Harlow played a saucy shopgirl who marries her boss (Chester Morris) and then, failing to win acceptance in his social circle, runs off with her chauffeur. Boyer played his role with a roguish charm, and it indeed might have led to bigger and better things but for the unfortunate circumstances that ensued.

Shortly after completing *Red-Headed Woman,* Jean Harlow married Paul Bern; and only a few weeks later, Bern committed suicide. The later scandalous disclosures were that Bern was probably impotent and probably a bigamist as well. But Bern had been Irving Thalberg's closest friend, and after Bern's suicide Thalberg suffered a physical collapse and went off to Europe to recuperate. With both Bern and Thalberg removed from the scene, M-G-M had no more interest in Boyer. There was also an economic retrenchment in Hollywood, because of some audience defection to radio, and the M-G-M bookkeepers were curious that Boyer was still drawing a salary. He said he never knew he was under an option contract at M-G-M until he was informed that his option wasn't being picked up.

He was "the most miserable actor in town, hating Hollywood with all the hate I could muster." There were no other offers from Paramount or elsewhere. Boyer believed that in this period, progress was not really possible for him because he simply did not know how to play the Hollywood game. He inquired at other studios but found that if they knew who Charles Boyer was, they hardly cared. He later believed that if he'd had a Hollywood agent at the time, he might have landed a lead in a Janet Gaynor picture that Fox had some difficulty casting. Instead he lost out to a countryman, Henri Garat.

Again he could endure the destructive waiting only so long. Submitting to his deepest gloom, he packed his bags to go home. This time he paid his own passage.

❉   ❉   ❉

The Charles Boyer who returned to Paris in 1932 was morose and inconsolable. Jacques Feyder told him there was nothing so remarkable about failing in Hollywood; after all, he'd done so himself. Boyer's retort was that surely no one else had failed there three times in three years. There was no cheering him—not by Alice Field with whom he resumed his stormy liaison, nor by his mother who came from Figeac to spend the Christmas holiday with him.

At this low point he may have really believed, as he later claimed, that his career was over. But Henry Bernstein rode to the rescue with a new play. *Le Bonheur* was a lush romantic drama which Bernstein had been hoping might attract Pierre Fresnay, until Boyer showed up again in Paris. It became an emphatic personal success for Boyer and that surprised him: he had never considered romance his theatrical forte.

But he didn't go onstage with *Le Bonheur* just yet. Marcel L'Herbier, who had brought Boyer into films thirteen years earlier in *L'Homme du Large,* had a screen project all ready to go. Pierre Blanchar had agreed to make *L'Epervier* for L'Herbier, but was detained in Bordeaux with another film unit; and André Benim reminded L'Herbier that Boyer was back in Paris.

While they were filming *L'Epervier* in and around Paris, Boyer had a fleeting romance with his leading lady, Natalie Paley. He also had a hunch that Marcel L'Herbier, at the peak of his long career as a film director, might be interested in the play he was about to do. Boyer showed him the playscript of *Le Bonheur,* and L'Herbier contacted Henry Bernstein to plan a screen version. So when Boyer returned to the Paris stage in *Le Bonheur,* he already knew he would also be doing it as a film. He still grieved over having not been in the *Melo* film, and this would be his first opportunity to repeat one of his stage creations in a picture.

Bernstein's *Le Bonheur* became the theatrical event of Paris in the spring of 1933. During its engagement, the *L'Epervier* film opened and was also proclaimed a hit, and the combination had the effect of regaining for Boyer whatever ground he might have lost. Then, immediately after the play closed, Boyer and his leading lady—Gaby Morlay, a splendid actress —made the *Bonheur* film that also attained a fair success.

Although the word "comeback" was not invoked, Boyer was experiencing a new success in his homeland. His absence had made native hearts grow fonder. Quite suddenly he was the man of the moment in Paris. Consequently he became a desirable actor for different projected film subjects, and he chose to follow *Le Bonheur* with *La Bataille*.

It was the play he'd done many years earlier, but in a secondary role. It had also been filmed as a silent with Sessue Hayakawa, who still resided in Paris and had been figured for the talking version as well. But Boyer's new topicality enabled him to secure the lead role of the Japanese naval commander in what was foreseen as a prestige picture. Also putting on oriental makeup for *La Bataille* was the young and lovely Annabella, whose promise had been noted in René Clair's *Le Million*.

Then *La Bataille* became a curious Anglo-French venture with financial assistance from Alexander Korda. The English version was shot immediately following the French, as an accommodation to Korda's darkly beautiful protégée, Merle Oberon. An all-British cast was planned for the second version, but Boyer sold himself to the producers as an English-speaking Japanese Frenchman and appeared in both versions. Critical and popular success was the resolution for both *La Bataille* and *The Battle*, and Boyer's tragic portrayal was the strength of both versions. He preferred the French, sensing director Nicolas Farkas's visual preoccupation with Merle Oberon—a slant-eyed stunner in the English edition.

Nothing went wrong for him now. To be in a position to select his own screen properties was a luxury. He felt that where others often made errors of judgment in what plays or films he should do, *he* would make no mistake.

Boyer believed that to visualize a film-to-be by reading its script was a common and dangerous folly. He said "One must make only a literary judgment of a script. It is the director's job to make it cinematic." Even when others had only praise for his films and his performances, Boyer was often disappointed from his own, distinctly literary perspective. He believed that a conventional leading-man assignment limited an actor, therefore he fought against them: "Only writers can create meaningful roles, which able actors may endow with characterization."

Only rarely had he been pleased with a role on either stage

or screen, and he had become increasingly aware of the shallowness in Henry Bernstein's run of protagonists. That even applied to his role in *Le Bonheur*, although he was no less grateful for its success at exactly the right time for him. And when his filmmaking activity continued almost without pause, he chose to follow *La Bataille* with Ferenc Molnar's *Liliom* for several reasons.

The Hungarian play had literary substance, and a real attraction for Boyer was the character of Liliom himself. The carnival barker was no stick figure but a character of both color and complexity, the sort of bravura antihero Boyer had long wished to play. Yet he said he chose *Liliom* over several likely filmscripts that dangled before him "really as a political decision"—his own protest against Nazi Germany.

Hitler's Third Reich had seized power in Germany, and the more perceptive observers already knew that to be a Jew in Germany was no longer safe. Throughout 1933 Paris became a haven for the new refugees—German Jews who stole across the western border into France. Among the refugees were leading artists, musicians, writers, and filmmakers. Boyer was already acquainted with Erich Pommer from his filmmaking chores in Berlin only a few years earlier, and he knew Fritz Lang by his reputation, which was extraordinarily high. Pommer was the foremost impresario of German films throughout the twenties and into the talking period, but he was Jewish; and because Lang's mother was half-Jewish by birth, the Nazis would have no further need of the director of such masterworks as *Dr. Mabuse, Metropolis,* and *M.*

Most of the refugee filmmakers eventually made their way to Hollywood by way of London, but Paris was the first stop. The French film industry was compassionate, making every effort to accommodate the fleeing artists. *Liliom* was produced by Erich Pommer and directed by Fritz Lang, and was the only French project for either. Pommer soon began a notable association with Charles Laughton in England, and Fritz Lang's next picture would be *Fury,* an American classic.

Boyer had despised Hitler and the movement that grew around him, ever since the Munich beer-hall putsch. But if he made *Liliom* as an act of political conscience, it was surely a practical consideration that Lang was a resourceful and creative director. Their *Liliom* film would eventually be reckoned an honorable failure, although not the disaster that an earlier American version had been—a primitive Fox talkie with Charles Farrell. The fantasy element in *Liliom*, so effective theatrically, has steadily confounded its moviemakers, and Boyer would later wish he'd played Liliom on a stage instead. Still, the screen rendering was uncommonly vigorous for him; and the critical opinion was that young Madeleine Ozeray, who played Julie with a deficiency of spiritual substance, was sadly overmatched by him.

The filming had barely gotten under way when someone on the production scene suggested that Charles Boyer really looked too old to be playing the young barker. It was a matter of encroaching baldness. Boyer's hairline, unusually high to begin with, had begun to recede early, and was thinning ever more noticeably in his mid-thirties. His first production shots for *Liliom* were scrapped, and throughout the filming he wore a wig. Thereafter he never appeared on stage or screen without an expensive, custom-made toupee.

He regretted in later years that even with artificial hair he was too old to make *Liliom* as an American film with Ingrid Bergman, who had played Julie on the stage and for whom the Molnar play was a special joy. Despite the limited success of the French film, Boyer on several occasions said that Liliom was his favorite of all the roles he had played on stage or screen. Transmogrified, it also became his favorite work in the musical theater. More than ten years after he made the picture for Fritz Lang, Boyer was in New York cheering the opening-night performance on Broadway of Rodgers and Hammerstein's *Carousel,* wherein Liliom became an American layabout named Billy Bigelow.

When the film of *Liliom* opened in Paris in 1934, Boyer was not on the scene and the critical reception was somewhat irrelevant. He was also about to prove that he could make a literary judgment between two scripts, and make a mistake.

He almost became involved with another refugee filmmaker from Nazi Germany; and then did, with yet another one. Anatole Litvak, a young Russian Jew who had become one of the leading directors of the German cinema before the Nazi take-over, was one of the first to flee and was making his way smartly in the French industry. He and Boyer had not yet become acquainted, but he had seen several Boyer screen projections and had admired the Boyer stage account in *Le Bonheur*. It was probably André Benim who brought them together, to consider a film project for which Litvak sought Boyer's participation. Boyer read a treatment for *Cette Vieille Canaille*, and was not favorably disposed toward the triangular drama that he said was one part *Pygmalion* and one part *He Who Gets Slapped:* elderly man transforms street gamine into a lady, but loses her to the young acrobat who has loved her all along. Boyer thanked Litvak politely, certain that he could find something more stimulating than the acrobat in *Cette Vieille Canaille*.

He had a change of heart, though, and perhaps a change of instinct, when he read in a newspaper that Harry Baur would play the character role in Litvak's forthcoming film. Baur was a powerful actor, a titan of the French cinema, just beginning to be challenged by the younger Louis Jouvet. Boyer was eager to play with Baur, and reached Litvak by phone to say he'd changed his mind. Another meeting was arranged; and on the information that the female role had not been cast, Boyer took Alice Field with him to meet Litvak.

Boyer would have made *Cette Vieille Canaille* but for the intervention of another refugee of sorts, although Erich Charell was not Jewish. In Germany he had gained some celebrity as a stage director, mostly of operettas. He had made only one film but it was an early-talkie blockbuster on an international scale: *Der Kongress Tanzt*, or *The Congress Dances* as it was known in America and England—a smart showcase for the British-born, German-bred Lilian Harvey, who was now a flop in Hollywood after arriving there amid much fanfare. Boyer had filmed with Lilian Harvey in Berlin, and while there had also met Erich Charell: an extravagant personality whose only film had emulated his own glitter.

When Charell met Boyer socially in Paris, he was en route to Hollywood to undertake his first screen venture since *Der Kongress Tanzt*. He boasted of an unlimited budget and other accommodations that were being made for him to create a masterpiece of a movie. He also summarized the plot, about the love life of an itinerant gypsy who also happened to play the violin. When Boyer asked what lucky actor would be taking that role, Charell said "I'd be happy to have Monsieur Charles Boyer in the part . . . furthermore, I can arrange it."

One might have supposed that Boyer would have resisted any effort to get him back to Hollywood. But generals defeated in war yearn to recapture the territory they have surrendered. Charles Boyer apparently believed that his success was synthetic until it had an indelible endorsement in Hollywood. And after all, the project was not as negligible as *The Magnificent Lie,* or as the role of Jean Harlow's chauffeur. The picture that Charell said would be called *Caravan* was what they called "major" and promised a prodigious star part that he could play.

He told Charell he'd like to do it, and Charell said he'd go on to Hollywood and make the necessary preparations. Boyer attempted to apologize to Anatole Litvak, as he bowed out of *Cette Vieille Canaille* on the very eve of its production. He protested that *Caravan* was simply a more substantial opportunity, one he'd be foolish to squander. But Litvak was furious.

Cette Vieille Canaille earned a considerable *succès d'estime* in France and around the world, and Boyer came to regard his defection as a major professional mistake. The picture was a triumph for Harry Baur, with whom Boyer had forfeited his only opportunity to work. There were other ironies: the female lead was played by Alice Field, whom Anatole Litvak took as his mistress; and the actor who replaced Boyer as the romantic acrobat was his friendly rival, Pierre Blanchar.

Caravan would be quite another story. Considering everything, however, when Charles Boyer went to Hollywood for the fourth time he got much more than he had bargained for.

4

They both remembered the day they met.

It was January 23, 1934, a Tuesday. Boyer could pinpoint the date because he had arrived in town on the weekend; and after taking rooms in the Hollywood Hotel, had checked into the old Fox studio on Western Avenue only the day before.

A small luncheon party was arranged at the studio, ostensibly to celebrate the completion of *David Harum,* a Will Rogers picture. But it was also an occasion for Boyer to meet some of the studio personnel, none of whom seemed to know he'd been in Hollywood previously. Winfield Sheehan, the production chief and luncheon host, introduced Boyer to some of the studio functionaries, as well as several actors— Will Rogers, himself; Phillips Holmes, who was to join Boyer in the cast of *Caravan;* and some players from a picture called *Bottoms Up* that was shooting on an adjacent set.

One of them was Spencer Tracy, an actor he recognized. Another was a blond young lady he was certain he'd never seen in a film. She had the unusual name of Pat Paterson, and all during lunch he couldn't keep his eyes off her . . . and was aware that she seemed to be staring at him.

By his account, they chatted informally. By hers, they hadn't spoken until she heard his mellow-accented voice on the telephone that evening, asking if she were free for dinner. By her account, she already had a dinner date but broke it, to give the Frenchman encouragement. By his, she kept her other date and put him off until the weekend—after which, however, they were seeing one another every night, besides which he was conspiring to be near her at the studio by day.

After that, their versions coincided. Theirs was a whirlwind courtship, and it was difficult to tell who was courting whom. It had taken them both quite by surprise.

It developed that Boyer had arrived in Hollywood sooner than he was needed. After Erich Charell had cleared Boyer's participation in *Caravan* and wired him to come on to America, the production was delayed indefinitely while Charell went off to find suitable shooting locations. Boyer wasn't idle in any event. He had to negotiate a contract with Winfield Sheehan, and he was also turned over to studio publicists and photographers to prepare the *Caravan* drum-beating well in advance. But he had time to spare, and the best use of it was to spend it with Pat Paterson.

The Boyer romantic history would seem to validate his claim that he'd never been in love before. It was some years later that he told the redoubtable Louella Parsons: "I believed I was past the age of falling in love. It was something that happened to younger men, and as a younger man I made every effort not to do it. I could not afford love, and I was selfish enough to avoid it."

There had always been women in his life, after his belated start as a *boulevardier*. When he became a preening Paris gentleman in tailor-made clothes, pretty women were a necessary adornment, a part of his costume. Beyond that, he was too discreet about his private affairs to invite a suspicion of serious involvement. In his days on the Parisian stage it was a pattern that his leading ladies fell in love with him but lost interest because he was not encouraging, or because he was stuffy, or for both reasons. He had briefly pursued Marie Bell, an emerging major actress in French films, but she was not receptive. There were brief minor romances in Berlin, Hollywood, and probably elsewhere, because he had come to enjoy the company of women. No meaning had been attached to any of them. The romance with Alice Field was more abrasive than sweet, and most remarkable for its off-and-on durability. But now, caught off balance, he was decidedly, excitedly in love.

It delighted him just to know they both were in surroundings as strange to her as they were to him; indeed, even stranger—she had preceded him to Hollywood only by a few weeks, and it was her first time in America. She expected to stay, however: she was the consensus favorite to be the next big star of Fox Films.

✽ ✽ ✽

Patricia Paterson was her real name, and she had been born in 1910 in the textile city of Bradford, in Yorkshire, thirty miles northeast of Manchester.

The Patersons were of the lower middle class, and her father was a wool merchant. She was Patricia only within her family circle; to everyone else she was Patsy or Patty, and then just Pat. A buoyant, demonstrative child, she was easily given to performing.

Her mother, seeking to capitalize on Patricia's aggressive charm and blond cuteness, pushed her onto the stage early. Pat was delighted; she loved anything that had to do with dancing, even the lessons. She started tap at age five and ballet at eight. Before she was ten she had joined the *Babes in the Wood* musical pantomime.

During the early postwar years it was a phenomenon in almost every British city. Pat stayed in the Bradford edition of *Babes in the Wood* for five years, evolving from a moppet into a willowy nymph. Her hair darkened only slightly. She remained a pretty blonde rather than a beautiful one, but *very* pretty: a mischievous pixie with dancing green eyes, who seemed tall only because she was so remarkably slender.

There was some trouble at home over her boy-craziness. Her father decided it was time to remove her from the show, even at the sacrifice of what was part of the family income. Instead Pat ran away from home with a boy in the company, and it was only years later that she was reconciled with her family. She and her young man struck out for London and she had what would later be recalled as "a typically tawdry misadventure," but only for a while. The boy deserted her.

Left to her own resources, she got work in a third-rate music hall, rented a cheap flat with another chorine, ate poorly, and put most of her slim wages toward dancing and singing lessons. She wanted to rise and be good.

She was good, and she rose. At seventeen she won a spot in a West End revue, *Stop Flirting*. In musical comedy she graduated from the chorus of *Queen High* to a featured role in *The Swordsman*, and was making a name for herself. Then she had a lead in one of the later André Charlot revues, and got into British pictures when the talkies came in.

She sang and danced in routine musical pictures—*Partners, Please; The Great Gay Road; Here's George*. She also proved herself a good-enough actress in sausage melodrama—*The Professional Guest; Night Shadows; Murder on the Second Floor*. By the time she was twenty-two she was a well-known player if not quite a star, with her own growing fandom—but only in England. The Hungarian immigrant Alexander Korda was only then beginning to transform the British film industry into respectability. British pictures were no match for their French, German, and Swedish counterparts, and comparison with the American product was humiliating. Few British films were exported, and American audiences had not caught so much as a glimpse of Pat Paterson until the summer of 1933, when *Bitter Sweet* was exhibited in the major cities.

This wasn't the later Jeanette MacDonald–Nelson Eddy version that so appalled Noël Coward, but Herbert Wilcox's proper English production with Anna Neagle and Fernand Gravet. Pat had a subordinate role but sparkled in it, and it was her first exposure in a lavishly scaled project. American audiences were rather indifferent to this *Bitter Sweet*, but Fox's Robert Kane believed that Pat had stolen the show—the only performer direct enough and bubbly enough to connect with American moviegoers.

Robert Kane was a studio gadfly who had once headed the Paramount operation in Paris but now was a Fox producer with tangent portfolio as a talent scout. Kane had taken on a specific responsibility to find a talented virtuoso performer— preferably a girl, young and unknown—to be developed as a star in Fox musical films. Musicals had been done to death in the first two years of the American talkies, and disappeared altogether—until Warner Brothers revived them with the Busby Berkeley cycle of backstage musicals initiated with *42nd Street* early in 1933. Musicals were restored to fashion, and every other studio was searching for a Ruby Keeler equivalent. Fox signed youngsters such as Dixie Dunbar and Sylvia Froos on speculation, as well as a blond thrush named Alice Faye and the five-year-old Shirley Temple. But when Bob Kane urged Winnie Sheehan and Fox casting director Phil Friedman to take a look at Pat Paterson in *Bitter Sweet*, they all agreed they'd found their star-to-be.

They signed her in London and it required no coaxing; almost every player in British films coveted nothing so much as a ticket to Hollywood. It was the new standard agreement, a seven-year contract with a one-year guarantee, and six options, beginning at five hundred dollars a week but with escalations, and clauses for renegotiation if stardom should be attained. Pat was delirious; it was more money than she'd ever hoped to earn. She said she didn't remember how she got to America, and supposed she'd just floated there.

There was fanfare on her arrival. She was billeted in the ostentatious Hollywood Hotel at the studio's expense until she moved into a new luxury apartment which they helped her find, on Van Ness Avenue near the studio. In November they introduced her to the Hollywood press, and she was set up for profiles in the fan magazines. Then she was thrilled by the announcement that she would be Spencer Tracy's leading lady in her first American picture. He had not yet moved into the front rank of movie players, but everyone in England knew who Spencer Tracy was, and she knew they'd be impressed. They began shooting *Bottoms Up* after the new year came in.

In January of 1934 she was undoubtedly ripe for a real romance. She had always enjoyed the company of men, and in England had rejected one marriage proposal after another. The career came first. She didn't rule out marriage, but said it must wait until she'd "arrived" in her profession. Now Fox Films had given her good reason to believe she'd arrived . . .

They wanted to get her into the public eye, and during her first weeks in Hollywood she was photographed in the fancy-dress nightspots, usually in the company of young bachelors also recently signed by Fox Films—a publicity ploy. Anyway, she had no special gentleman friend when she went to the little studio party and bumped into Charles Boyer.

They were their own proof that opposites attract, and they certainly complemented one another. Boyer was soft-spoken, never boisterous, given to sly little smiles, an acknowledged introvert. Pat Paterson was not loud, but she was merry, laughing when there was nothing to laugh about, and talking, talking—always directing the conversational traffic. She was talking, too, in the most beguiling English accent Boyer had listened to. And then there was *his* accent: Pat said it made her fall in love with him before she knew anything else about him.

Her only disappointment had been that he had never heard of her; but then, she'd never heard of him, either.

* * *

Twenty-two days after they met, they got married. It was an impulsive thing for both of them, and rather a lark; on the drive to Yuma, neither really expected to go through with it.

It stunned the people at Fox Films, who didn't even realize that Pat Paterson had entered into a romance with the French actor. The only person in whom Pat had confided was Herbert Mundin, a British character actor in the picture with her, and a self-appointed surrogate father. After their affair attained a nocturnal stability, Boyer ceased to inhabit the *Bottoms Up* set by day, so as to discourage suspicion of what was really happening.

The romance had a clandestine aura. At the end of the day's shooting he would wait for her in his car at a discreet distance from the studio gate, and drive her home. Pat had no car and couldn't drive until he taught her, in their first weekend together. A Plymouth roadster had been entrusted to him by Fox Films, and they made long evening drives up the Pacific Coast Highway.

They also dated conventionally and fashionably, with dinner and dancing, and they saw some movies; Boyer was distressed that there was practically no legitimate theater in all of Los Angeles. Boyer renewed the few social contacts he still had in the filmland, and introduced Pat to Maurice Chevalier. They also dined out with Adolphe Menjou and his fiancée, Verree Teasdale. But wherever they went by themselves they were unrecognized, because neither was a familiar face for American moviegoers.

Mostly they just talked while sipping white wine in Pat's apartment. She told him about industrial Yorkshire and he told her about pastoral Lot. He told her about Paris and also Berlin, Rome, Bucharest, and all the places where he'd lost money gambling. She told him about London, which he hadn't visited except in transit.

They talked about their aspirations as artists. He confessed his disappointment in what he had achieved as an actor; he had envisioned a much higher artistic attainment. Pat had known no disappointment, and indeed no setbacks. She was less idealistic than Boyer, and not really an actress but an entertainer. If she could entertain and get rich doing it and be famous, that would be enough. She was excited about *Bottoms Up*. American moviemaking was easily superior to the British, and the Fox regimentation awed her. She rated *Bottoms Up* as the best thing that had happened to her, a likely professional turning point. Boyer counted on *Caravan*'s being as vital for himself, and Pat remarked that they were really in the same boat. He said yes, but one of us is so much older.

He was thirty-four; she was twenty-three.

Pat said they also talked about marriage—not about getting married, or about being married to one another, but more abstractly about marriage itself. Each had decided that marriage had no place in their lives. Boyer said the only possible reason he would marry would be to have children; every Frenchman wants to have a son. Pat liked children, but said she had a "dancer's premonition" about not being able to bear children.

They decided they had every reason not to get married . . . and then they did it. *Bottoms Up* finished shooting on a Saturday in that era of the six-day moviemaking week. There was another party at the studio, but without so illustrious a presence as Will Rogers. Winfield Sheehan was again present and rather surprised to see Boyer there as Pat's guest. Boyer also met the *Bottoms Up* director, David Butler, and some of the other cast members—among them John Boles and Thelma Todd, as well as Spencer Tracy and Herbert Mundin. It was a rollicking affair, indicating that most of them thought they had a hit. Sheehan had a present for Pat: a two-week vacation before she was to report for her second Fox picture. Leaving the party, Boyer said "I suppose that means we have to get married right away."

They joked about it, and almost applied for a license. Through what was left of their second weekend together they talked about what if they were married and making films in different countries. They resolved nothing, but on the following Wednesday they decided to drive across the border into Yuma, Arizona, where they could get married without a wait . . . simply because it was Valentine's Day and it seemed appropriate.

They were married by a justice of the peace and spent their wedding night in a Yuma motel. Pat believed that in the three weeks of their acquaintance and hectic courtship, not one disagreeable word had been issued by either of them: "No, we never really had a fight until the next day, on the drive back from Yuma." Even such minor tiffs that they both insisted were few would almost never be witnessed by a third party.

The newlyweds notified the studio and a few friends. Maurice Chevalier, the champion bachelor, gave them a reception a few days later. An announcement was prepared for the press by Fox Films, but subsequent newspaper stories were brief and not prominently featured; neither party was known to the general public. Pat Paterson's status as a new Fox player was noted, but not Boyer's. He had not resolved the terms for his participation in *Caravan,* but the novelty of getting married made that seem a less important matter to him.

He moved out of the Hollywood Hotel and into Pat's apartment, until they could find a suitable larger place. And Pat wanted a house.

*   *   *

Before they were married, Boyer marked time during Pat's shooting schedule by finding a Hollywood agent. If he was not well-known to the American public, he was an international show-business figure to reckon with. All the agents knew who Charles Boyer was, and many sought to represent him in his American dealings. Knowingly, he put them into competition with one another. He met with all the leading filmland agents—Nat Goldstone, Arthur Landau, Frank Orsatti, Leo Morrison. He was not merely interested in learning what they might do for him, or by what methods. He wanted to know something of their character. Adolphe Menjou urged him to affiliate with Joyce-Selznick and introduced Boyer to Myron Selznick. With Frank Joyce as partner, David Selznick's brother ran the agency that had the most bargaining clout and the filmdom's most illustrious client list. Boyer sensed that what Myron Selznick did for his clients would always be motivated by a drive for personal power. He did not have to tell Menjou that he didn't *like* Selznick, who, in the first place, had not really offered to represent him.

But he liked Charles Feldman. In a partnership with the Sam Jaffe who wasn't the actor, Feldman operated a middle-sized agency with a small but select client list that included Claudette Colbert, Richard Barthelmess, Joan Bennett, Elissa Landi, Leon Errol, and Samuel Goldwyn's new Russian import, Anna Sten. Unlike most of the agents Boyer assessed, Feldman seemed to have read a book or two and perhaps could distinguish a dry wine from a sweet one. They had a handshake agreement, and Boyer invited Feldman to negotiate a one-picture contract with Fox Films. Under no circumstances would he sign a term contract that would bind him to the company beyond the *Caravan* project.

The free-lance player was almost nonexistent in the star circle. Fredric March left Paramount in 1934 to become the first successful free-lancer among players in the top rank, and Irene Dunne and Cary Grant were only a few years behind him. But they were all solidly established. If Boyer had a discernible track record in Hollywood it was a negligible one, and the people at Fox gave Charles Feldman a hard time. They could be generous financially, but for a multi-picture arrangement, not just one film. Boyer, though, was a gambler by avocation, and so was Charlie Feldman. They both understood the nature of bluffing. Boyer realized that he might eventually sign for two or three pictures, for nothing was going to prevent him from making *Caravan;* but he wouldn't capitulate until it was necessary. And it never became necessary. Erich Charell, who had become Erik for American consumption, had returned to the studio screaming that Boyer was indispensable and had to be signed; why had they brought him there in the first place? So Feldman proposed an unreasonable fee for *Caravan,* and there was a compromise. Boyer would receive forty thousand dollars for what would probably amount to seven weeks of work. That was considerably more than Pat Paterson would earn under her Fox contract for a full year; and pro-rated on a weekly basis, it was comparable to what America's leading box-office stars were earning.

The contract was signed in early March, but with Charell still making elaborate preparations, including a lot of purely scenic photography, the summons for the actors was still a month away. There were casting items in Louella's column: Jean Parker would appear with Boyer in *Caravan;* then, so would Loretta Young in what was being shaped as a desert-based romantic triangle drama.

Charles did not mind the wait: he and Pat had more time together than they had counted on. Pat was to have returned from her vacation and honeymoon to take a second lead in *Change of Heart,* a Fox item reuniting the team of Janet Gaynor and Charles Farrell. It was a big-budget picture and Pat was supposed to "get" James Dunn, another prominent Fox player, in the end. Instead Ginger Rogers got James Dunn. Sheehan notified Pat that she was being replaced in *Change of Heart* while another musical more on the lines of *Bottoms Up* was made ready for her. She wasn't told openly that Fox officials were apprehensive about her showing in the debut film.

Bottoms Up had been edited and previewed in the fast, efficient rhythm of the studio operation, and the preview audience reaction was mysterious. They hadn't disliked *Bottoms Up,* but hadn't liked it either; and there was no negative comment about Pat Paterson but also not *enough* comment about

Newlyweds Charles Boyer and Pat Paterson in Hollywood in 1934.

Publicity photo of Pat Paterson as an aspiring Hollywood actress.

Pat Paterson in a musical turn with John Boles in *Bottoms Up*, her American screen debut for Fox Films.

The Boyers aboard ship in 1936, returning from Europe after the filming of *Mayerling.*

Charles and Pat photographed with Norma Shearer at a sneak preview of *Tovarich* at Warners' Hollywood Theater in October 1937.

The actor with his mother, Louise Durand Boyer, in Hollywood.

Boyer and Gary Cooper mingle with servicemen as wartime camp entertainers.

Boyer with Adolphe Menjou, for many years his closest friend in Hollywood, until their political estrangement.

Boyer with friend and costar Ingrid Bergman at the Brown Derby in 1947.

On Broadway in 1953: Boyer and Mary Martin in *Kind Sir*.

The annual stockholders' meeting of Four Star Productions in 1954: Dick Powell, Charles Boyer, and David Niven.

Boyer with S. N. Behrman, his *Lord Pengo* playwright, in 1963.

Michael Boyer in 1964.

her. And that was the case when the picture went into national release toward the end of March. Neither a hit nor a flop, it was an enjoyable but forgettable musical, certainly not one to linger in the memory as the Warner extravaganzas did. It had an appealing score by Burton Lane and Harold Adamson, but the songs as delivered mainly by Pat Paterson and John Boles failed to become hits. The box-office response to the picture proved only ordinary.

Spencer Tracy wasn't Pat's "leading man" after all, playing what was very nearly a character part as a show producer—top-billed but functionally in a subordinate role, and distinctly unhappy about it; Tracy was an embattled actor at Fox with a periodic drinking problem, and his days there were numbered, although at M-G-M he would soon become one of the glories of his profession. Pat's leading man in *Bottoms Up,* and a rather bland one, was the John Boles who appeared to have just stepped out of a collar ad. Mainly, though, the picture clearly had been shaped around Pat, and her employers were puzzled that there was no apparent public reaction to her. They continued to "build" her, and finally put her back to work in a musical entitled *Call It Luck* that might have been a lot like *Bottoms Up* but was produced on a smaller scale, a distinctly minor musical. The one after that would be even smaller.

It wasn't immediately seen that she was a flop, but in pictures that was finally what you were if you weren't a hit. It could not have occurred to her or to anyone else in 1934 that her screen career which was thought to be just beginning was nearing its end.

It also would not have occurred to her, because it was done innocently and without conscious design, that she was commencing the transformation of Charles Boyer.

❋   ❋   ❋

Where *Bottoms Up* had been the sort of mildly disappointing picture that comes and goes and leaves no unpleasant aftertaste, *Caravan* was something else. More than a failure, it was a horrendous flop, one of Hollywood's fabled disasters of the thirties.

That resolution did not come as a shock to Boyer who had seen it coming all along, from the beginning of production. Only a few interior scenes were filmed in a studio, at Fox's Movietone Center. Most of the picture was shot in sandy California and New Mexico deserts, and the production was chaotic, to Boyer's utter bewilderment. Samson Raphaelson's script possessed a certain literacy that had appealed to Boyer, but it was melodramatic hokum and he knew it. His difficulty, which finally translated into deadly conflict, was with Charell, who kept urging Boyer toward a gaudy kind of acting that lacked motivation, and to scowl a lot and make grotesque faces.

The other players shared his discontent, but it was not so important to them. Loretta Young, although only twenty-one, had started early in pictures and had already been in scores of them; she'd been in some hits and misses, and could survive *Caravan* and other misadventures without jeopardizing her standing. Jean Parker was also an established player at a more modest level. Phillips Holmes, who had started promisingly but faded quickly, was just hanging on and might easily have reasoned that *Caravan* could be no worse than his picture that preceded it, Anna Sten's disastrous *Nana*.

Loretta Young was the countess who fell in love with the gypsy fiddler, Jean Parker was his Romany sweetheart, and beyond that it was difficult for the players to know what their picture was about—and more difficult still for the Fox executives to comprehend after they had put it all together and given it a screening. Uncertain over what to do with it, they deferred its release until September. They made a game bid to sell it as an offbeat prestige picture, and prepared display ads that were impressive feats of draftsmanship. They even managed to get a picture of the curly-wigged Charles Boyer into *Vanity Fair*.

All to no avail. The *Caravan* episode passed into history, and Fox may have been grateful that it wasn't obliged to use Boyer in any more pictures. It finished off the amazing Erik Charell, whose career as director showed one international smash hit and a comparable flop.

In later years Boyer was mildly philosophical about *Cara-*

van: "Everyone should have a flop, to know what it's like. Besides, had I not come to Hollywood to make *Caravan*, I would not have found Pat. As for the picture—well, I suppose they believed they might make capital of a man whose eyes could look as if they mirrored all the sorrow in the world. But really, I wasn't the type to play mad music in cinema moonlight."

He wished he were home; but there was his bride, toiling in the modest fare of a failing Hollywood studio. They had a wobbly agreement that each should travel wherever necessary for professional purposes, with no obligation to the other. His emotional disposition, however, was that he could not presently face the prospect of being away from Pat even briefly. He might have been suicidal but for her support in his darkest professional hour. She consoled him with British stiff-upper-lip assurance that things would surely get better for him.

Boyer was considerate of his wife's own struggle as well. Before *Caravan* was released, Pat's second picture had been shot, edited, and exhibited, and had passed into oblivion—the inconsequential *Call It Luck*, in which she played opposite Charles Starrett, later a cowboy star. It was directed by James Tinling, definitely of the Fox scrub team, and he was also in charge of her next one. It was *Love Time* with the fading Nils Asther; and Boyer could see, if his wife couldn't, that Fox had lost interest in her. *Love Time* wasn't even a musical.

Charles Feldman was unable to generate any interest in Boyer at other studios. There were offers from distinctly minor producers but distinctly minor salaries came with them, and Feldman wouldn't consider them; he agreed with Boyer that it was better to make no picture at all than to enter into a bad one knowingly. Pat finished shooting *Love Time* shortly before marking her first contract year; and Boyer, speculating that her option wouldn't be renewed, suggested that they both kiss Hollywood good-bye and go off to Paris. But when Pat confronted Winnie Sheehan to determine her future, she was reassured that they were still interested, still "building" her. They picked up her option and scheduled her for a more appealing project—*The Lottery Lover,* and he was Lew Ayres.

Boyer had a minor compensation. The English version of *La Bataille* that he had made a year earlier with Merle Oberon and John Loder was a critical success in its belated American premiere as *Thunder in the East.* Feldman hoped to translate that into renewed marketability for his client and was trying to develop a "package" for Boyer and Maurice Chevalier, whose own American career had taken an uncertain turn. The idea eventually bore fruit in *Folies Bergère,* which proved to be Chevalier's last American film for more than twenty years. Boyer wasn't in it, however. Walter Byron took the secondary role that Boyer had considered playing, until he received a bid from Marcel L'Herbier to come to France and make a film called *La Route Impériale.*

It seemed the right thing to do at the time, as even Pat agreed. He made train and steamship reservations, and actually had his bags packed. His departure was set for the end of November; first he would spend the Thanksgiving holiday with Pat.

Then fate came knocking at the door, or Walter Wanger did; and Boyer stayed a while longer in Hollywood.

5

❋❋❋❋❋❋❋❋❋❋

A college man was a rare thing among Hollywood executives, but Walter Wanger was something extra—a bona fide Ivy Leaguer, Dartmouth '16. Before he turned to moviemaking he had been an aide to President Woodrow Wilson at the Paris Peace Conference, in the aftermath of the World War. A latecomer to Hollywood, he was nearly forty when he joined M-G-M as a Thalberg associate—actually Paul Bern's replacement, following Bern's suicide. Like Bern, he knew how to fold a napkin and where to place the fork on his plate. The studio needed a token gentleman who could impress foreign visitors in the parties that were held in the Marion Davies bungalow.

Walter Wanger is now on his way to being forgotten, but for a time—from the mid-thirties to the early forties—he almost attained the Goldwyn-Thalberg-Selznick-Zanuck-Wallis level as a creative and decidedly independent producer. Charles Boyer might eventually have scored in Hollywood without Wanger's intervention, but his emergence surely would have been different. It was primarily Wanger who marketed Boyer successfully to the American public; and whether or not Wanger was consciously a catalyst, the Boyer screen persona was formulated in the pictures he made for Wanger.

It might not have happened at all, had not Wanger been sailing home from Europe on the *Île de France* in the 1934 autumn. He and the wife he would soon divorce were fellow voyagers with their good friends Alfred Lunt and Lynn Fontanne. Their regular ritual of sailing was to retire to the ship's theater after dinner and drinks to watch the evening's movie. On one occasion the picture was *La Bataille,* the French original with Boyer and Annabella. And they were impressed.

The Lunts in particular were impressed by the subtle power and ultimately by the tragic force of the actor Boyer. Lynn Fontanne asked, "Who *is* that marvelous Japanese?" Boyer had fooled her completely. The Lunts probably saw few films, but the cosmopolitan Wanger had been watching Boyer films regularly for several years. No doubt he would have been curious about any actor who could so regale America's preeminent acting couple; but the timing was perfect. Wanger was seeking an actor with a *different* quality, and even though he knew all about *Caravan,* he sensed he'd found his man.

Walter Wanger had left M-G-M and organized his own producing unit, for release through Paramount. His first independent venture, *The President Vanishes,* was a newly released hit and he was returning to the United States to get his second one going, but lacked a male lead. He had purchased a Phyllis Bottome novel called *Private Worlds* because its environment—a mental hospital—hadn't been depicted in an American movie and offered good melodramatic possibilities. His difficulty was in interesting a suitable male star in the role of the troubled doctor. Fredric March and Warner Baxter had both rejected the part, and M-G-M wouldn't loan Robert Montgomery, who wanted it.

Wanger had a top female star to play the woman doctor— Claudette Colbert, reaching her peak with the recent *Imitation of Life* and as DeMille's *Cleopatra,* and just about to grab an Academy Award for *It Happened One Night.* Wanger reasoned that by obtaining box-office insurance in the second leads, he could cast an unknown in the star role, or even a presumed commercial liability such as Boyer. So he also signed two rising and attractive players, Joel McCrea and Joan Bennett, casting them as inmates; then he proceeded to fall in love with Miss Bennett, who was married. (The producer was also married, but within a few years Joan Bennett would become the second Mrs. Walter Wanger.)

When Wanger offered the role, Boyer resisted it; his bags were packed. A few weeks earlier, yes; but with L'Herbier's film awaiting him in Paris, definitely no. But Charles Feldman pleaded with Boyer to meet with Wanger and discuss it. Boyer grew truculent, but after Pat echoed Feldman's request, he said all right, he'd meet with Mr. Wanger.

The Boyers and Wangers dined together at Perino's and then went to the Wanger home for a nightcap. Boyer was polite but in no way encouraging. He believed he'd made his position quite clear. When Wanger conspired with Pat to get him to read the script, Boyer slipped out of propriety and had some sharp words for Pat, saying she was behaving selfishly, accusing her of trying to keep him in Hollywood against what was in the best interest for his career.

After an awkward silence, Boyer became contrite and graciously suggested they take a look at the script. Mrs. Wanger excused herself and went off to bed, but soon the two Boyers and Walter Wanger were reading the *Private Worlds* script together. Pat took all the female parts; Wanger read the men other than Boyer's doctor role. Wanger sensed Boyer's growing interest while they read Lynn Starling's dialogue. Boyer's reading grew less perfunctory and more actorly, and he paused to ask who was directing. The name Gregory La Cava was meaningless to him.

He liked the script very much. He had no serious reservations, even assessing the psychiatrist role as exactly right for him but also a challenge. Before their long night had ended, he had accepted the part and had begun to forget all about L'Herbier's *La Route Impériale*.

Finally, though, he accepted *Private Worlds* not because he liked the script, but because in one evening he came to like Walter Wanger so much. To Boyer, Wanger was an atypical American filmmaker, although he was like Thalberg in some ways, and articulate like Thalberg, as most other Hollywood folk weren't. Very soon he and Wanger would have a strong and valuable friendship. But perhaps their relationship was never again so good as on that first night.

* * *

The Boyers rented a medium-sized house in Beverly Hills, considering their filmland status still too tentative for any thought of buying a home.

They proceeded to accumulate a menagerie of cats—Persians and Siamese, and they wouldn't turn away the occasional authentic alley cat that came poking around Beverly Hills. Boyer wore down his wife's partiality to dogs, which fitfully resided with them but were usually outnumbered and otherwise intimidated by the felines.

Adolphe Menjou taught them bridge and the Boyers became regular cardplayers—often, for a while, with the Wangers. Boyer purchased a Duesenberg, but it was an inexpensive used one; and he also bought a Dodge coupe for Pat to drive.

When their shooting schedules coincided, they breakfasted together at 4 A.M. to make the early-morning calls. Pat had an easy drive to the Fox studio but Boyer drove all over town to film on various locations, since most of *Private Worlds* was being shot elsewhere than at the Paramount studio. They would come home exhausted, then regain vigor by sharing the day's experiences. Pat's morale was up; she expected *The Lottery Lover* to turn into a nice little picture. For the first time she had a director—William Thiele, a Jewish refugee of high accomplishment in pre-Nazi Germany—who was giving her helpful advice on acting, particularly in the playing of light comedy.

Boyer's first reports on the *Private Worlds* filming were less encouraging—indeed, they were rather glum. Now that the director had taken over it was hardly the charming Walter Wanger's picture, and Boyer wasn't getting on well with Gregory La Cava.

La Cava could offend the sometimes thin-skinned Boyer quite easily by merely mispronouncing his name, although most Americans were doing that. When La Cava first called him Boy-yer with the first syllable accented, the actor said with his typical formality, "I beg your pardon, but that is not my name." To all who erred he would politely explain that the correct pronunciation was Bwah-yeah with both sylla- bles stressed; and that furthermore it wasn't Tscharles, but Sharl, with no final "s" sounded. He became more annoyed when La Cava avoided the "Sharl Bwah-yeah" issue by addressing him pointedly as Mon-sewer. It also got back to Boyer that La Cava had told someone he wasn't going to take any crap from a Frenchman.

Gregory La Cava was then in his mid-forties, a Hollywood veteran apprenticed in many routine silent and talking fea- tures. He had steadily acquired the faculties of a skilled craftsman, to be parlayed with a creative instinct he probably had all along. He had begun working into quality pictures only recently, beginning perhaps with *Gabriel Over the White House*—the first picture he made for Walter Wanger, and Wanger's first at M-G-M. It bothered Boyer that he and La Cava were becoming antagonists, for he could see that in most ways of directing a film La Cava knew what he was doing. He also sensed La Cava's dissatisfaction with his per- formance and respected the director for that, for he knew he wasn't "getting" the part, was not feeling it.

On a morning still in the first days of shooting, La Cava kept ordering repeat takes of a scene between Boyer and Joel McCrea. And Boyer knew La Cava's displeasure was not aimed at McCrea. But after the scene went about as well as Boyer thought possible, La Cava shrugged and said "All right, let's try it again." Then he paused, posed, and en- deavored to pronounce his actor's given name correctly for the first time:

"Sharl, permit me to ask you, in what language are you thinking?"

Boyer was puzzled. "I do not know what you mean."

"I mean, Sharl, that you're saying your lines in English, which isn't good English but will have to do . . . but maybe it would do better if you were also *thinking* in English."

"But I must think in French . . . because I *am* French."

"Well, I say it's asinine to think one language and speak another. Miss Colbert is also French and can speak it very well, but ask her how she *thinks*."

Suddenly, it seemed so simple. By thinking in his own language, Boyer knew he had forfeited the aspect of nuance for acting in another one. It had made him ridiculous in *Red-Headed Woman* and ludicrous in *Caravan*.

He would often cite it as his most important breakthrough, without which he could not have met the competition in English-speaking films. He found that thinking in English was indeed an easy thing; he only needed to train himself to do it. He would begin to think in English when he was acting, or buying a new hat, or making love to Pat.

It turned *Private Worlds* completely around for him, and most of the shooting became an entirely pleasant experience as he took command of the psychiatrist role. He and La Cava sensed a mutual gratitude, and became quite friendly.

When the picture had its prerelease screenings in February of 1935, Wanger and his satellites weren't sure what they had. La Cava, probably the most conservative person on the scene for having been in Hollywood longest, liked the picture but didn't believe it would sell. They all agreed it was different.

Released in March, it remained an enigma. Most reviews were strangely evasive. There were a few raves, but more notices that were unarguably hostile. When *Private Worlds* built into a hit, it was quickly forgotten that the reviews were mixed. If it had seemed a bold departure, a picture ahead of its time, audiences were ready for it. Its reputation grew and historically it became overrated very quickly; today it can hardly suggest thematic daring, although it remains a watchable picture.

Yet Walter Wanger and many other wise folk realized soon enough that it wasn't thematic substance that put *Private Worlds* over. Quite definitely it was Charles Boyer. It was a positive outing for Claudette Colbert, who picked up a second successive Academy Award nomination. Joan Bennett and Joel McCrea were good enough within their limitations. But the movie world and its patronage love a new star, and especially one who may be called unique. The American screen had no other actor quite like Boyer, or like him at all.

Most foreign accents are a liability, but for Boyer the accent was an advantage, his own trademark, part of the charm inhabited in a vocal quality that was itself unique.

And those eyes! It was soon evident that they were melting hearts. *Private Worlds* gained identity as a "woman's picture." It was women who adored it, and Boyer was the object of their adoration. It was also apparent that while every aspect of Boyer's performance was praised by the critics and endorsed by the audience, the scenes that stirred them were the ones in which Boyer made anguished love to Claudette Colbert, doctor to doctor.

He was a new "find." The people who had seen *Caravan* could find it very convenient to forget that he had been in it; after all, this was an entirely different actor. But actor wasn't the word that came immediately to mind. It was lover.

* * *

If Charles and Pat had been better-known screen personalities at the time of their marriage, there would probably have been widespread speculation within the film colony that the union wouldn't last; observers more than likely would have "given it six months."

The cultured and debonair but prim and somewhat arrogant Frenchman; and the vivacious but largely unlettered girl from a British chorus line—it didn't figure. It especially didn't figure when the persons involved had approximately equal dedication to their respective careers. For the two-career marriage to work, one finally had to take precedence. Eventually Pat would abandon her own ambition and move entirely within the Boyer shadow, but not without a bitter struggle—with him as well as with the fate that stalled her professional progress in a quicksand.

Although they had agreed early on that each was entitled to an individual pursuit in theater or films, after they were married Boyer's Old World point of view was brought to bear, both on Pat's career and on their own domesticity. Without resorting to a fund of platitudes, he seemed really to believe that a woman's place was in the home, certainly if it was *his* home; that whatever else Pat might do, her principal function should be to accommodate *him*. He probably did not appreciate, then, that Pat always met him considerably more than halfway—of necessity, since he wouldn't budge.

One of their friends once noted that if they bought a piece of furniture together, Charles's choice prevailed. They would buy the sofa Pat had picked out if he liked it; otherwise they would choose another . . . and Pat had little veto power over his selections.

They began collecting art in those years of the Great Depression when even Old Masters could be privately obtained by the almost rich. Charles favored the post-Impressionists; Pat's taste was eclectic; and he would reject her whims and perhaps thoughtlessly remark that she knew nothing about art.

Yet it was the travel issue on which they were increasingly strained. Once Boyer had satisfied his stubborn pride and made good in Hollywood, he sought to formulate himself as an international star who could commute between Europe and America and accrue professional royalty in both hemispheres. But as Pat's career became a hindrance to that design, he started belittling her shabby attainments in Fox films. Had she been alternating, say, between Hollywood and London, he surely would have felt no duty to be her camp-follower. Yet he believed she should follow *him,* if he wanted her to.

He planned a return to Paris after completing *Private Worlds,* believing it vital to retain continuity in the French film activity. He sensed that his earlier tenures in Hollywood had cost him some standing at home. He prodded Pat to make her own preparations to accompany him, but she was reluctant to leave. For one thing, she believed her Fox pictures were better than Boyer rated them. *The Lottery Lover* might well have been her best American exposure to date, as she believed. Still, it was only a "programmer," released on a minor scale just before *Private Worlds* registered its substantial hit. Boyer suggested that she simply quit Fox and go to Paris with him, believing that Pat could have a more gratifying career in Paris. She had learned French quickly and well under his tutelage, and he could fix her up with an agent. But Pat wasn't about to leave. She had acquired for herself an

American agent—the aggressive Leland Hayward—who was already conniving to renegotiate her Fox contract. So in early 1935 Boyer prepared to return to Paris without Pat, and was sullen about it.

He changed his mind and stayed, but not out of consideration for Pat. Charles Feldman got hold of him and advised him to stick around, something was about to pop. It looked as if Boyer could make a picture with Katharine Hepburn . . . and didn't he want to?

* * *

In Hollywood there were the "Big Five" among producing organizations that maintained large studios and had extensive theatrical holdings. Just about everyone in America could quickly identify four of them as M-G-M, Paramount, Warner Brothers, and Fox. They were likely to trip over the fifth one, however. Was it Universal, or Columbia? No, they were the "Little Two," busy producers but of generally more modest fare, besides which they owned no theaters. The company completing the major pentagon was RKO Radio, actually giant-sized after a series of mergers that involved several earlier companies (including the American branch of Pathé) with the Radio-Keith-Orpheum theater circuit.

RKO seemed just to plug along, maintaining a fair production standard while never quite acquiring the knack for marketing it effectively as did the four other behemoths. That RKO failed to achieve a popular "image" was linked to its failure to develop stars. In the talkie era it had brief success with Ann Harding, but she began to fade after too many lachrymose vehicles. Irene Dunne bloomed brightly but settled her contract and began to free-lance smartly among all the studios. Then there was Katharine Hepburn. The undisputed sensation of 1932 and the Oscar-winning actress for 1933, she became the shining glory of RKO Radio and then its thorniest problem. After four hit films in a row, she sustained two dismal film flops that were sandwiched around a disastrous return to Broadway in *The Lake*—the occasion for Dorothy Parker to observe that "Miss Hepburn ran the gamut of emotions from A to B."

Miss Hepburn remained a film critics' darling, and the more discerning moviegoers swore by her talent and individuality; but too many moviegoers either didn't like her, or didn't care to see her pictures. But among screen actors, most of whom didn't know the oddly reclusive Hepburn personally, she was something of a deity. It was still reckoned an honor to be in one of her pictures. Boyer's friend Adolphe Menjou had worked with her and rated her the most exciting personality in films, and Boyer himself knew that in France she was the young American actress who commanded the greatest attention.

Just when RKO was beginning to have difficulty exploiting Katharine Hepburn, they put under contract a young Czech on whom they counted to be something RKO had not experienced—a male superstar. They gave Francis Lederer the biggest buildup this side of Samuel Goldwyn's Folly, Anna Sten. As Franz Lederer he had been an especially promising film player all over the European continent, and Boyer had met him briefly when Lederer worked for Julien Duvivier in Paris. A fussed-over Broadway success in *Autumn Crocus* cleared his passage into American films, where he proceeded to flop as resoundingly for RKO in *Man of Two Worlds* as Boyer was flopping for Fox in *Caravan*. Lederer then made two more 1934 pictures and both were received rather warmly by the critics, who also had fair tolerance of his fussily mannered performances. But despite Lederer's darkly strong handsomeness, American audiences weren't responding to him.

Now the RKO strategy was to put Katharine Hepburn and Francis Lederer together in a picture, theorizing that two commercial wrongs could make a right. RKO producer Pandro Berman prepared a production that would have quality appointments in every department. The married writing team of Sarah Mason and Victor Heerman, which had scripted Hepburn's joyously embraced *Little Women*, was put to work on a feminist drama about a girl musician-composer who falls hopelessly in love with a famous conductor. As a gesture to Miss Hepburn, Berman brought in the illustrious Philip

Moeller of the Theatre Guild as director. Then they started shooting the picture.

The fireworks were immediate. Hepburn had a reputation for being temperamental, but Lederer was more so. The conflict wasn't between them but between Lederer and Moeller. The firebrand was Lederer, who approved of no part of Moeller's direction but was especially irked that Moeller was rather consciously making a Hepburn picture, while he believed it should be a Lederer picture as well. Lederer shouted on the set for several days, and in the second week of shooting made a stormy departure. He may have given an either-he-goes-or-I-go ultimatum. Moeller, in any event, offered to withdraw; but it may have been feared that if Moeller left, so would Hepburn, and then where would they be? Moeller was retained, Lederer refused to return, and *Private Worlds* was a brand-new hit with another continental actor making a fine showing.

Boyer accepted the assignment and reported immediately, but not without first reading the Mason-Heerman script and liking it. He was pleased to find that the conductor was something of a cad. He was vain, humorless, selfish but charming: Boyer wondered if he could play such a role. The conductor would dally with the girl, treat her unjustly, dump her, and then become contrite and take to drink. The title conveyed the mood: *Break of Hearts*.

Boyer and Hepburn endured an uncertain period of several days during which they slowly warmed up to each other, then started enjoying their work in what was largely a two-character drama with distended duologues. Boyer said Hepburn was the most dedicated actress he'd met in any country, and in one of the rare interviews Hepburn gave during that period she paid him similar compliment. Boyer also found Philip Moeller to be a splendid director of actors, as well as a decent and gracious fellow.

But Francis Lederer was vindicated, to some extent, when *Break of Hearts* was released. Moeller's direction was overbearingly theatrical. The picture was an effective acting piece, but the picture was also static—totally deficient in cinematic fluidity. The intelligent screenplay became only a marathon of talk with cigarettes. A national magazine called it "basically a smoking contest between Hepburn and Boyer." Many years later the Briton Leslie Halliwell would rate it as "Well-acted soap opera, not really worthy of its stars."

The RKO experiment had clearly failed. *Break of Hearts* was another misfire for Katharine Hepburn, despite her excellence in it, because the cash register wasn't jingling. Hepburn's status had grown even shakier, although she would regain much lost ground in her next outing, as Booth Tarkington's *Alice Adams*. Ironically, though, *Break of Hearts* proved a plus for Charles Boyer. Released only three months after *Private Worlds*, it verified that he was an actor of depth and considerable dimension. It fortified the impression of emotionally romantic substance. He was besieged by fan mail as he hadn't been in Hollywood, or even in France. He was a Very Hot Property.

He was also committed to another American film before *Break of Hearts* had been wrapped, and he was under a multi-picture contract.

In the early wake of *Private Worlds*, Walter Wanger put the then-potent writing team of Gene Towne and Graham Baker onto a melodramatic story especially for Boyer, and it was Wanger's instruction to make his character vaguely oriental, still remembering how *La Bataille* had so impressed the Lunts. Towne and Baker developed a script built around a half-caste, a Eurasian who would fall in love with an American girl—a miscegenation melodrama reminiscent of the Sessue Hayakawa silents. Boyer also found the *Shanghai* script perilously reminiscent of *Caravan*, but decided he would do it. After *Private Worlds* and *Break of Hearts* it would be a shrewd change of pace to avoid the typecasting trap, for it was also a sort of action picture—to be shot largely on Catalina Island, which was then the usual shooting location for Hollywood films set in the Orient.

Film offers now logically were coming to him from France in abundance, so Boyer planned definitely to travel to Paris after the *Shanghai* business was over. He had expected to go alone, but even before shooting his first scenes for *Shanghai* he knew Pat would be going with him, and without a fight. Pat was no longer a Fox employee, and Fox Films had ceased even to exist.

The sprawling Fox concern, ancient as movie studios went, had been increasingly in financial difficulty during those years of the Great Depression. So early in 1935 the industrial gadfly Sidney Kent orchestrated a capitulative merger giving Joseph Schenck and Darryl Zanuck control of Fox. Only two years earlier, they had formed 20th Century Pictures as an independent company, distributing its product through United Artists. They had put together a string of prodigious hits with few misses in between—the likes of *The Bowery, The Call of the Wild, The House of Rothschild,* and the March-Laughton *Les Misérables.* Fox revenues had declined despite the emergence of the surefire Shirley Temple.

So there was a new corporation, called 20th Century–Fox. Zanuck was in charge of production, with Schenck as chairman of the board. Right away they instituted a retrenchment program, jettisoning a substantial portion of the contract-player list. Pat Paterson was one of the casualties. The little time remaining on her active contract was settled and her option dropped. Just before that action was taken, she had been put to work in a B picture, but of a slick order—*Charlie Chan in Egypt*—and all the Fox Chans with Warner Oland had a guaranteed popularity. Also in the cast and also dropped from the contract list was the newcomer Rita Cansino, who later would be rechristened Rita Hayworth.

Pat completed her fifth and last Fox film in a state of shock, and only then did Boyer begin to realize how important Pat's career was to her. Leland Hayward tried peddling her services to other studios but found no takers.

Then, surprisingly, Boyer signed a four-picture contract with Walter Wanger. Although Wanger had suggested a multi-picture pact earlier, he didn't insist on one because he understood Boyer's wish not to be tied down. Charles Feldman, though, believed that at this stage of Boyer's American career he needed the security of firm commitments, particularly for effecting more practical shuttling back and forth between the continents, as Charles seemed determined to manage. Right after *Private Worlds*, Boyer might have obtained a generous term contract with any of several companies but for his lack of interest in one. There was a definite renewal of interest by Irving Thalberg, although now he was only an autonomous M-G-M producer and no longer its production chief.

Boyer reaffirmed that he would agree to no term contract with a studio, and it wasn't only a desire to remain independent: he believed he could make more money on a per-picture basis, negotiating each contract separately, and he wanted to make a lot of money. But he intimated to Feldman that he might now consider a multi-picture arrangement with Walter Wanger, whom he trusted. It was only because Wanger was the producer that Boyer had agreed to make the dubious *Shanghai*.

Wanger and Feldman drafted a proposal for Boyer to consider: a four-picture deal would supersede the one-shot contract for *Shanghai*, and would commence with that project. Financial escalations were provided for. Boyer was hesitant, but perhaps not about the dollars. In a confidential discussion with Wanger (a confidence betrayed by the producer some years later), Boyer resorted to mild friendly blackmail, asking Wanger what might be done to aid Pat's career. Boyer signed for four pictures because Wanger said he'd try to do something for Pat.

Shanghai was produced with routine efficiency. The journeyman James Flood directed Boyer and Loretta Young in formula hokum—one of the pictures Boyer would later wish he'd never made. It was a statistical fact that the domestic return for *Shanghai* exceeded that for Wanger's earlier, better *Private Worlds*, but that was no clear indication of Boyer's having become a draw. Titles dipped in oriental geography inevitably clicked at the box office. There were other signs, though, that he was now a name familiar to American moviegoers.

Thunder in the East was put back into circulation, and the Franco-English picture performed better than in its previous go-round. Then there was *Liliom*, which had failed to obtain American exhibition earlier, but on the strength of Boyer's name was now playing art-house circuits in the larger American cities. An enterprising distributor even secured an English-language print of the thing he'd made in Berlin with Lilian Harvey—called *The Only Girl* in Britain but making the American rounds as *Heart Song*. All of this amounted to a Boyer explosion on American screens in 1935.

So he went back to France somewhat redeemed and certainly richer. The financial measurements of his contract with Wanger were not revealed, as Boyer became increasingly secretive about that aspect of his profession. It was hinted, though, that he had been seeking a hundred thousand dollars per picture, and was getting very nearly that.

If he was not quite the toast of America, he would find upon returning to his homeland that he was quite the toast of France. Pat would go with him to share his triumph, and her growing hope was that in the world's most romantic city they might still be able to conceive a baby.

6

It was a great era of French cinema.

This was the hour of Jean Renoir and René Clair at their pinnacles, but also of Marcel Carné, Marc Allégret, Julien Duvivier, and the enduring Jacques Feyder. Carné and the brilliant screenwriter Jacques Prévert were collaborating on a string of works that would all earn classic status. Allégret was emerging as France's preeminent star-maker, beginning with Simone Simon and Michèle Morgan. Duvivier was creating the melancholy *Pépé le Moko* and envisioning the episodic, influential *Carnet de Bal*. And Feyder had made the exquisite, supremely comical *La Kermesse Héroïque* with Rosay and Jouvet, which regaled America as *Carnival in Flanders*.

Measured against such accomplishment, Boyer's attainments in both France and America had been very ordinary, and it mystified him that he was the man of the hour. Much was being made, on his return, of his fabulous success in American films, interpreted as a triumph for France itself. So exalted indeed was America in the motion picture world! It could be noted that Maurice Chevalier's return to Paris only months earlier, and after half a dozen years abroad, had caused much less excitement. Chevalier's Hollywood career had been glorious in the beginning, but had declined steadily from its high point. He returned to France only because of his diminishing Hollywood prospects, the opposite case from Boyer. His homeland welcomed Boyer as its brightest cinema star—more glorious than Blanchar or Fresnay or the comparatively new, splendid Jean Gabin who was *Pépé le Moko*.

Boyer again embraced all of them, and also Philippe Heriat whose career had faltered, and Pierre Brasseur, now rising belatedly into the top class. Pat met them all, and she also met Gaby Morlay, Marie Bell, Alice Field . . .

He made many new friends, among them Madeleine Renaud and her younger husband, the enchanted Jean-Louis Barrault, who had marked his striking screen debut in Allégret's *Les Beaux Jours*. The Boyers were being entertained by the imposing Marcel Pagnol and the great Raimu, whom Charles had never met.

They were a grand fraternity, these players and other creative artists who had a unity—and a unity of purpose—that Boyer believed was never approached by their Hollywood counterparts. And now, around them all, Boyer was a young lion, to whom even Jouvet and Baur and Michel Simon paid homage. They didn't expect to keep him in Paris forever, and didn't believe they should. To have an unofficial French ambassador in Hollywood was necessary to them; and with Chevalier no longer there, Boyer had inherited the diplomatic portfolio.

Boyer now knew where the real money was, and saw these occasional returns to France as indulgences of his vanity. There had been great curiosity over his British-American wife and he was proud of Pat's clever handling of the Paris press, delicately in French. He was gratified, too, that his mother was in Paris now, luxuriating in her son's eminence. Those considerations aside, he wanted to make one new French picture of such excellence as would validate all the attention he was receiving.

There were many offers, but the most intriguing one came from Anatole Litvak. That was a surprise, for Litvak had been enraged by Boyer's last-minute defection from *Cette Vieille Canaille* a few years earlier.

Litvak was a loner on the Paris production scene, not of the mainstream. But occasionally he delivered stunning and adventurous cinema, and his latest film was the big new hit in Paris when the Boyers arrived there. That was *L'Equipage* with Annabella and her much older husband, Jean Murat. It had been written by Joseph Kessel, the vintage Boyer friend who had become France's leading novelist. Now Kessel had also written what Anatole Litvak said was the world's best screenplay, and it was called *Mayerling*.

In 1888, in the Austrian hunting lodge called Mayerling, there occurred the double suicide of the Crown Prince Rudolf von Habsburg and his mistress, Marie Vetsera. Litvak rated it the world's greatest romantic tragedy and perhaps the greatest love story as well—superseding, most certainly, the fiction about Romeo and Juliet. He already had his Marie Vetsera—the delicately beautiful Danielle Darrieux, a major French star. Litvak said half a dozen top actors were anxious to play the prince, "including Blanchar except now he is much too old and never handsome enough to be matched against Darrieux." When Boyer said why not Pierre Fresnay, Litvak said why not Charles Boyer?

"Fresnay could play Rudolf if there were no Charles Boyer. But for Charles Boyer there can be no substitute. I will not make the picture without you."

Not that Boyer was resisting. After a little cat-and-mouse game with Litvak, he was pleased—indeed, he was ecstatic in his subdued way—over the opportunity of *Mayerling*. But he was curious that he had suddenly come to be regarded as one of the world's handsomest men.

He said, "I do not know when I became so nice-looking as they all say. I suppose it was when I lost my hair and began experimenting with the toupees. In silent films, I looked like a bandit who eats little children."

Boyer with toupee was a handsome Habsburg prince all right. Yet other factors made him the mandatory Rudolf, as the director later revealed. If *Mayerling* emerged as a work of art, fine, but not even that was its director's primary objective. Litvak wanted a smash hit not only in France but in America, and even more especially there. He calculated that of all the French actors, only Boyer could be a box-office magnet for *Mayerling* in America. Furthermore, Litvak wanted a whopping financial success that would be his ticket to Hollywood, always his goal.

All of these things would come to pass.

They certainly thought it was a work of art in France in 1936, and in America the following year. *Mayerling* was beautifully photographed, tastefully directed, and acted with subtlety and intelligence by Boyer and Darrieux. Boyer's anguish was most convincing, indicating that Litvak had him pegged. If Boyer had rather suddenly and somewhat unexpectedly emerged from Hollywood as a "great lover," Litvak believed it was no fluke but the delayed occurrence of something that should have happened sooner. He said *Mayerling* couldn't have been as strong without Boyer because "it is sublime tragedy and Charles Boyer is, in essence, a tragic artist."

❀   ❀   ❀

With *Mayerling* finished, the Boyers spent the Christmas of 1935 with Charles's mother, and welcomed the new year with Pat's family in England.

Mme. Boyer still had her house in Figeac but would alternate her residence, preferring thenceforth always to be in Paris when her famous son was there. Charles bought an elegant Paris apartment for his mother, and hired a full-time housekeeper and a personal maid to watch over her. He had the money.

After Pat introduced her husband to members of the family from which she'd grown so distant geographically and emotionally, they stayed several weeks in the British Isles, motoring throughout England, Scotland, and Wales. They took in all the London shows, and it would become an annual habit with them. Boyer was mobbed in England as he had been in Paris, suggesting that his fame was now worldwide. Just occasionally, someone would pay token attention to his wife. Press accounts of Boyer's visit to Britain tended to give the report that he was "accompanied by his wife Pat Paterson, formerly an actress."

Back in Hollywood, they started doing things as they hadn't done them before.

They took their furniture out of storage, intending to place it in another rented house. Then they sold all of the furniture at auction, other than their paintings. They remained in

Beverly Hills not as renters but as homeowners. Capriciously they bought one residence after another, selling each one in turn, until they more or less settled in a two-story Mediterranean house at 930 North Alpine, which they had custom-decorated with discreet lavishness. It was in the Beverly heights near Pickfair, the mansion that was still Mary Pickford's and had once also belonged to Douglas Fairbanks.

Along with new furniture, new cars, a cabin cruiser, and a beach cottage, they bought complete new wardrobes. They continued buying a lot of clothes and not just everyday wear —scores of evening dresses, dozens of conservative business suits. Then they started showing off their finery in public, as if having agreed that now they both wanted to "go Hollywood."

For one thing, Boyer had decided to stop working so hard —even though, for a while, it was a resolution to be broken. He reasoned that an actor going from picture to picture could burn out, talent and inspiration blunted. He also believed that overexposure was a primary hazard of the film star's career— a hazard that the shrewd Greta Garbo didn't invite. He would prefer a regimen of working only half the time, with long rests between assignments. With Pat not working at all, there was ample opportunity to organize their leisure.

Before, they had been stay-at-homes, their social life restricted to a few intimate friends who hadn't always mixed well. Pat had her friends, he had his; the more sociable Pat collected them indiscriminately in droves, while the more selective Charles had fewer but deeper associations. Now they were joining the larger party, the continuing serial that played at Ciro's, the Mocambo, the Trocadero . . .

Boyer had always shunned athletics; his most strenuous competition had been at the bridge table. He kept a membership in the Beverly Hills Tennis Club but had never been on the court. Now, however, he was taking tennis lessons with Pat from the club pro. He'd try golf and dismiss it as utterly boring, but learning to ski gave enjoyment to them both. The Boyers did almost everything together. Periodically they motored to Las Vegas during its early, primitive development as a gambling mecca. Boyer kept his passion for gambling under smart control. A business manager provided him with a gambling allowance, and it didn't matter if he lost it all, it merely angered him.

Besides a business manager, he had a broker, other financial advisers, and his professional mentor, Charlie Feldman, whose talent agency was gaining imposing dimensions under its new name, Famous Artists. Boyer's own entourage now included the personable Irving (Fig) Newton as his permanent stand-in. Where the Boyers earlier had employed only one or two servants and sometimes none at all, they now had an expanding household staff. Boyer employed a succession of secretaries to manage his appointments and personal correspondence. His fan mail alone was a triviality that had to be dealt with. As a free-lance actor he had no studio assistance for such details, and Pat was no longer interested after the novelty of his popularity wore off.

His money was being invested in stocks, bonds, commodities, and real estate. This was the way the rich get richer, and he was investing his money even when it purchased art works for display in their home. The Boyer collection was being supplemented by his own creations—Charles the artist, and rather a good one as Sunday painters go.

His disposition had altered remarkably—toward Hollywood or the United States, and probably toward both. In the fall of 1936, Mr. and Mrs. Charles Boyer made their first application for U.S. citizenship. Even if they couldn't vote, the liberal Boyers would help out in the Roosevelt re-election campaign.

They were also making inquiries about adoption agencies. Nature appeared to be letting them down.

◦ ◦ ◦

Boyer had expected soon to be making another picture for Walter Wanger, but now that was off in the future. Wanger presently had more than he could handle. While seeking to retain his own autonomous producing unit, he had also been placed in charge of production at Paramount but was not pleased with the arrangement. Soon he would be making a complete break from the studio, bent on achieving total independence, and believed his next Boyer project should be delayed a few months for that eventuality. Besides, he wanted the next one to be much better than the lackluster *Shanghai.* His writing boys, Gene Towne and Graham Baker, believed that this time they were hatching a good one.

Wanger soon made his break from Paramount. Irving Thalberg didn't make his from M-G-M. Dissatisfied there after his relationship with Louis B. Mayer deteriorated, Thalberg had obtained the blessing of Loew's Inc., the parent company to M-G-M, for distributing his own independent projects through Loew's—as Irving G. Thalberg pictures, without the M-G-M logo. In June of 1936 Thalberg told Boyer to give some thought to becoming one of his company's charter players. That was the last time they met, and three months later Thalberg was dead. He was Boyer's own age.

Younger by four years than Boyer was David Selznick, Thalberg's friend and jealous rival, who had already made *his* break from Louis B. Mayer, who was his own father-in-law. Selznick had been a young producer at Paramount and then was production chief at RKO before being lured by his father-in-law to M-G-M, where he produced a dozen or so glossy successes. He conceived his independent Selznick International Pictures "in the tradition of quality," and was putting its first exhibit—*Little Lord Fauntleroy,* with Freddie Bartholomew—into national release early in 1936, when he was also getting in touch with Charles Boyer.

For several years Selznick had been planning a version of the Robert Hichens novel *Garden of Allah,* which in the early years of the century had been a worldwide sensation, selling almost a million copies. At M-G-M he had envisioned it for Garbo. Now, projected as his second independent effort, he had Marlene Dietrich on loan from Paramount. He sought Charles Boyer to play the strange fellow who loves and marries her without revealing that he is an escaped Trappist monk. Boyer knew the novel and thought it outdated for modern screen fare, but he also knew that David Selznick was a quality-obsessed producer who possibly had never made a poor picture. If Boyer needed an additional hint that Selznick was pulling out all the stops, the picture was to be shot in the recently perfected three-color Technicolor process. He said he'd do it, although some advised him against it because, they said, Dietrich is through.

Marlene Dietrich, much like Katharine Hepburn, had not lost her prestige but had lost her following, perhaps never numerically a strong one. Again like Hepburn, Fräulein Dietrich dazzled those moviegoers who look beneath the film-star surface to find mystique. Yet the American public at large had never warmed up to her, although her Paramount pictures generally drew throngs in their European bookings. She arrived in Hollywood in 1930 to continue the spectacular association with her Svengali, Josef von Sternberg, after their sensational, German-made *The Blue Angel*. Six of her eight American films had been directed by Sternberg but their association had ended, and Paramount was weary of her. She owed them one picture, after which the contract wouldn't be renewed, but she didn't expect to be out of work. By pairing her with Boyer, Selznick had just about the most exotic star combination that could be devised in the Hollywood of that era.

Although *The Garden of Allah* was to win some acclaim for its advanced use of color, Boyer was undoubtedly right about its old-fashionedness. It was also a picture he'd wish he hadn't made. Critics were tolerant of both stars while ridiculing the high-pitched love story—which, even with its lush adornment, did not find a large audience. It was confirmed that Dietrich was slipping or had slipped, although three years later she would charge back in *Destry Rides Again* and have a whole new career. But it was also suggested that since Boyer hadn't saved her at the box office, his own popularity might have been overestimated. Some alarm was attached to mounting evidence that while women adored Boyer, American males were indifferent or were becoming hostile toward him. He was already aware of that theory while filming *The Garden of Allah*, and that may have influenced his behavior.

That it had a stormy production is confirmed in *Memo*, Rudy Behlmer's valuable compilation of David Selznick's official correspondence pertaining to his film projects. At one point Selznick considered Boyer a troublemaker, as well as Dietrich. Unlike most producers, Selznick insinuated himself into the creative process of all his pictures, interfering officiously with his directors. While Richard Boleslawsky directed the *Garden of Allah* players in their Arabian desert on a patch of Arizona (near Yuma, where the Boyers were wed), Selznick interfered from his Culver City office, where he was involved in the early planning of *Gone With the Wind.* Selznick wrote a long and enraged letter to Boleslawsky during the shooting period when he learned that Boyer and Dietrich were resisting orders—giving Boleslawsky a very hard time about orders that came through him but were actually from Selznick.

Boyer always spoke favorably of Boleslawsky, a product of Stanislavsky's Moscow Art Theater and a director often favored by actors with theatrical backgrounds. No matter who was giving whom a hard time, Boleslawsky was probably the one who suffered most. *The Garden of Allah* was the last picture Boleslawsky completed; months later he was dead of a heart attack at forty-eight.

The Selznick correspondence also reveals that while he never sought to use Dietrich again, Selznick remained covetous of Boyer, who at one point agreed to appear in *Intermezzo* opposite the new Selznick import from Sweden, Ingrid Bergman. Why Boyer withdrew or was withdrawn in favor of Leslie Howard is not made clear, but Selznick also helped arrange Boyer's participation opposite Bergman later on in the M-G-M *Gaslight.*

After *The Garden of Allah* completed shooting in June, it was edited and screened for a dissatisfied Selznick who ordered retakes in August, with release delayed until November. The salvage job apparently didn't work, and Boyer was also irked that the scene he considered his best one was excised from the final version. By that time, however, he knew that *The Garden of Allah* couldn't possibly kill his American career, if it could harm it at all. He was making a picture with Jean Arthur, and set up to make one with Greta Garbo.

* * *

Before Walter Wanger had his next Boyer picture set for shooting, and before he had extricated himself from Paramount, he let Raoul Walsh talk him into buying a script that Walsh himself had written. It was adapted from a story by Eric Hatch, one of whose comical yarns was the basis for a current smash hit, *My Man Godfrey*. Wanger rated *Spendthrift* a fair gamble, so he elected to produce it personally for Paramount with Walsh as director.

When Boyer returned from the desert location where Pat had been with him throughout the *Garden of Allah* shooting, Wanger gave them a small dinner party that seemed a bit strange to Boyer, since they knew none of the other guests. They knew Joan Bennett, who was not yet Mrs. Walter Wanger; but they weren't acquainted with the Raoul Walshes or with Henry Fonda and his new bride, Frances Brokaw.

Pat had caught a glimpse of the young Henry Fonda when he checked in at Fox, just before the fateful merger. Repeating his stage role, he'd made *The Farmer Takes a Wife* opposite Janet Gaynor, as his first film. He was one of the more promising of the newer screen actors, and Wanger now had him personally signed for a multi-picture deal similar to Boyer's, but probably for less money. Wanger also had Joan Bennett under personal contract, as well as Sylvia Sidney with whom Fonda had made a recent hit of *The Trail of the Lonesome Pine*. Boyer suspected Wanger of plotting to get him into a picture with one or perhaps all of his other new chattels.

Instead Wanger asked Pat how she would feel about making a picture with Hank Fonda for Paramount. After being initially flustered, Pat said she'd be delighted, supposing she was accepting a secondary role. Instead she was Fonda's leading lady, and she was also meeting her director. It was all very pleasant. After that it got rough.

She hadn't filmed in eighteen months. It was like starting over, and she was rusty, and they did things differently at Paramount—where, in any event, she wasn't coming in trumpeted as their next big star. *Spendthrift* was on the sound stages very soon after that dinner party, and Raoul Walsh became impatient with Pat not much later. When she delivered a piece of dialogue matter-of-factly, Walsh bellowed, "Pat, can't you recognize a comedy line?" She answered with her own exasperation, "Well, not *that* one!" And it went on that way, with Henry Fonda unenthusiastic about any of it.

Before submitting himself to retakes for *The Garden of Allah*, Boyer haunted the *Spendthrift* set until he decided it was a bad idea. He had something other than a proprietary interest in Pat's career, sensing that Wanger was doing him a favor, and that Wanger feared he'd taken a risk. Pat was distraught throughout the five-week shooting schedule; she was certain that all of her Fox pictures had been better than this one. She didn't alter her opinion after they screened the rough cut.

When Boyer sought Wanger's own assessment in confidence, the producer avoided making personal judgment but said "Raoul Walsh doesn't think she's another Lombard." At that point and in that picture, Fonda also failed to impress anyone as a second William Powell.

Wanger made his exit from Paramount while studio hands were putting the final touches on *Spendthrift*, after which William LeBaron had it cut down to seventy minutes and released it as a B. *Spendthrift* was no flop. It wasn't anything at all; few people knew it existed, or if they knew, they forgot about it eight minutes after they'd seen it. It was a swiftly played trifle that prompted little laughter, as the audience shared Pat's inability to find anything funny.

When Boyer curtly remarked, "She's not supposed to be Carole Lombard . . . Pat is a musical comedienne," Wanger calmly said "All right, I'll get her into a musical." He truly believed that *he* had let Pat down.

He was confident that he hadn't let Boyer down with *History Is Made at Night*. From its inception it was shaped as a love story with trimmings that were at first comical, then melodramatic. Boyer liked it from the start. After his mournful desert monks and gypsies and Asiatic half-castes, he was delighted to be in spiffy modern dress, in a subject that afforded him some lightness for at least part of the distance. He had to think back all the way to *Red-Headed Woman* for an American picture of his that afforded some gaiety.

Wanger had checked the dismal grosses for *The Garden of Allah* and had heard the talk about Boyer attracting only the women patrons. It was with some cunning that he borrowed

Jean Arthur from Columbia to be Boyer's paramour in *History Is Made at Night*, and not only because Miss Arthur was capable of balancing comedy with drama quite expertly. It was already evident that Jean Arthur was a man's star. She was no raving beauty, but men liked her directness and her good-pal personality, often revealed in her roles as a working girl in a masculine environment. Although long in films, Jean Arthur was a new vogue, having recently soared to the top star class in the screwball merriment of *The Ex-Mrs. Bradford* with William Powell, and in two very different pictures with Gary Cooper, as the girl Mr. Deeds met when he went to town, and as Calamity Jane to Cooper's Wild Bill Hickok in DeMille's *The Plainsman*. She would subsequently be illuminated in some of the best works of Frank Capra and George Stevens, and as the prototypical Hawksian woman in *Only Angels Have Wings*. Yet she would retain a fondness for *History Is Made at Night* as her most elegant and sophisticated exposure. Boyer had been warned she would be a terror to work with, and found her just the opposite.

He was a debonair *maître d'*; she, the wife of a scheming paranoid played by Colin Clive, the original Dr. Frankenstein. After equal parts of light and heavy, it was resolved by a *Titanic*-like shipwreck in which the lovers survived, to share their tomorrow. It could have gone either way or several ways, but Frank Borzage was a resourceful veteran director who could have it *every* way, with the assistance of virtuoso players. Borzage was an unreconstructed romantic, and it is the observation of Andrew Sarris that "*History Is Made at Night* is not only the most romantic title in the history of the cinema but a profound expression of Borzage's commitment to love over probability."

To achieve such profundity, an actor of Boyer's romantic conviction was an absolute requirement. *History Is Made at Night* is not the immediate reference point for Boyer that half a dozen other pictures may be, and is forgotten but for an enduring cult who cherish it. But more than any other screen subject, it offers the quintessential Boyer in his charm both serious and light, in his emotional depth, and in his elevated amorousness—facets that make timeless a picture that seemed at least slightly corny even when new. To some undetermined extent, the assignment also rescued him.

This was a high point for Wanger, too. His first independent film for United Artists release, *You Only Live Once,* was Fritz Lang's stunning tragic melodrama with Henry Fonda and Sylvia Sidney. *History Is Made at Night* was an agreeable contrast that marked Wanger as "the new Samuel Goldwyn," and he would stay at that level a little while longer, despite such misadventures as *Vogues* and *52nd Street*—both of which followed *History Is Made at Night* on Wanger's release schedule for 1937.

Boyer's next Wanger picture would have been *Vogues,* but for his refusal to do it. It had musical elements, and Wanger had a key supporting role designed for Pat Paterson . . . and she also rejected it. Joan Bennett had the lead, and the role Pat didn't want was taken by a brunette named Dorothy McNulty, who was soon to change her hair color and her name. As Penny Singleton, she would enact Chic Young's Blondie in a dozen popular minor film farces, and also enjoy long-running success on radio. She almost stole *Vogues,* as Pat might also have done, except there was not much to steal. Boyer wanted no part of it, obeying his old principles; it was a literary judgment. Although Wanger had the respected farce-writing team of Bella and Sam Spewack on the script, the comedy and other interest were deficient; otherwise the prospect of Boyer as a fashion designer might have seemed logical. Warner Baxter took the role, and it was released as *Vogues of 1938,* although it came and went in the 1937 autumn. Seeking another new film atmosphere as he had with *Private Worlds,* Wanger had a story built around rival fashion houses. He hired a chorus of John Robert Powers models, and then incongruously brought in the Group Theater's Harold Clurman to give them motivation to *act.* This was Wanger's most expensive production of the thirties, "enhanced" by Technicolor in gaudy register, and he had counted on Boyer as box-office protection. Boyer's contract did not give him script refusal—an oversight, he insisted—so Wanger tried every tactic to change Boyer's mind. Well, not every tactic, they were friends after all; but not as good friends as before.

Wanger prepared *52nd Street* on a less lavish scale and had a more entertaining musical film—still, a too easily forgettable one. Many moviegoers may have thought it was a revival of an old Warner Brothers musical; for whatever their reasons, few came to see it. A likely reason was that although it offered an array of top-notch entertainers of the day—Ella Logan, Kenny Baker, Jerry Colonna, ZaSu Pitts—it had no pedigreed "stars." The male lead was the Englishman Ian Hunter, and playing opposite him—she didn't turn this one down—was Pat Paterson. *52nd Street* bore a striking resemblance to the Fox *Bottoms Up* that had brought her to America, and also was shaped around Pat, almost a "vehicle" . . . and perhaps Wanger was rankled that Boyer didn't appreciate what he was trying to do for his wife.

Boyer was not unappreciative, but he was very apprehensive. Pat was terrified during the *52nd Street* shooting ordeal, the old confidence all gone. She was near to tears, telling her husband she was too damn rusty. She hadn't kept up her dancing lessons, and it wasn't like riding a bicycle, something that could be picked right up. On the screen she appeared to be getting all the steps right for the dances Danny Dare had devised for her; she knew she was still more graceful than Ruby Keeler! But it was very hard work now, so hard it stifled Pat's own bubbliness.

Boyer thought she was quite wonderful—the best thing he'd seen her do. But Pat said it wasn't fun anymore. She'd wanted to keep her career and he hadn't given nearly enough encouragement; in the end, though, she was walking away from a career against his urging.

He was saying "Pat, I want you to be *happy*."

And she was saying "I guess I had no idea how happy I am just being your wife."

While she was filming *52nd Street*, the movie theaters were showing *History Is Made at Night* and Charles was over at M-G-M playing Napoleon, opposite Garbo. On professional terms the Boyers hardly suggested a match. She conceded once and for all that he'd won the competition.

※　※　※

This was his peak year, the *annus mirabilis*.

In spring it was *History Is Made at Night*. In the 1937

summer it was the American release of *Mayerling*, the most successfully exhibited foreign-language film of the decade. Fall brought *Conquest* and his personal triumph as Bonaparte. And for winter there was *Tovarich*, a Christmas special, directed by Anatole Litvak.

He later remarked that if he'd made *Vogues* for Wanger, he could not have been Napoleon to Garbo's Marie Walewska. That wasn't exactly true. The two pictures were shot at the same time, but M-G-M would have waited for him. They'd been waiting for years to find a Napoleon who wouldn't wither in the bright rays of Garbo's sheer presence.

It had been a dormant project for years. It has been calculated that M-G-M purchased over two hundred story properties as vehicle possibilities for the divine Garbo during a twelve-year period in which she made fourteen talking pictures, several from the public domain. The Polish novel *Pani Walewska* had gathered dust on the story-department shelf because there was no one to play Napoleon. Various writers worked on a script intermittently in speculation that a Napoleon would materialize—probably not from the star ranks, because it was not foreseen as a costar role. *Marie Walewska,* as it was called in its prehistory and shooting schedule before the late title change to *Conquest,* was a Garbo vehicle, plain and simple, based on Napoleon's most interesting and admirable mistress. The Polish countess had an adulterous affair with Bonaparte, bearing him a son who would not be acknowledged officially, yet would be a credit to the late emperor when he emerged as a leading French diplomat in the mid-nineteenth century. There was no star actor *short* enough to play Napoleon, and the closest they had come to getting the problem resolved was to use Claude Rains. It was finally decided that Rains was a shade too old to be playing Napoleon, or to make love to Garbo—although Rains did play Napoleon in 1936 in a Marion Davies picture for Warner Brothers.

With Charles Boyer's substantial emergence in 1935, the M-G-M project was reactivated, again on speculation; they certainly didn't tell him about it. It was assigned to Thalberg's unit but had no specified time, and Thalberg may well have intended to defer the project until he had his own company, targeted for 1938. Thalberg discussed the project with Boyer in their last meeting, shortly before Thalberg's death, but even then it wasn't definite.

S. N. Behrman had worked on the script in one of its early treatments, and returned for late revisions before and during production—revisions that he said were immediately logical with the knowledge that Boyer was playing the role. Behrman wrote, "One may study even the final shooting script and see that the Emperor is not fully or satisfactorily developed, not as the Countess is. What Charles Boyer accomplishes in his portrayal is the issue of his own intelligence and his own magic. He didn't have a lot of help from the script, although he had help, or inspiration, from Garbo, as I'm sure Clarence Brown would tell you."

Clarence Brown was considerably more than "Garbo's Man Friday." He was one of the few M-G-M directors capable of endowing a film with his own visual conceptions and his personal humanity, so that they appeared to be directed and not merely produced in the M-G-M trademark high gloss, although most of his films had that too. Brown directed Garbo in seven films, of which *Conquest* came last, and was less a Garbo vehicle than any other only because the leading man was not overwhelmed by her.

Boyer's contract with Wanger was non-exclusive, so it was not necessary for him to obtain permission in order to accept the role—which, anyway, he didn't do when they first asked him. He didn't second-guess the substance of the property, but had serious doubt that he should play Napoleon. It was not a fear of challenge, although he recognized the challenge:

"I would have been hesitant if someone had asked me to play Jesus. I mean no disrespect to the Christ, but Napoleon has a more powerful historical presence, where Jesus is a powerful spiritual presence. Which would be the harder role to play? For a Frenchman, I believe it would be Napoleon. I was fearful that to the French people, no performance of Napoleon Bonaparte, not even a *perfect* one, would be satisfactory."

On the other hand, they were calling him a great actor in

France, where he had yet to give proof of that. He decided to play Napoleon, in earnest hope of providing that proof.

He sensed how badly M-G-M wanted him, and came to realize that the picture probably would not be made without him. He extracted an undisclosed but presumably enormous fee when he signed the contract, even before he had shot his first scenes for *History Is Made at Night*. With that chore discharged, Boyer pursued a close acquaintance with Greta Garbo before their own production cycle began, so their coexistence on the closed set that Garbo demanded could be relaxed when it had to be. It was often tense, he said, not because of temperament or any possible problem between them, but because Garbo's commitment was as serious as his.

Conquest is not a classic. Over the years it has held up well, as most of Clarence Brown's films do; and the Garbo performance now seems stronger, perhaps, than it did in 1937. It was never a weak account, and the Garbo intangibles are inherent. But the story plods. It owes its strength to its stars—the supporting players are also decidedly able—but a consensus response is conveyed by *The New Yorker* review stating that for the first time, Garbo had "a leading man who contributes more to the interest and vitality of the film than she does."

Garbo's M-G-M costars had been such as John Gilbert, Clark Gable, Robert Montgomery, Melvyn Douglas, John Barrymore, Herbert Marshall, and a callow Robert Taylor in the nonetheless glorious *Camille* that immediately preceded *Conquest*. Some of these were very able actors or quite effective screen personalities, but even Barrymore was no match for Greta Garbo in *Grand Hotel*. The finest actor she had worked with was probably Fredric March in the *Anna Karenina* also directed by Clarence Brown, but March was a pallid, miscast Vronsky. So might Boyer also have been, although even at thirty-seven he *should* have been her Armand Duval. But *Conquest* presented the actor who was precisely right for the exacting role.

There were some reservations voiced. The Boyer conception was found to be too sympathetic; the crueler aspects of Bonaparte were believed not properly illumined. Boyer was imparting a psychological and emotional depth that made his strong characterization more complex and more believable, and quite naturally more sympathetic because of that. His triumph was not that he played Napoleon imperially, but that he made him a human being. Not a great picture, but a great performance.

When the torrents of praise came, Boyer was relieved, and gratified to have been solemnized, but also embarrassed. He did not know what to say when they asked him about his performance, as they *were* asking—he was the topical interview subject, although woefully reluctant. He said "What can I do? I tell them my performance as Napoleon could have been better and they think I am posing, they think I am being modest in a calculating way. How can I make them understand—how does an actor do that? I know my Napoleon could have been better. It *should* have been better . . . which is not to say I am disappointed with the performance, I am not disappointed but pleased. But it should have been better. Do you understand me?"

While *Conquest* was filming, Boyer watched the "dailies" or "rushes" for the first few days—the raw exposure of the footage just shot in the working day. He didn't have a habit of watching the rushes elsewhere, but at M-G-M it was a tradition, an end-of-the-day sociable thing. Greta Garbo liked to watch the rushes, liked to comment on the image of herself, whom she always referred to as "she." For Boyer the rushes only brought awesome frustration—he was always seeing ways in which he could have improved the performance.

He was an actor in a way that Greta Garbo was not an actress. He conceded that it was reasonable for some people to have said that she didn't know what she was doing; but what she did, she did instinctively, sometimes innocently but usually magically. Boyer also believed that she could not comprehend her magic—who could?—and that it worried her, hastening her early retirement.

Years later, he reflected on his *Conquest* costar: "Today there are no actresses like her. Some have more acting ability, but Garbo had a guarded mystery about her and was enchanting to be with, to work with. The most beautiful nose

and face, and you could read on it all the thoughts that came
to her. Her ability to project what was within was unique."

When the 1937 Academy Award nominations were announced early the next year, Charles Boyer was nominated as
best actor for playing Napoleon in *Conquest*, Greta Garbo as
best actress for *Camille*.

＊　＊　＊

When *Mayerling* appeared on U.S. screens in 1937, its fame
had long preceded it. Samuel Goldwyn was reputed to have
said that it had "worldwide success throughout Europe." It
played throughout Europe, indeed, throughout 1936, and was
still in general distribution there when it crossed the Atlantic.
Americans were the last to see it. So when the major American commercial success that Anatole Litvak craved had finally
been attained, the director was already in America.

In the immediate European celebrity of *Mayerling*, Litvak
contacted every major film operation in Hollywood to inform
them of his availability. From several likely offers, he accepted one from Warner Brothers and checked into the studio
in Burbank late in 1936, with even shriller fanfare than had
greeted Fritz Lang on the latter's arrival at M-G-M earlier
that year.

Litvak's first project was an American version of his *L'Equipage*, the Annabella–Jean Murat film so much admired by
Boyer. A new title was inevitable and *The Woman I Love*
was chosen, to capitalize on the recently voiced pronouncement by Great Britain's Edward VIII, abdicating his throne
even before his coronation. Some moviegoers were quite
disappointed to arrive at the theater and discover that
Miriam Hopkins was *not* playing Wallis Warfield Simpson.
The Woman I Love was by no means a flop in its April 1937
release, but it was regarded as a considerable disappointment.
Certainly it was not another *Mayerling*, nor had it properly
served the eminence of its leading players. The status and
reputation of both Paul Muni and Miriam Hopkins would
decline in the years ahead, but in 1937 both were prestige
stars—M. Emile Zola and Miss Becky Sharp. The custom
had been to be rather more impressed by their pictures.

Litvak had charged into the filmland with panache and a trace of arrogance, telling everyone how great he was. Some Hollywood veterans were given to hoping that this Humpty Dumpty would take a fall. He hadn't yet, really, but he was wobbly after *The Woman I Love,* and sensed that his next Warner Brothers stint had an obligation to be very, very good. He wanted to do an American version of *Cette Vieille Canaille,* again with Muni and Hopkins, and notified Charles Boyer that he could have just one more chance to play the acrobat. But Robert Lord of the Warner hierarchy forbade another remake of a Litvak French success because it seemed a risk, and gave Litvak a choice from among several properties already owned by the company.

Litvak selected *Tovarich,* a current hit on Broadway as adapted by Robert E. Sherwood from a French play. The Warner folk were pleased that Litvak *knew* he could get Charles Boyer, who was much in demand. Litvak supposed he could, as eventually he did, but it was a titanic struggle. Boyer gave one of his unequivocal no's, and it was a long time before he wavered. He welcomed an opportunity to work again with Litvak, was even anxious to do so, but in some other property: "He is a Russian, and I am French! Furthermore, they are in Paris. It would be idiotic for me to play a Russian around people who are supposed to be French."

But in 1937 Hollywood a tree was a tree and you shot it in Griffith Park, and foreign accents were interchangeable and indistinguishable, just so long as they were real foreign accents . . . and they didn't even have to be real if you were a good faker. It was a moviemaking convention that Charles Boyer would *never* come to terms with, but he would compromise many times. He compromised on *Tovarich* "because I thought it would make a good picture, and that to follow Napoleon with a comedy was a wise thing."

Boyer negotiated an expensive free-lance contract that Robert Lord said had blown the budget so high that they could no longer afford Miriam Hopkins, whom Litvak desperately wanted in the other lead role. Hopkins was not then a Warner contract star and had taken to free-lancing after her recent release from Samuel Goldwyn, but Warner Brothers had paid both her and Goldwyn quite handsomely to be the woman Paul Muni loved. Litvak said he understood economics very well, so he'd accept some other actress. Meanwhile, he married Miriam Hopkins and for the two years of their union it was Hollywood's stormiest by near-unanimous opinion. So what did Robert Lord do? He hired Claudette Colbert, who was surely more expensive than Miriam would have been. Colbert was on loan from Paramount, so it meant another double fee. Hal Wallis had wanted to get Bette Davis, a Warner contract star then working for a modest weekly salary, into *Tovarich,* but abandoned the idea because it would have forced them to delay *Jezebel.*

Boyer must have been pleased with the arrangement. Claudette Colbert was one of his favorite people, and he hoped that his third picture with her wouldn't be their last. (It was.) *Tovarich* would prove a contrast to both *Private Worlds* and the entirely forgotten *The Man from Yesterday.* Boyer and Colbert—although the formal billing was reversed —would play White Russian royalty, exiled by the 1917 revolution, and taking jobs as servants with a French equivalent to the American family in *My Man Godfrey,* who don't know their servants' real identities. Colbert was an established stylish comedienne who smartly alternated her portrayals between light and heavy. The surprise would be Boyer the light comedian.

History Is Made at Night in its early passages had given more than a mild hint that he could handle high comedy, but *Tovarich* was sustained nimble froth, giving the appearance of an actor who'd been doing comedy all his life—as Boyer seldom had. The supporting cast was unusually strong, and the matter of the accents was partially resolved by having the key French characters played by stylish Britons with impeccable English speech—Basil Rathbone, Isabel Jeans, and Melville Cooper. But there was the Frenchman Boyer passing off his accent as Russian, while the Frenchwoman Colbert's Russian accent sounded one hundred percent American.

No one minded. *Tovarich* was an unqualified critical success that attracted and delighted a large national audience and also did especially well in France. Many American patrons still couldn't figure out what the title meant. What *Tovarich* meant was that Hollywood was safe for Anatole Litvak, and vice versa.

❖   ❖   ❖

When Boyer was in France to film *Mayerling*, he met a young man named André Daven who had no artistic pretensions but who loved films as a member of the lay audience and wished to be involved with them as a producer. Boyer admired Daven's frankness and his sincerity, and his reading background—it was Daven who convinced Boyer that he *had* to read Proust, after he had consciously avoided Proust for so long. Boyer introduced Daven to Joseph Kessel and they developed their own strong friendship. They became possibly Boyer's closest friends in Paris, although Kessel was only a part-time Parisian. If Kessel was on the scene during Boyer's visits to Paris, they inevitably became a threesome with Daven, deriving rare fulfillment just by sharing long hours of talk—about film and theater, world affairs, but primarily about literature.

In 1980 André Daven said in Paris: "Few people knew how well-read Charles was. He didn't boast, he was very modest about it. He spoke, often in great complaint, of what he had *not* read. There was so much that he wanted to read, and he was running out of time. But he read everything—fiction of every type, the classics but also the modern novelists, the serious ones. He was partial to the Germans—Hans Fallada and Stefan Zweig. But he read more history than fiction—histories of all places and of all periods. He was so curious.

"Even his good friends joked about him behind his back, and he knew that. They said he was . . . the American expression is stick-in-the-mud. They believed there was no joy in him but that was not true. There was joy, it was all inside. It was difficult for most people to see. But his wife saw it. She must have, because they had . . . a rhythm in their life, always when they were together. She read a lot, too, but not the same things. She read *Gone With the Wind* and I suppose *Forever Amber*. She wasn't deep and he loved her because she didn't pretend to be. But somehow she penetrated him.

Charles couldn't help it that he was such a moody person, but Pat understood his moods perfectly."

André Daven believed also that Boyer's fabled fiscal conservatism was misunderstood: "People said he was such a tightwad. That was because they wanted him just to give his money to them, and he would not. But he was a generous man, when there was a purpose. And he was generous in other ways, certainly toward me . . ."

In 1936 Boyer counseled Daven, giving him his own knowledge of the tricks of the trade, encouraging him to become a producer for the screen. Daven produced his first important film the next year, after some apprentice efforts. He interested Marc Allégret in *Gribouille*, and in an incredibly beautiful girl who changed her name from Simone Roussel to Michèle Morgan when Allégret gave her the lead role opposite the incomparable Raimu.

Earlier Allégret had shaped the considerable French stardom of Simone Simon, an actress of sparkling personality who went to America and became Darryl Zanuck's equivalent of Sam Goldwyn's Anna Sten, unable to come to terms with the Hollywood system. With Michèle Morgan, Allégret would be credited with even greater success; she is by common agreement the French screen actress *par excellence* of all time.

When the Boyers arrived in Paris in 1937 after *Tovarich* was in the can, Daven and Allégret told them about *Orage*, for which a mature male actor was needed to appear opposite the very young Michèle Morgan. Boyer said he would be happy to do it before he knew what the story was about— such was his faith in the people involved. It was an illicit affair between a properly married businessman and a footloose young girl, the sort of thing that might be done by Jean Gabin and Brigitte Bardot in a later era. *Orage* obtained American distribution (as *Storm*) because Boyer was in it. Allégret did not consider it one of his estimable works. Michèle Morgan hated it—no, she hated her performance, which was not received enthusiastically. She later indicated that she had been off balance, awed by Charles Boyer who had become a god. He wasn't mean to her and was really quite considerate, but she was intimidated by his very presence . . . although she hadn't been intimidated by the towering Raimu. She forgot to act, or forgot how to, while Boyer created a character.

Like Simone Simon before her, and like Micheline Presle and so many others after her, Michèle Morgan went to Hollywood and did not catch on there—another example of America's inexplicable resistance to France's actress-beauties. *Mayerling* was Danielle Darrieux's passport to Hollywood; but although critics praised her performance in *The Rage of Paris* (1938), audiences were small, and so she returned to France. Boyer assisted Darrieux's passage to Hollywood, and was helpful while she was there. With Morgan, later, he also played a behind-the-scenes role, assuring her of the security of a lavish term contract, arranged by Charles K. Feldman even before Michèle's arrival in California.

André Daven also made it into Hollywood during the war years—only because Boyer, as Daven said, "was so generous a man."

7

Charles Boyer owed Walter Wanger two pictures. Only one would be made; the remaining commitment was canceled by mutual consent when their differences became irreconcilable.

The one that was made and released—well, it was historic, and is.

Algiers is a classic. It is not even nearly a great picture, although it is by no means a bad one. A motion picture becomes a classic when it is retained in the public memory, and *Algiers* is a part of American culture, a staple of filmland folklore.

It is the picture in which Charles Boyer did *not* say "Come wiz me to zee Casbah" to Hedy Lamarr.

By now just about everyone knows that the line was never spoken, much as "Play it again, Sam" was never delivered precisely by Humphrey Bogart in *Casablanca,* that other piece of fabulous Hollywood–North African folklore. Boyer and Lamarr were *in* the Casbah in most of their *Algiers* scenes, and they *did* have an important scene in which they were not in the Casbah, but the dialogue was nowhere close.

The line that never was eventually became the most popular association with Charles Boyer, and was the ironic residue of a picture he fought against making.

A story goes with it.

Boyer, like Anatole Litvak and perhaps some other transplanted cinema artists, nurtured ambitions to remake in Hollywood some of his own French successes, or other titles from the wondrous fund of European film classics. In the mid-thirties Boyer tried to interest Walter Wanger and other producers in filming his modestly successful French film *L'Epervier* as *The Lovers,* long before Louis Malle used that title. He even hired his own writers to adapt *L'Epervier* and to prepare a new treatment based on *Le Capitaine Fracassé,* the silent picture he had made with his lifelong friend, Pierre Blanchar. In the mid-forties Boyer even entertained notions of an American version of *Orage,* despite its modest reputation in both hemispheres.

Wanger had his own ideas about pictures he wished to produce, and about those he believed Boyer should do. His priority project was getting Boyer and Sylvia Sidney in a picture together; and he proposed yet another version of Boyer's *La Bataille,* with Miss Sidney projected for Annabella's old role. Boyer refused even to consider it. He said "If I act the same role in another language, I am not repeating myself. A different language spells a different characterization, inevitably. But to repeat a performance in the same language would be absurd. One could not be creative at all." He had done *La Bataille* in both French and English, and was not eager to undertake yet another exotic portrayal.

He apprised Wanger of some other good French films, particularly a lovely Feyder item called *Le Grand Jeu.* Wanger purchased an option on *Le Grand Jeu* but was not enthusiastic about it. He was rather more eager to produce another French subject he had acquired—*Pépé le Moko,* a much-praised Julien Duvivier film. Boyer rated it highly, but said "Not for me, surely!" when Wanger sought his interest in the title role. Boyer did not wish to play Pépé or any other role that Jean Gabin had played: "Gabin is too special. He is unique. When he plays a role, it stays played. Others should not tamper. I will not tamper with a Gabin performance."

Wanger said he would drop the subject; he wouldn't ask Charles to take an assignment he wouldn't enjoy. Then, while Boyer was filming *Tovarich* for Anatole Litvak and the Warner company, Wanger obtained the Ben Hecht–Charles

MacArthur adaptation of *Wuthering Heights* and rejoiced that he'd found the ideal property for Boyer and Sylvia Sidney.

Hecht and MacArthur were prolific screenwriters throughout the thirties, often but not always in collaboration, and had even directed some of their own original screenplays for Paramount. Hecht later revealed that over several years a "Sunday pastime" for him and MacArthur was a script derived mainly from the first half of Emily Brontë's *Wuthering Heights*, a novel they both adored. They had planned to produce and direct their own picture, but Paramount refused to commit the necessary budget, after which Hecht and MacArthur left Paramount and failed to obtain a directing function elsewhere. Hecht might have sold the screenplay to his friend David Selznick but for Selznick's preoccupation with *Gone With the Wind* and other important properties. Selznick suggested that Hecht and MacArthur try Walter Wanger; and Wanger purchased the script which he perceived as first-rate.

Charles Boyer also admired the Hecht-MacArthur screenplay, and was strongly attracted to the role of the brooding, embittered Heathcliff. Sylvia Sidney was thought to be ecstatic over the Catherine Earnshaw role which, amidst its elegant English trappings, could deliver her from a wearying run of drab American working-class heroines. Boyer agreed to the project, Wanger issued the production and casting announcement to the press, and then Boyer had second thoughts. Although Heathcliff also rated as something of an exotic, he was supposed to be a gypsy boy raised from childhood in the Earnshaw home. Therefore Boyer's French accent would be incongruous and, he believed, inadmissible. Wanger said that problem could be resolved easily with just a few explanatory lines of dialogue. Boyer didn't believe it was that simple. He also heard the community gossip, which ridiculed the casting of Boyer as Heathcliff.

Wanger, meanwhile, was beset with economic problems. The spotty commercial returns for his recent pictures made bankers reluctant to finance a production of the scope required for *Wuthering Heights*. Wanger needed the immediate proof of a major box-office success, and reasoned that he would have to put the prestige-courting *Wuthering Heights* on a back burner while he concentrated on a money hit.

To Boyer he proposed first one likely commercial prospect, then another, each as the picture to precede *Wuthering Heights,* which presumably would conclude the Boyer-Wanger contract. Eventually Wanger made both *Trade Winds* and *Eternally Yours* without great success, and without Boyer who rejected both. Boyer believed Wanger's idea for *Trade Winds* was ludicrous. Tay Garnett, Wanger's director, possessed a lot of fancy scenic footage that had been photographed during an around-the-world cruise. Wanger and Garnett planned to shoot a neat little melodrama in front of a continually changing scenic background, with most of the action occurring on an ocean liner—essentially, a ninety-minute "process shot" that could make an inexpensive film resemble an extravaganza. To Boyer, it was a most dubious creative impulse. Wanger did manage to get Fredric March for the detective role Boyer rejected, opposite Joan Bennett; and David Niven was Boyer's "replacement" in the romantic trifle that was *Eternally Yours,* opposite Loretta Young. Boyer rated *Eternally Yours* as a comedy without either likable people or funny lines. Against such humdrum material, *Pépé le Moko* looked like strong stuff to Boyer when Wanger again proposed it.

Wanger pleaded that the way of the independent producer wasn't easy. His operation was in financial trouble, and his speculation on both the traveloguelike *Trade Winds* and the studio-bound *Eternally Yours* was mainly economic. Wanger's *You Only Live Once,* with its tragic resolution, had been a critical success but a financial failure. Although *History Is Made at Night* was a hit, its profit was modest. Wanger expected to break even with *Vogues of 1938* but had lost money on *52nd Street*. His and Garnett's *Stand-In* with Leslie Howard, Joan Blondell, and Humphrey Bogart was very popular, yet first returns were sluggish for *I Met My Love Again* with Wanger's other contract stars, Henry Fonda and Joan of the sisters Bennett. Wanger also hoped to put into production a John Howard Lawson story about the Spanish Civil War, with Fonda and Madeleine Carroll. This too would be a financial gamble. Indeed, *Blockade* would prove Wanger's courage to make an uncommercial property because he had a political conscience. Despite his being one of the most dedicated and ambitious independent filmmakers, Wanger was undercapitalized and fighting for his life. And he had not one prospect of a major box-office success.

Boyer, apparently stirred to compassion, agreed to make *Algiers* for Wanger. *Algiers* was the producer's title for *Pépé le Moko*. Wanger briefly had even considered making the picture with Fernand Gravet—historically the first in a long line of "second Boyers" auditioned in Hollywood. Boyer knew that his own performance as Pépé inevitably would be compared with Jean Gabin's and that thought still galled him; but he believed *Algiers* would make a splendid picture and could give Wanger his needed "smasheroo."

That concludes what was only the first installment for a three-act melodrama. After intermission and a smoke, Wanger showed Boyer and the film community his two new "discoveries." If both qualified as authentic discoveries indeed, neither had been discovered by Walter Wanger.

The first was Sigrid Gurie, whom Sam Goldwyn claimed to have discovered in Norway but who was later revealed to be a Brooklyn girl. Goldwyn had given her the "introducing" treatment in *The Adventures of Marco Polo*—wherein Gary Cooper, of all people, enacted the thirteenth-century Venetian. The Gurie girl failed to stir a public response; but then, how could she? The Marco Polo picture was one of the flops of the age. It had *just* flopped, and Sam didn't know what to do with his "siren of the fjords." So he loaned—no, he *gave* Sigrid Gurie to Wanger, begging Walter to take her. Wanger assumed the girl's contract, probably believing that she deserved another chance, but also knowing that he could cash in on all the publicity manufactured in her name over recent months by the Goldwyn machine. Sigrid Gurie would play Gaby, Pépé's faithful guttersnipe, in the Casbah—his sweetheart until he finds the other, beautiful, woman.

The other, beautiful, woman had been "discovered" often. For Hollywood's purposes, she had most recently been discovered in London, personally, by none other than Louis B. Mayer.

She was Hedy Lamarr. And a story-within-the-story goes with it.

＊　＊　＊

In 1933 a twenty-year-old nubile beauty named Hedwig Kiesler pranced around totally nude, swimming part of the time, in a ten-minute sequence in the Czech film *Extase*, directed by Gustav Machaty.

The film was a worldwide scandal but in America was accorded respectable art-house distribution, as *Ecstasy*. Yet Hedwig Kiesler dropped out of sight. She made no more films because she had married a munitions tycoon who made a vain effort to buy up and destroy every existing print of *Extase*. It remained in continuous international exhibition for thirty years.

The Viennese Kiesler was discovered again in court, divorcing her husband. Then, in 1937, Louis B. Mayer was in London on some other business matters while also signing Greer Garson, whose true discoverer he was. An agent brought Hedwig Kiesler to meet Mayer, because she wanted to get back into pictures. The story goes (and may be apocryphal) that Mayer didn't realize she was the naked girl in *Extase* until after he had signed her, and that the sanctimonious Mayer's aides were afraid to tell him. In *The Lion's Share*, Bosley Crowther quotes an exchange between M-G-M publicity chief Howard Dietz and the newly signed Kiesler: "Did you appear in the nude?" "Yes." "Did you look good?" "Of course!" "Then it's all right, no damage has been done."

Louis B. Mayer believed that the most beautiful of Hollywood actresses was the deceased star of silent films, Barbara LaMarr. He changed Hedwig Kiesler's name to Hedy Lamarr and took her to the M-G-M studio in Culver City, where she languished nearly a full year, inactive but drawing salary. By an incredible coincidence, M-G-M had also contracted Gustav Machaty, her discoverer-director for *Extase;* and the studio had planned to have Machaty direct her again, in a

remake of *Within the Law*. But when her screen tests revealed a stunning beauty whose acting potential, however,
was near zero, that idea was abandoned. Machaty showcased
another M-G-M newcomer, Ruth Hussey, in *Within the Law*,
while Mayer plotted to lend Lamarr to some other company.
It would be a way to see what she could do, without
compromising an M-G-M picture. She was offered to Goldwyn for the *Marco Polo* foolishness, but Sam chose Sigrid
Gurie because maybe *she* could act . . . a little. Paramount
also rejected Lamarr for Ronald Colman's *If I Were King*.
Then Walter Wanger accepted her at a cut-rate price, but
beauty *was* a factor.

End of story-within-story. Wanger introduced Sigrid Gurie
and Hedy Lamarr to Charles Boyer, and also to John
Cromwell. In agreeing to star in *Algiers*, Boyer had requested
and been granted "director approval," because he was not altogether confident with either of Wanger's men, Tay Garnett
and Irving Cummings. Cromwell was Boyer's choice and
Wanger signed him as the best director available, but grudgingly, because he was relatively expensive.

John Cromwell was an actor's director, and a fine actor
himself with a solid theatrical background. Of the quorum of
Broadway directors imported by Hollywood at the dawning
of the talkies, Cromwell and George Cukor were the only
ones to attain undisputed success in pictures and find a permanent niche. Cromwell eventually made more films for
David Selznick than any other director—eight all told, at Paramount, RKO, and for Selznick International—because he
wasn't intimidated by Selznick or his memos, and could handle him diplomatically. When Cromwell directed Leslie Howard at RKO in *Of Human Bondage*, he insisted on borrowing
Bette Davis from Warner Brothers to play Mildred, so in a
way he was her catalyst. As the director contracted for *Algiers*, he was just coming off the wonderful Selznick offering
of *The Prisoner of Zenda* with Ronald Colman, Madeleine
Carroll, and the younger Douglas Fairbanks, whose career
Cromwell resuscitated by casting him as Rupert of Hentzau.

That introduces John Cromwell, now the speaker:

"She was a nice girl, or she was then. Hedy didn't make

trouble, didn't have an ego problem. The problem was that she couldn't act, and we knew it before we started shooting or even rehearsing. After you've been in the business for a time, you can tell easily enough right when you meet them. I could sense her inadequacy, Wanger could sense it, and I could see Boyer getting worried even before we started talking behind Hedy's back. I'm talking about *presence*. It's difficult to explain, or it's difficult for some people to understand. Spencer Tracy had presence. Bogart had it. Cary Grant. Gary Cooper never understood a thing about real acting but had the most marvelous presence. Among the girls? Hepburn and Davis, of course. I may be the only person to have directed both Kate and Bette, can't think of anyone else that did. I never directed Norma Shearer but she had that special command, and Irving knew he could shape a great career for her—it had little to do with acting. Barbara Stanwyck had great star presence, and I'll add a special favorite, Irene Dunne, underrated on every count. All of these people could act, some better than others, but the aspect of presence gets closer to what a real star is.

"Sometimes the word personality is interchangeable with presence although they aren't the same thing. But the principle applies, and Hedy also had no personality. How could they think she could become a second Garbo? Good God, I forgot all about Greta! She was tops for presence and personality both, and had something else the others didn't, whatever the hell it was. But where presence is something that can be acquired to some extent, as Joan Crawford did, you cannot endow someone with a personality. They have it or they haven't. Carole Lombard wasn't bereft of presence, but she may have been number one for personality. Hedy Lamarr had a more discernible presence from picture to picture, call it a persona if you will, and she also learned to act. Sort of. She gave some decent performances later on, was very good in a Marquand thing. She still had no personality. Hedy always got star billing, but she wasn't a star. She was a beauty.

"Well, we got the picture going, and we did all right. The critics saw she couldn't act but she got by, and they sold the picture by gushing how beautiful she was. I'll take some credit for making her acting passable but can only share credit with Boyer fifty-fifty. I rate my accomplishment with Lamarr in *Algiers* above what I did with Davis in *Of Human Bondage* because Bette could have done it on her own without me. Hell, all I did was cast her and say roll 'em. So I'll say Boyer's was a finer accomplishment than mine. I didn't have to act with her; he did. He proved himself a gentleman of grace and courage, and excellent poise. If you were in a group of people and saw an atomic bomb falling down on you, Charles Boyer would be the one not to panic.

"He pulled Hedy through so delicately. He sensed a lack of confidence, but was more concerned about the little confidence she *did* have, which was sometimes revealed in the slightest arrogance. He didn't want to destroy that, but he never lied to her. He didn't tell her she was bad, but he didn't say she was good. He acted with sincerity and with integrity, and she responded to it. Any actor, good or bad, responds to another actor's level. Look at Lana Turner, probably the very worst actress that ever made it to the top. But when she acted in the Garfield picture she was very good, because she was playing off him. In *Algiers* Hedy plays off Boyer, and he's incredible. The love scenes are so strong that you don't see it's all *him*.

"And yet . . . and yet *Algiers* is the cross he had to bear, and kept on bearing years afterward. They say Ingrid Bergman was so mystified by *Casablanca* being such a hit that she wouldn't talk about it for years. That was the case with Boyer and *Algiers*, except he *had* to talk about it, for a kind of catharsis. It was all the fussing over the love scenes and the come-with-me-to-the-Casbah lunacy. I say the love scenes are strong, but Boyer made high demands on the art of acting and he was embarrassed by them, he thought they were so bad. To him it was a cruel irony that *Algiers* and the lovemaking with Hedy was what he was most famous for, and would be remembered by. I almost forgot Jean Arthur, a remarkable screen personality. A difficult person out in the street, so they say—I never knew her—but everyone who went to the movies *liked* her, and that's unusual. Every movie star is disliked by some people—Gable, Crawford, Dietrich certainly, even Garbo, Ronald Colman—but everybody liked Jean Arthur.

"I got onto this because she and Boyer made a picture that had wonderful love scenes. They're something to watch— much better than *Algiers* or anything else I can think of except Tracy and Hepburn and other examples where they really *are* in love. Boyer and Arthur, Borzage said, got on well enough on the set, very businesslike, thoroughly professional. No chumminess, though. But in their scenes you'd swear they're the absolute real thing, and it's not Harlow and Gable bouncing around all steamy, but an inner thing. You'd suspect he had something going on the side with her, but then you'd have to say no, not Charles Boyer, and definitely not with Jean Arthur. They just stored up a lot and saved it for the cameras and sang their duet. That's it, a duet—scenes not just to be watched, but listened to. Boyer and Arthur had two of the truly supernatural or paranormal voices, and if you close your eyes and listen, they're a musical composition—some harmony, some counterpoint, everything orchestrated by Frank Borzage, God rest his romantic soul. *History Is Made at Night*, I think it was. Not an awfully good picture, just so-so, with hokey sinister triangle stuff. But it has scenes that represent the pinnacle of Boyer's art, or that part of his art relating to the great lover, which on the screen he truly was. The Arthur movie is a good example, but with Boyer there are many others. He made pictures with Margaret Sullavan whose voice was sort of a cousin to Jean Arthur's voice, and Maggie could also act with great emotional conviction. Boyer did some beautiful things with Irene Dunne, too—there's no end of it, and then the French pictures also have to be considered.

"Well, *Algiers* really *is* a pretty good picture. I've never been ashamed of it. I believe it was Walter Wanger's pride and joy. He did *Stagecoach* right after, and that's one of the greatest pictures ever made, as *Algiers* certainly isn't. But Walter gave John Ford full credit for *Stagecoach* because the whole thing was Ford's idea, and the creative conception was entirely the director's—just like *Foreign Correspondent*, which is never called a Wanger movie, always a Hitchcock movie. But *Algiers* was something Walter believed he'd created. He signed me to direct—well, Boyer *asked* me to direct—and I would not claim to be the picture's creator, nor was Boyer. But Wanger didn't create *Algiers,* either. Julien Duvivier did. And that was Boyer's anguish . . ."

✻ ✻ ✻

The *Algiers* shooting script was being prepared by John Howard Lawson from a story treatment by James M. Cain, based on Julien Duvivier's French screen adaptation of the story "Pépé le Moko," authored by "Detective" Ashelbe. Lawson and Cain were first-rate Hollywood hacks as well as authentic literary figures—one a playwright, one a novelist. They are co-credited for an *Algiers* screenplay, which neither of them wrote, but whose functions had been contracted by Walter Wanger. Both Lawson and Cain could converse in French, variably, but neither knew it well enough to translate, literally or creatively, the original French screenplay. Wanger hired someone else to accomplish that function, after which John Howard Lawson paraphrased the translated dialogue into workable English.

Lawson's shooting script was either thrown away, burned, stuffed into a wastebasket, or otherwise discarded; or possibly it was bound in leather and placed in a bookshelf, where it may be gathering dust today and tomorrow. In short, it was never used. At some point after John Cromwell was brought in to direct *Algiers*—after casting had been completed, but before a scene had been shot—Walter Wanger had the sudden inspiration to duplicate the French *Pépé le Moko* shot by shot, using its shooting script as a guideline.

Charles Boyer was stunned, nonplussed, aghast; he couldn't believe it; he certainly didn't understand it. If the original production was to be duplicated visually, he would be straitjacketed in the Jean Gabin performance, helpless to create his own. Furthermore, the comparison with Gabin would be unavoidable.

This was Act Three of the *Algiers* theater piece, which

wasn't a soap opera and smacked of melodrama but which Charles Boyer believed was a tragedy.

Wanger explained that it would reduce the production cost substantially, even enormously—perhaps by as much as Charles Boyer's own handsome salary that Charles K. Feldman had escalated quite dramatically. To duplicate the original shooting script, with every scene, shot, and camera angle specified may not really have been Wanger's own inspiration, after all. David Selznick dropped strong hints that he had enlightened Wanger on the economic advantages of a duplicate version. This is revealed in Selznick's correspondence, at a time when he was proposing his new star from Sweden, Ingrid Bergman, for the *Algiers* role Hedy Lamarr would finally play.

A visually creative director might have walked away from the project. John Cromwell wasn't Josef von Sternberg, and he had suffered under Selznick, and was a philosophical fellow. Sure, he was disappointed, feeling rather deprived of a director's toys; but he still possessed his favorite toys—his actors, two of whom might melt from the heat. Cromwell was an actor's director who would discharge his assignment dutifully, with pleasure and gratitude for the opportunity to work with Charles Boyer.

Cromwell, always pronouncing it Bwah-yeah, said "Boyer was the unhappiest man in southern California. He felt doomed to imitate a Jean Gabin performance, and never appreciated how different his own Pépé was from Gabin's. Boyer showed something like genius to make it different. It was a triumph of nuance. The shots are the same, the dialogue has the same meaning, but Boyer's Pépé and Gabin's Pépé are two different fellows, but in the same predicament."

The predicament is that Pépé, a master criminal, is a wanted fugitive but has sanctuary in the sinister Casbah quarter of Algiers, where wise policemen never go. His drab workaday existence is compensated by lively companions for whom he is a sardonic major-domo, and by a mistress with whom he could have no complaint, until the beautiful married woman appears in the Casbah. They meet, they fall in love, an illicit relationship is implied; she goes out of the Casbah and he follows her, forfeiting his safety; and there is a tragic resolution.

Algiers was a critical success upon its national release in June of 1938. Reviews were favorable, thoughtful, respectful; they were not raves. It was a hit, but less than a smash; it was not near the top of *Variety's* list of the year's big moneymakers. In that era, ten pictures were nominated for the Academy Award as the year's best, and *Algiers* was not among them. Comparing the American and French versions was and is academic. Neither is great, both are good, each has its own superior characteristics. John Cromwell believed that he had much the better cast, leading ladies perhaps apart, with strong character contributions from Gene Lockhart (who informs on Pépé), Joseph Calleia, and Alan Hale. Cromwell's direction is impressive within its prescribed limitations, and the more discerning reviewers cited a triumphant mood piece, very French in its spirit.

But a motion picture does not have to be great to be extraordinary. It is that when it simply has something out of the ordinary, as Hedy Lamarr certainly was. Reviewers almost unanimously declared her a deficient actress, then took a brief pause before spending long paragraphs on her exquisiteness.

If a poll were taken today to determine the most beautiful woman of all time in American films, Hedy Lamarr would probably win. Many frivolous contests revolve around such matters, and Hedy in her heyday won most of them. The best-known contest was conducted by *Look* in 1944 to determine the most beautiful woman in American films at that time, and it was unresolved, with four current stars in a tie; but the four were displayed, in order, as Hedy Lamarr, Ingrid Bergman, Gene Tierney, and Linda Darnell.

Hedy Lamarr's beauty was a national preoccupation in 1938 that existed apart from how good *Algiers* was or was not. Everyone knew who she was, and didn't have to see *Algiers* to know what she looked like. The resourceful Louis B. Mayer got his hirelings to bombard the news media with Lamarr features in the immediate wake of her loan-out success. Her visage was everywhere, in still photographs—those moist luminous eyes, the sublimely tapered nose, that perfect mouth with its ample sensuous lips, and a geometrically amazing face with serene cheekbones—all crowned by the black silk of her hair with its natural widow's peak. Mayer knew how to pick 'em, and perhaps Walter Wanger did too.

Algiers earned its lasting fame, first, for having introduced Hedy Lamarr. Only a few years later, when many other decently good films of its era had been almost or entirely forgotten, *Algiers* was remembered because of that. Then came another development, an even more flukish one.

Because Charles Boyer had a secure position in America and the rest of the world, and because he was an exotic with a singular voice and a unique accent, a Boyer impersonation became a standard in every nightclub impressionist's repertoire. *Algiers* perhaps hadn't been his best picture, but because of the Lamarr factor it was one generally known to the public, and therefore a logical nail on which to hang one's Boyer imitation.

Argument cannot be resolved over who devised the line or said it first. It has been attributed to many, and claimed by many others. No matter, they all picked it up, and it wasn't just "Come wiz me to zee Casbah"; the classic delivery became "Hedy . . . Hedy, come wiz me to zee Casbah." In the film the Lamarr character certainly was not named Hedy, which only points up the travesty aspect. Nor was the vocal mimicry accurate. Boyer never made such pronunciations as "wiz" and "zee." He made the *th* sound clearly and correctly, and his "inimitable" accent was basically the result of every syllable being stressed in his English speech. Rather than a valid impression, the Boyer imitation became outright parody, a piece of comic shtick.

Boyer didn't take it gracefully at first, and later it continued to infuriate him. Friends cajoled him, as usual, for being unable to take a joke, but were finally made to see that his fury was not over being mimicked with a line not actually spoken. He believed that the parody demeaned his integrity as an actor, even creating the supposition that he was *not* a serious actor. He believed the whole thing had been carried altogether too far when one of the best-known Boyer imitators proved to be that American original, Mr. Bugs Bunny.

To the bogus impersonation he also attributed the myth, as he called it, of the great lover—or "lovair."

"Mostly I've played other parts, but even when I've played other parts people see me differently. In America, when you have an accent, in the mind of people they associate you with kissing hands and being gallant. I think this has harmed me, just as it has harmed me to be followed and plagued by a line I never even said."

It is also likely that with *Algiers* the main body of American moviegoers interpreted the "great lover" identity as a limitation of Boyer the actor. The very nature of parody is to define a limitation, and the British scholar David Thomson, in his *Biographical Dictionary of Film,* notes that "It is no small accomplishment (for Boyer) to have maintained his intimations of Gallic passion in the face of constant imitation and parody."

Had *Algiers* been a more pleasurable experience for Boyer, he might have been more tolerantly disposed toward its ironic fame. But he had been miserable throughout the filming, equating it with *Caravan* as a consistently frustrating chore. Furthermore, *Algiers* estranged him from Walter Wanger artistically, if not on personal terms. They maintained a civil association, but their friendship was sorely strained by Boyer's decision not to appear in *Wuthering Heights.* He rejected *Eternally Yours* almost simultaneously, giving Wanger a hint that Boyer wished to be released from his contract. The terms of that contract stipulated another salary increase for Boyer with the final picture commitment, so it was Wanger's own suggestion that they terminate the agreement.

At about the same time that Wanger parted company with his intended Heathcliff, he also lost his Catherine Earnshaw. In the view of the industry, Sylvia Sidney had become a box-office liability, and the rumor mill held that Wanger had dropped her for that reason. Miss Sidney's departure from Hollywood was entirely voluntary, and she returned to Broadway because she was weary of picture-making. According to one report, the ordeal of working for William Wyler in *Dead*

End had destroyed Sylvia's confidence. In any event, Wyler provided an account of how Samuel Goldwyn, and not Walter Wanger, came to produce *Wuthering Heights:*

"When I was directing *Dead End* for Sam, Sylvia Sidney showed me the *Wuthering Heights* script and wanted my opinion on it. She was apprehensive about it, and not at all sure she wanted to make the picture if Charles Boyer was going to play Heathcliff. Right away I saw a terrific script with wonderful visual possibilities. Then when Sylvia quit pictures for a spell, and Wanger also lost Boyer, I told Goldwyn about the Hecht-MacArthur screenplay for *Wuthering Heights.* I knew Sam was looking for a property for Merle Oberon. He had a large investment in Oberon but she hadn't caught on with the American public. I said she'd be a perfect Cathy, and that prompted Sam to just buy the screenplay outright from Wanger. And then Sam, wouldn't you know, was all hot to get Charles Boyer to play Heathcliff. Sam could be persuasive, and he might have talked Charles back into it, except Charles hadn't enjoyed Oberon when they made a picture earlier. So I held out for the actor I wanted."

The actor Wyler wanted was an Englishman who, rather like Charles Boyer, had been a flop in his first visits to Hollywood—Laurence Olivier.

*   *   *

Although *Algiers* won no Oscars, it was accorded four Academy Award nominations: James Wong Howe's cinematography, a clear improvement on the French; Alexander Toluboff's art direction; the supporting actor performance of Gene Lockhart; and for best actor, the Charles Boyer portrayal of Pépé le Moko.

The other nominated actors were James Cagney, Robert Donat, Leslie Howard, and Spencer Tracy. Although it rated as a wide-open race, Boyer finally lost out for the second successive year to Tracy, who followed *Captains Courageous* with his Father Flanagan role in *Boys Town.*

Nevertheless, back-to-back nominations helped to certify Boyer as one of the more prestigious actors in Hollywood's top-star nucleus. Without having penetrated the circle of leading box-office attractions, he rated as a "bankable" star. He was *hot*. In Hollywood you're hot when every major producer covets your services, for practically everything. In 1937 and 1938 they even proffered for Boyer's consideration several conventional American or English protagonists. If he was interested, it would be simple enough to add a few lines of dialogue to make the fellows French, or perhaps some other foreign substance.

During the period of his non-exclusive contract with Walter Wanger, the actor received a barrage of overtures from Paramount, M-G-M, Warner Brothers, and 20th Century–Fox— the Big Four—all of whom sought a piece of him. They proposed many pictures that never got made once he had rejected them. Samuel Goldwyn even tried to tempt Boyer into playing Dmitri in *The Brothers Karamazov*, which Sam had planned years earlier with Anna Sten projected as Grushenka, and which remained on the shelf. That Hollywood still had some fuzzy notions about Boyer's essence and perhaps his range is attested by some roles he might have played, in films that *did* get made. Strange as it may now seem, Boyer at one point was apparently considered interchangeable with such disparate screen personalities as England's Ronald Colman and Herbert Marshall, and the American stalwarts Melvyn Douglas and Tyrone Power, all of whom at least twice took assignments that earlier had been proposed for Boyer.

Perhaps no producer was so covetous of Boyer as 20th Century–Fox's Darryl Zanuck. Years earlier, before welding his independent 20th Century unit to the Fox empire, Zanuck had produced the tearjerking *Gallant Lady* with Ann Harding. He wanted Boyer for the remake, called *Always Goodbye*. Boyer admired Barbara Stanwyck, who was projected as his costar; but he liked neither the script nor his intended role, which Herbert Marshall eventually played opposite Stanwyck. Undismayed, Zanuck proposed other subjects for Boyer, including the prestigious *Suez*—about the French engineer Ferdinand de Lesseps, who built the great canal. Boyer was intrigued, especially when Zanuck decided to import Annabella from France to appear with him. But Boyer's "literary judgment" of the screenplay caused him to refuse the bait; whereupon Tyrone Power, the new young superstar groomed personally by Zanuck, took the De Lesseps role. Boyer's evaluation proved astute, for *Suez* was a notable failure and was believed the only American film of 1938 that lost money, mainly for being an expensively mismanaged project. It was not a total loss for Tyrone Power, however: he married Annabella.

Power also played another 1938 role that had been figured for Boyer, if somewhat bizarrely—as Count Axel de Fersen in *Marie Antoinette*. As early as 1932, when Irving Thalberg purchased Stefan Zweig's famous biographical novel about the unfortunate French queen, a lavish M-G-M production was in planning for Thalberg's wife, Norma Shearer. Boyer recalled that while he was chauffeuring Jean Harlow in M-G-M's *Red-Headed Woman*, Thalberg had slotted him in the role of the wily Duke of Orleans, eventually played by Joseph Schildkraut. Later, when Boyer achieved American fame opposite such actresses as Colbert, Hepburn, and Dietrich, Thalberg had considered him for the role he truly ached to play—the tragic, ineffectual Louis XVI, whom Robert Morley was destined to portray beautifully. Louis had been foreseen as the primary costar role, and Boyer insisted betimes that he *was* a character actor, after all; but apparently he was no longer considered for Louis after Thalberg's death in the fall of 1936.

When the project finally came to fruition in 1938 with Shearer's emergence from mourning, everybody at M-G-M wanted Boyer in the French Revolution spectacle as Shearer's leading man—the Swedish diplomat Fersen. Louis B. Mayer, who once had rejected a Thalberg notion of Boyer as a prospective M-G-M star, nevertheless took full credit for having lured Boyer into *Conquest;* and producer Hunt Stromberg, becoming a good friend to Boyer, intimated that Mayer wanted Boyer to "protect" the possibly fading Shearer at the box office. A French historical subject had sure appeal for Boyer, and there was general expectation that *Marie Antoinette* would be a great picture, but he simply did not wish to play Fersen. Boyer pointed out that if he did, he would be the only real Frenchman in the cast, portraying virtually the only character in the film who was *not* French. He resisted to the end, and M-G-M ultimately borrowed Tyrone Power from Zanuck in a trade for Spencer Tracy, who could then be in Zanuck's *Stanley and Livingstone*. Power may have protected the box office for a somewhat disappointing major M-G-M production; but as Fersen, he was the only negative charge in an otherwise positively acted film.

Nevertheless, the M-G-M folk were persistent in their efforts to bring back Boyer for an encore to his Napoleon portrayal at the same studio. Indeed, Boyer and Garbo were filming *Conquest* when Jean Harlow's sudden death invalidated writer Richard Schayer's conception of a picture to costar Harlow and Boyer. After that, Boyer rejected the M-G-M offer of *The Toy Wife*, who was Luise Rainer. Then Frank Borzage, the director of Boyer's *History Is Made at Night* and now an M-G-M contract director, sought Boyer for *The Shining Hour*. Boyer knew that his good fortune in having appeared with a succession of household-name actresses had enhanced his standing, and *The Shining Hour* offered the prospect of *two* ranking female stars, Joan Crawford and Margaret Sullavan. Could any actor ignore such opportunity? Boyer could, when the script did not beguile him. He saw his intended role as a cardboard projection within the conventions of female-dominated soap operatics. Melvyn Douglas was Boyer's "replacement" for *The Shining Hour*, as he had also been for *The Toy Wife*. And there was yet another effort by M-G-M to get Boyer into a picture with Luise Rainer.

The Viennese actress was a thorny problem for the august studio. After a showy debut in *Escapade* made her the talk of Hollywood, she played Anna Held in *The Great Ziegfeld*, wherein a smiling-through-tears telephone scene helped her snare an Academy Award as best actress in only her second picture. Then Thalberg cast her in *The Good Earth*, which proved to be his last production; and Rainer contributed an affecting performance as O-Lan. In early 1938, while Boyer was filming *Algiers*, Luise Rainer became the first two-time Academy Award winner, picking up her second successive

Oscar. Yet ironically, the word already was circulating throughout the filmland that she was "through."

Two Rainer pictures released after *The Good Earth* had been all-around fizzles, and she had completed two others (including *The Toy Wife*) that awaited release without optimism for their prospects. Louis B. Mayer calculated that the Rainer stardom might still be salvaged—if not by her second Oscar, then by her scheduled appearance in a project that was especially pampered by Mayer himself—*The Great Waltz*, the story of the younger Johann Strauss. Since Hollywood had a way of equating all non-Americans, Mayer wanted the French-foreign Charles Boyer to play the Austrian-foreign Strauss in *The Great Waltz*. To make the offer more tempting, Mayer brought over from France one of Boyer's closest friends to direct—Julien Duvivier, reaching the height of his reputation with *Un Carnet de Bal* as the follow-up event to *Pépé le Moko*. Boyer was tempted, too, by a strong focal role, to which even Luise Rainer would play a support function.

Again he was bothered by an illogicality. Rainer, after all, was an authentic Viennese; and Miliza Korjus, the coloratura assigned the other female lead, had at least been trained in Berlin. Even Duvivier believed it would hardly matter, but Boyer said yes it does, because now all the American people *know* I'm French. Yet when he turned down *The Great Waltz*, the Strauss role was given to the Belgian Fernand Gravet, who had come to Hollywood as a "second Boyer" after success in French plays and films. On the Continent his name had been Gravey, but it was further Frenchified by the Warner Brothers, who feared that the American people might call him "Gravy."

Even before Boyer had made *Tovarich* for the Warner company, an effort had been made to get him into the Warner fold for one of the title roles in *The King and the Chorus Girl*. The story had been conceived by none other than Groucho Marx, who may have sensed comical possibilities for Boyer's soulful Frenchman before anyone else. Marx and Norman Krasna produced a farcical script built around an often-inebriated foreign monarch, distracted by Broadway pulchritude. After giving Marx initial encouragement, Boyer backed off, saying he didn't believe a bombardment of one-liners was the kind of comedy best suited to his style. Failing Boyer, Warner Brothers brought Fernand Gravet from France to be king to Joan Blondell's chorus girl. They put him under contract, and at one point Gravet was also "announced" for *Tovarich* before Claudette Colbert, according to rumor, held out for Boyer. When *The King and the Chorus Girl* failed to click at the box office, there was a studio effort to remove Gravet from the projected *Fools for Scandal* in favor of Boyer. The bait was Carole Lombard, a leading comedy star of the period, but Boyer wouldn't nibble because he didn't like anything he read. Indeed, it became the only unargued flop of Lombard's big-star period, although both she and Fernand Gravet worked hard to pump life into it. After it thudded, the Warner company dropped Gravet, who would have returned to France but for the intervening opportunity of *The Great Waltz*. It was the last of Gravet's three American films, any and all of which Boyer might well have played.

Although Boyer successfully resisted every effort to get his signature on a regular studio contract, he came closest to signing with Paramount. William LeBaron, the production chief, regularly dangled properties that Boyer found interesting, such as the role of François Villon in *If I Were King*. It was believed that only Boyer's refusal to sign a three-picture deal kept him from playing Villon, before Ronald Colman insinuated himself into *If I Were King*—which then became his own *Algiers* equivalent, the foundation for later Ronald Colman impersonations.

Boyer liked the Paramount setup. It was a "director's studio" in contrast to such a "producer's studio" as M-G-M. He apparently reconsidered a Paramount offer after completing *Algiers* and severing his association with Walter Wanger, although *If I Were King* was no longer in the offing. Money talked, and Paramount was in a generous mood. Charles Feldman worked out terms for a three-picture pact that was to be initiated with *Zaza* and followed by *Midnight*, with Claudette Colbert figured as his top-billed costar in both ventures. Boyer was not enamored of either project, and his last-minute decision not to sign with Paramount was prompted by picture possibilities elsewhere that held more appeal for him. So Herbert Marshall was slotted as Colbert's leading man in *Zaza*, which failed; while the Paris-based *Midnight* was a considerable hit, with Don Ameche as the "French" cab driver in Boyer's stead.

Boyer now was superintending his own career. The picturemaking activities of most leading stars in that era were governed by committee. Clark Gable and Spencer Tracy at M-G-M, Gary Cooper and Bing Crosby at Paramount, James Cagney and Errol Flynn at Warner Brothers—all of them trusted the sagacity of studio minds that had formulated their star images. Only rarely would a studio make a mistake that could damage one of its valuable properties. For a star player, a well-oiled studio system could be a form of insurance, an element of quality control that the free-lance player did not possess. Left to his own resources, Boyer did all right.

Fredric March, who cleared the path for free-lance actors in the talking period, gave Boyer full credit for enhancing his own career through keen judgment of material: "A free-lance actor with star status gets every kind of junk thrown at him. It's important to be able to distinguish gold from dross in a script, or to sense what a certain director may or may not be able to do with a dubious property. I had a good knack, but I'm sure Boyer's judgment was more sound. I made *Trade Winds* which he'd refused, and he was probably right. I made some other mistakes that Charles wouldn't have made, like something called *There Goes My Heart*, just the sort of thing he was forever turning down. He really has always managed his own career, which might have been a very different career if he'd accepted some of the garbage they threw at him."

Yet there were some pictures in which Boyer had wished to appear but didn't, for different reasons. In 1935, when his standing was still uncertain, he failed to secure a leading role in *Under Two Flags*. Darryl Zanuck planned a remake of Ouida's adventure story about the French Foreign Legion as an American debut vehicle for Marc Allégret's French discovery, Simone Simon, who actually filmed a few scenes before Claudette Colbert replaced her as Cigarette. Boyer sought the part of the mysterious Corporal Victor, but lost out to Ronald Colman—the most dramatically imposing male star of the mid-thirties. Later, when Boyer was solidly established and had even been cast as Napoleon, he courted a leading character role in Paramount's *Ebb Tide*, without success. The Robert Louis Stevenson story appealed to him but he was vetoed in favor of Oscar Homolka, hardly a box-office magnet; and if Boyer had made *Ebb Tide*, he might not have had *Tovarich*.

Later still, there was *Good Girls Go to Paris*, which Boyer rated as superior to the similarly constituted *Midnight* when both were in the planning stage. He preferred to follow *Algiers* with a comedy turn in any event, and romantic comedy trifles were a specialty of the Columbia studio. When Columbia's Harry Cohn offered Boyer a shot at *Good Girls Go to Paris*, the actor perceived a likely screwball winner and welcomed another outing with Jean Arthur, now Columbia's leading star. Although *Good Girls Go to Paris* did eventually achieve smart comedy success, it did so without either Boyer's or Arthur's participation—which gave it the look of a smaller picture, ably acted in by Melvyn Douglas and Joan Blondell.

Sometimes a free-lance actor had to choose between subjects that were almost equally desirable. Boyer decided that as much as he liked *Good Girls Go to Paris*, he liked *Love Affair* even more.

8

❊❊❊❊❊❊❊❊❊❊

C harles Boyer's determination to remain independent in an era of studio-governed actors was thought to be professionally motivated, to give him free choice between picture prospects of all the companies. That was only a part of it. In an interview given at very nearly the peak of his career, Boyer remarked that "If you are contracted to a motion picture company, that company owns your mind and body. The studio decides not only the roles you will play; it also attempts to control every aspect of your life. A contract artist has absolutely no privacy. The studio follows him everywhere, even into the bedroom."

The Boyers had a private life. Socially they were a highly visible couple. They attended functions all over town and were often photographed together—everywhere, it seemed, except in their own home. The Boyer residence was declared off limits to newspaper and magazine photographers. Boyer was not difficult about granting interviews but never gave them at home.

In retrospect, it is curious that he retained major stardom for many years without ever becoming a familiar presence in the fan magazines. For every magazine puff about Boyer, there would easily be a dozen stories about, say, Clark Gable. This was an indication of the intricate involvement of the studios with the fan magazines during what was a heyday for both. Indeed, Boyer was very nearly the least publicized major star of that period, the only likely exception being his fellow free-lancer Fredric March; and March had earlier been common fodder for the fan magazines during his Paramount contract years. Furthermore, Boyer did not enlist a press agent of his own, considering one both a nuisance and an unnecessary expense.

Charles and Pat maintained cordial relations with Louella Parsons and then also with her subsequent rival, Hedda Hopper; yet they never "reached out" to woo those brokers of public favor. By exercising gracious diplomacy from a discreet distance, the Boyers seemed never to acquire enemies in the film community. Their abundance of good friends may once have been separately labeled "his" and "hers" but in time became truly "theirs," if still somewhat separate and compartmentalized—the British set, its French counterpart, and a distinctly American element.

The permanent British "colony" was quite small within the Hollywood sphere, but scores of English actors and actresses were often in temporary residence there. It was Pat Paterson Boyer's chosen task to orchestrate them socially. Diana Wynyard, Frank Lawton, and Evelyn Laye were Pat's chums while she and Charles were honeymooners; and when they returned to England, others arrived to supplant them—Ian Hunter, Richard Greene, Anna Neagle, and Herbert Wilcox for a few years, and Reginald Gardiner permanently. Leslie Howard, Edna Best, and Roland Young rated as trusted friends to the Boyers, as did a later-arriving mature couple, Gladys Cooper and Philip Merivale.

When Laurence Olivier made good on his third try in Hollywood as Sam Goldwyn's Heathcliff, he surprised everyone by bringing his girl friend with him . . . and then *she* surprised everyone by snaring the "role of the century" as Scarlett O'Hara in David Selznick's tumultuously produced *Gone With the Wind*. Vivien Leigh thrived on intimate friendship and had known Pat Paterson when both were trying to break into British films. In Hollywood they drew closer and pooled their friends, giving definition to a vibrant English clique. Its centerpiece undoubtedly was the rising young

David Niven, who rather suddenly had become the most popular man in town, of any nationality.

More than just another of Pat's buddies, Niven soon established a strong, devoted friendship with Boyer. To the casual observer they were not at all alike, other than to appear equally at ease in a tuxedo: Niven the trigger wit, the life of every party; and Boyer the quiet, preoccupied intellect. But Niven could provoke Boyer to roaring laughter when no one else could, and Boyer was a divining rod for Niven's seldom-glimpsed serious side. Their friendship flourished, Boyer said, "when we discovered that we both despised the Nazis about equally."

Besides keeping social congress with such long-assimilated French folk as Adolphe Menjou and Claudette Colbert, Boyer in his unofficial ambassadorial capacity was a shepherd in the filmland for players newly arrived from France, most of whom were young actresses—Simone Simon, Annabella, and his *Mayerling* costar, Danielle Darrieux, who stayed only long enough to make one inconsequential picture in 1938. Boyer would be a more vital intermediary in the war years ahead, when many of his exiled countrymen would get to Hollywood. But before that, French and British patriotism brought the two Boyer "sets" into one, bound by their common abhorrence of the Hitler regime in Germany. While native Americans in Hollywood as elsewhere awoke slowly from a long sleep of isolationism, the foreign contingents were watching the European developments keenly, and with deep concern.

In Hollywood, Boyer was one of the more vocal opponents of the Third Reich. While much of the world and most Americans applauded the Munich conference of September 1938 with its hollow promise of "peace in our time," Boyer denounced the resolution of appeasement and had not been in favor of negotiation with Hitler in the first place. He had been mistrustful of the Nazis since his 1931–32 tenure in the Berlin studios, when he worked for a Jewish producer who still regarded the Nazis as a joke, as most others also did. But Boyer recalled: "I was in Switzerland not much later, when Hitler became chancellor, and the Jewish refugees began to stream out of Germany. I believed then that there would be chaos for the world if the Nazis weren't stopped very quickly."

More than merely contemplative, Boyer was a political activist on an international scale from the mid-thirties on, but that facet of his life was not generally known by the workaday Hollywood journalists who tried to find things to write about him. Not that his political stance would have interested them; star-watchers were distracted primarily by the subjects' love lives. They really wanted to get the lowdown on the Boyer marriage; but if there was any dirt, no one had found it.

✿ ✿ ✿

An actress who played a supporting role in one of Boyer's 1939 films spoke forthrightly about the man who had become the screen's "great lovair."

"I don't know of a woman who has made a picture with Charles without enjoying the experience. Women are comfortable with him, because they sense right away that their bodies are safe, he isn't hell-bent on screwing them. This is more important than most people realize. Sex on a movie set is almost taken for granted, and any actress has to keep her legs crossed unless she just doesn't care. Maybe not every man is after it, but it's pretty much a custom, and easy as pie for a male star. Charles is one of the exceptions, though. Women become his friends because they trust him, and because of that trust, actresses play well with him. Whether he's being informal on a set, or acting for the camera, Charles does know how to handle women."

He had not always known how to handle women. Anatole Litvak could reflect that "In France, Charles seldom had a satisfactory relationship with a woman, if he was acting with her or if she was someone with whom he thought he had fallen in love. I thought he hated women. But in America he became a different person entirely. It could be seen that he enjoyed women. Being married must have changed him greatly."

Hollywood has always had an abundance of "happiest marriages" that terminate in the divorce courts, where the relationships often are revealed to be something other than they have seemed. The Boyers were one of those couples unblemished in the public view, which Pat found ironic "because none of our friends thought we would last even a year." But after four years of marriage, they suggested a couple thoroughly adjusted to each other, and their friends believed their only differences had been settled early. Pat often remarked that "We have our little fights, but we keep them entirely to ourselves. Even our spats have become only a little game we play. We fuss around and then I give in, and that makes Charles happy, then he becomes very considerate of me . . . as he wouldn't, if I hadn't given in."

Such "problems" as they had experienced had occurred mainly and unevenly during their honeymoon year, while each was managing a career. When Pat withdrew from the moviemaking scene and eased into her husband's shadow, there was no evidence of tension between them, nor any indication that Pat had regrets about her abandoned career. She insisted that she didn't miss performing, while admitting that she had expected to.

The Boyers' long holiday following the *Algiers* filming ended, however, not with Boyer taking on a new screen role, but with Pat's unexpected return to the cameras after a layoff of more than a year. It was all a lark. Hunt Stromberg, a friendly M-G-M producer, asked Pat to take a small role in *Idiot's Delight*, which had accommodated the Lunts on Broadway and would serve Norma Shearer and Clark Gable on film. In an ironic comedy that imparted a strong antiwar message, Gable was song-and-dance man Harry Van, and Pat was enlisted as one of "Harry's Girls," of whom there were half a dozen in chorine turns. Clarence Brown filmed it in the autumn of 1938, and Pat enjoyed the activity because now the pressure was off. As an early 1939 release, *Idiot's Delight* had a mixed reception, but within the film community there was a widespread acknowledgment that Pat Paterson in her limited opportunity revealed a distinct sparkle, such as had been perceived years earlier in her British pictures. She expressed a willingness to make a picture at any time, on the same basis, if anyone should ask. No one did, ever again, and she really didn't mind.

❊ ❊ ❊

Throughout his career Charles Boyer protested gently that he was basically a character actor, and that the people who tabbed him a great lover had it all wrong. He became increasingly uncomfortable with the label, which, however, he had prompted directly by his free choice of material. His two 1939 releases came near to formulating him, and they were subjects he selected from surely many possibilities.

The standard Boyer image now emerging was a contrast to the historical Napoleon of *Conquest*, but also to the engaging fugitive of *Algiers*. The Boyer of *Love Affair* and *When Tomorrow Comes* was a cosmopolitan gentleman, a gracious fellow of breeding and sophistication, with social and artistic status, always impeccably attired in smart but conservative business suits—indeed, the Boyer screen projection was drawing closer to the essence of Boyer himself. For such an image, the bittersweet love story was a natural habitat.

Boyer's special niche was clarified during the American screen's finest hour. It is the judgment of history that 1939 was Hollywood's greatest year, with a sudden flowering of quality pictures that have stood the test of time remarkably well. Dozens of titles from the 1939 inventory retain status as classics more than forty years later, including one and possibly both of the unabashedly romantic items that teamed Boyer with the genteel Irene Dunne.

The best-known titles are reference points of our popular culture. A list that could begin with William Wyler's *Wuthering Heights,* Frank Capra's *Mr. Smith Goes to Washington,* John Ford's *Stagecoach,* and Ernst Lubitsch's *Ninotchka* would climax inevitably with those two fabled works credited to Victor Fleming, *The Wizard of Oz* and *Gone With the Wind.* Within that sphere are others almost as good—*Dark Victory; The Women; Love Affair; Gunga Din; Of Mice and Men; Destry Rides Again; Bachelor Mother; Goodbye, Mr. Chips; Young Mr. Lincoln; Midnight; Only Angels Have Wings; Intermezzo; Drums Along the Mohawk; Babes in Arms; The Story of Vernon and Irene Castle; The Old Maid;*

Red-Headed Woman (1932). Boyer as Jean Harlow's amorous chauffeur in his early false start at M-G-M.

Thunder in the East (1934). That's the American release title for the English-language version of *La Bataille,* with Merle Oberon, John Loder, and an oriental Charles Boyer.

Private Worlds (1935). Boyer's breakthrough film, in a mental hospital with fellow doctor Claudette Colbert.

Break of Hearts (1935). John Beal, Katherine Hepburn, Jean Hersholt, and Boyer in a romantic drama about musicians.

Garden of Allah (1936). Boyer and Marlene Dietrich as Hollywood's most exotic star team in a Selznick production filmed in early Technicolor.
Mayerling (1936). Boyer and Danielle Darrieux in a subject for international acclaim. Seventeen years later they were reunited in the magnificent *Madame de...*

History Is Made at Night (1937). Boyer, Jean Arthur, and Ivan Lebedeff in the climactic shipwreck sequence.

Tovarich (1937). Another success with Claudette Colbert, and Boyer's first comedy role in any language.

Conquest (1937). Boyer as Napoleon, and Greta Garbo as his most sympathetic mistress, Maria Walewska, for M-G-M.

Algiers (1938). Boyer isn't entreating Hedy Lamarr to come with him to the Casbah, but he might as well be.

Love Affair (1939). Boyer's own favorite film and a triumph all around, with Maria Ouspenskaya and Irene Dunne.

When Tomorrow Comes (1939). An immediate reunion with Irene Dunne in a picture almost as good.

All This and Heaven Too (1940). Boyer costars with Bette Davis at her peak in a gloomy drama trumpeted by Warner Brothers as a major event.

*Golden Boy; The Roaring Twenties; Union Pacific; Stanley
and Livingstone . . .*

Most directors employed by the leading studios had been
"picture people" since the silent days, but many had developed their craft slowly. The end of the vibrant thirties decade
seemed to bring creative maturity to both the veteran moviemakers and the newer men apprenticed in the sound era.
Cecil B. DeMille, Lewis Milestone, Clarence Brown, Henry
King, Howard Hawks, John Stahl, Sam Wood, Edmund
Goulding, Raoul Walsh, Rouben Mamoulian, Michael Curtiz,
Leo McCarey, George Stevens, John Cromwell, George
Cukor, Garson Kanin—all had one or more substantial hits in
the watershed year. They had evolved into a creative Estab-
lishment, but hardly more so than the stars themselves.

During Charles Boyer's early, frustrating tours of the Hollywood studios, the American screen's leading stars still had
been such as Douglas Fairbanks and Mary Pickford, John
Barrymore and Gloria Swanson, Richard Barthelmess and
Lillian Gish—although an evident trend favored personalities
of more modern vintage. By 1939 the sands of stardom had
shifted and then resettled, to reveal a new hierarchy. A handful of veteran stars remained undimmed—Ronald Colman,
William Powell, and the M-G-M distaff triumvirate of Garbo,
Shearer, and Joan Crawford. Yet the screen's dominant images more often were players developed essentially or entirely
during the talking years. They appeared regularly in the
screen's more imposing features and commanded its choice
roles—Bette Davis, Barbara Stanwyck, Katharine Hepburn,
Irene Dunne, Carole Lombard, Claudette Colbert, Jean
Arthur, Myrna Loy, Ginger Rogers; and Clark Gable, Spencer
Tracy, Gary Cooper, Cary Grant, James Cagney, Fredric
March, Bing Crosby, Fred Astaire—and Charles Boyer: he
had already attained the highest level, and among Hollywood's male starring elite he was the only true exotic for
whom English was a second language.

Coming into their own were such relative newcomers as
James Stewart, Margaret Sullavan, Henry Fonda, Alice Faye,
Errol Flynn, Rosalind Russell, Tyrone Power, Ann Sheridan,
John Garfield, and the precocious Mickey Rooney and Judy

Garland. Just getting started in American films were Ingrid Bergman and Greer Garson, along with Hedy Lamarr. In the second rank of players were some who would soar higher in the years ahead—Humphrey Bogart, Olivia deHavilland, Bob Hope, Rita Hayworth, William Holden, Jane Wyman . . .

Stars were "bigger" in that era than they have been in subsequent cycles, because the well-oiled studio machinery defined and formulated the more engaging personalities. Almost everyone went to the movies then, and audiences of dispositions saw the same features without the necessity of a rating system. A restrictive production code prevailed, but accomplished moviemakers could employ innuendo and other resources of imagination to produce distinctly adult entertainment—to which, however, younger and less sophisticated moviegoers could respond at their own levels.

It can be noted that many well-remembered 1939 pictures were remade years later, without a single instance of the original success being duplicated or even approached. Part of the enduring appeal of a well-made movie is its manner of conveying vintage, of distilling the feel of the time in which it was made. Old movies remind us of the way we were, in our national attitudes toward life and love, when they were made. The 1939 cornucopia reveals movie gems of every type and persuasion, but the body as a whole clearly indicates a national preoccupation with romance. In the grand design of Hollywood, the undisguised love story had an important place, and was widely appreciated whenever it was discharged with skill and integrity, as in both of Boyer's 1939 assignments.

Although different studios produced them, both pictures enlisted Irene Dunne as the female star—the only instance in the Boyer career of successive appearances with the same leading lady. Both pictures were love stories by precise definition, and each was an uneven mixture of humor and pathos. If each was a "woman's picture," one was more specifically that. One is an unargued classic, the other less certain in its permanent rating despite its fervent champions. *When Tomorrow Comes* always had one point in its disfavor: it wasn't nearly as enjoyable for the general audience as *Love Affair,* which preceded it and obligated the Dunne-Boyer reteaming, but also made comparison of the two pictures inevitable.

As late as 1965, Boyer still identified *Love Affair* as his personal favorite among all his American films. It rates as a curious choice, for his role was overshadowed by his costar's, if subtly so. Their parts were more or less equal in size, but *Love Affair* was seen mainly from the perspective of its leading lady; it was a carefully shaped vehicle for Irene Dunne, and hers was the Academy Award-nominated performance. Boyer admired *Love Affair* "because, for what it was, it was almost perfectly executed . . . it came closer than any of my other pictures to being exactly what it had hoped to be." He liked his role of errant artist Michel Marnet because he liked the fellow on personal terms. Boyer created a man of more natural warmth than perhaps any of his previous roles had contained. There was also very little doubt that Irene Dunne was his favorite leading lady.

❋ ❋ ❋

Leo McCarey conceived *Love Affair* expressly for Dunne and Boyer, but derived his inspiration from Boyer's appreciation of earlier McCarey pictures, and of Miss Dunne herself, although Boyer had been only slightly acquainted with both his new costar and their writer-director. Boyer had a nodding acquaintance with McCarey earlier when they had worked in Paramount's Hollywood studio at the same time, but they moved in different filmland circles. Yet Boyer's rating of McCarey as an unappreciated major artist was perceived by the director, and may have set *Love Affair* in motion.

The Boyers' Beverly Hills mansion had its own small built-in movie theater, complete with projection booth. Showing just-completed pictures in one another's homes was a pastime of the more established Hollywood folk, but the Boyers also began to collect prints of pictures one or both of them adored. Among his own works, Boyer retained a print only of *Liliom*. The modest collection included some German silent pictures, a few French and English items, and only four or five American pictures—two of which, however, were directed by Leo McCarey. Boyer himself cited Charles

Laughton's *Ruggles of Red Gap* as an unusual picture with an artful alternation between high comedy and knockabout farce, modified by occasional sobriety. Pat's own favorite movie for a time was the marital comedy *The Awful Truth,* which Charles also rated as a total delight, against which he compared even *Tovarich* unfavorably. Boyer also admired McCarey's tragicomic *Make Way for Tomorrow,* although he did not own a print of it; but he and Pat often screened *Ruggles* or *The Awful Truth* for their guests. At other times Boyer would watch snippets of both films, to study the ways in which the comedic and emotional turns were set up visually, and to behold the smart comedy playing—particularly by Irene Dunne and the emerging Cary Grant in the latter exercise.

Although *The Awful Truth* was from the 1937 ledger and earned Academy recognition for McCarey as "best director" in that year, it was his last completed picture prior to *Love Affair.* Throughout much of 1938, McCarey was involved—or was *supposed* to be involved—with *The Cowboy and the Lady,* the idea of which he had sold to Samuel Goldwyn for fifty thousand dollars, without so much as a script—because it seemed a likely bet for bringing together Goldwyn's two contract stars, Gary Cooper and Merle Oberon. McCarey was the intended writer-director but excused himself from both functions when he lost his enthusiasm, although he was screen-credited for an original story he never actually wrote. *The Cowboy and the Lady* eventually employed more than a score of writers and became a minor scandal in the industry. Boyer must have heard all the talk and was probably cautious when McCarey got to talking about the story he was "writing" especially for Boyer and Irene Dunne. But when they were all brought together socially to discuss the prospect of *Love Affair,* Boyer elected to cancel his half-made plans to film for Paramount or Columbia or both, and go with Dunne and McCarey. By the time *Love Affair* went before the cameras for RKO in the fall of 1938, they were all very good friends; and Boyer's rapport with Irene Dunne already rated as extraordinary.

Excepting only some acknowledged friction with Lilian

Harvey when he filmed with her in Berlin, Boyer customarily maintained at least a surface compatibility with all his leading ladies. With many of his illustrious costars there were also friendships that went beyond mutual professional admiration. Yet the closeness they developed usually spanned only the shooting schedules of the pictures that concerned them. Irene Dunne was the most notable exception. The filming of *Love Affair* initiated a friendship that deepened over the years. Miss Dunne had long been married to a physician, Francis Griffin; and the Boyers and Griffins became a comfortable foursome socially. At one time Pat could state it as "a fact" that the two doctors retained by the Boyers were both married to Charles's costars, for Claudette Colbert's husband was Joel Pressman, also a Boyer physician.

In 1977, when Irene Dunne appeared before a glittering audience in Washington's Kennedy Center following an American Film Institute screening of *Love Affair*, she refused to name a "favorite leading man" of her film career, but narrowed the contest to Boyer and Cary Grant, with each of whom she made three pictures. She said they were as different as two men could be: Cary was "a cut-up, full of mischief," and to make a picture with him wasn't work but play; while Charles was "such a dedicated actor that it *was* work, but such an agreeable challenge." She called Boyer "the perfect gentleman," and for many years it was the consensus view of the film colony that Irene Dunne was herself the perfect lady.

Gregory La Cava, one of her directors, once remarked that "If Irene Dunne isn't the first lady of Hollywood, then she's the last one." In retrospect Miss Dunne may be seen to have been an unusual and highly original star, a woman of gracious and dignified bearing both on and off the screen, who demonstrated extraordinary versatility without ever playing an unsympathetic role.

Another unusual aspect of Irene Dunne was her maturity. She was Boyer's own age and already well past the ingenue phase when she entered pictures in 1930, a musical comedienne when musicals were an early fad of the talkies. Possessing a lovely lyric soprano, she was in musicals on Broadway and in national stock throughout the twenties, and a favorable impression as Magnolia in a *Show Boat* road company was her ticket to Hollywood. When an overdose of musicals killed the genre for a few years, she emerged as a strong dramatic actress in *Cimarron,* exhibiting a substance of nobility and graceful fortitude. While soap operas were a Hollywood mainstay she was in her element, in the original *Back Street* and numerous phosphates. Her career might have washed away in a torrent of suds—the fate of both Ann Harding and Ruth Chatterton—but for Irene's keen ability for reading movieland trends. She returned to musicals and became Jerome Kern's favorite interpreter of his melodies, in no fewer than five films, but without again acquiring primary identity as a musical actress. Most important, when screwball comedy became the new vogue of the Depression years, Irene made the varsity in her maiden effort with *Theodora Goes Wild.*

Her enduring success owed much to her own shrewd career management. After several years as an RKO contract star, Irene really came into her own when she was *on* her own, selling her services to four companies more or less simultaneously—Columbia, Universal, Paramount, and her old RKO studio, in limited pacts with all of them. She alternated high-class soap operatics (*Magnificent Obsession*) with more screwball magic (*The Awful Truth*), while not quite abandoning the musical format. Again as Magnolia, she gleamed in the second of the three *Show Boat* screen musicals, the one most easily earning classic rating. She was at the peak of her career when she made *Love Affair,* which would remain her own favorite film as well as Boyer's. In all their appearances together, Irene took the lead billing.

But for his congeniality with Miss Dunne and their mutual trust in the quixotic McCarey, Boyer might have found *Love Affair* an ordeal to rival *Algiers.* He was a methodical actor, given to early memorization of all his dialogue; but McCarey advised Boyer against memorizing a script that wouldn't be used. McCarey liked to improvise. That wasn't Boyer's style, but actor and director were in fundamental agreement that the *Love Affair* script had a lot of problems.

McCarey wrote the original story about a club singer and

an artist with playboy tendencies, who have a shipboard romance while each is somewhat grudgingly betrothed to another. Delmer Daves developed a scenario, for which the redoubtable Donald Ogden Stewart supplied additional dialogue—mainly bright banter for the shipboard sequences. McCarey intrigued both his stars with the notion of a trick picture that would be mostly rollicking in its first half and mostly serious in its second; but after they started filming he said "I don't think it will work, not with this script."

The change of mood was too abrupt for being not properly set up in the screenplay. For accomplishing that, it was Boyer's own suggestion to build up a scene with Maria Ouspenskaya as his grandmother into a substantial midpicture sequence. As played, it became the pivotal scene that made all of *Love Affair* work. It defined three players and their respective roles in spiritual terms; and by enabling Boyer to express a loving relationship with his grandmother, it also removed most of the actor's misgivings about the role he was playing.

Excepting only *History Is Made at Night*, this was the first occasion of a role fashioned especially for Boyer. McCarey gave him license to alter the part according to his own actorly instincts, and the artist evolved into an entirely decent chap with whom Boyer could more easily identify. The fellow became a philanderer only by inference. In the initial scene wherein the voyagers meet, McCarey sneaked in a playful comment on Boyer's now-certified "great lover" image, having Irene Dunne remark that "I know all about you . . . every woman does." Yet there was no hint of a rogue in any aspect of the Boyer portrayal. Even the heartfelt "affair" with Miss Dunne's nightclub singer was remarkably chaste to every appearance.

They made changes daily, embellishing parts of the script while abandoning whole chunks and devising new material; it was a complete reversal of the *Algiers* experience. The costars set their own rehearsals that were most often prodded by Boyer's interest in motivation, which was never a concern of their director. At other times Boyer was a solitary figure in rehearsal, taking long walks around the studio to find the proper mood for his character in the scenes about to be shot.

They all sensed they had a winner when the rough cut was screened in January, two months before the national release. Yet *Love Affair* attained a success that may have taken even its creators by surprise. Immediately it achieved a box-office endorsement commensurate with the critical superlatives. There was some general agreement that the first, lighter half was more exceptional than what followed, and was mainly responsible for the healthy commercial return. Yet the second half contained Buddy DeSylva's "Wishing" (will make it so), which became the nation's most popular song of the 1939 summer, further enhancing the *Love Affair* mystique. Irene Dunne seemed to be singing "Wishing" with some orphan girls, but the voices on the soundtrack were the Robert Mitchell Boys Choir—a gentle suggestion of the Hollywood magic. Earlier, in a nightclub setting, Miss Dunne also had an effective presentational solo, "Sing My Heart."

Sensing the depth of their love at the conclusion of their voyage, Michel Marnet and Terry McKay put themselves to a six-month test while apart. They agree that if their feelings have not changed, they will meet at an appointed time atop the Empire State Building. He keeps the appointment; she doesn't, but only because she is struck by an automobile and crippled while en route to their rendezvous—which he doesn't know, of course. Yet his love for her has regenerated Boyer's sometime artist, who now is inspired to become a serious painter. After other complications are dispensed with and they are finally reunited, Irene Dunne's blithe assertion that "If you can paint, I can learn to walk" assures the audience that she'll be out of her wheelchair in no time. *Love Affair* remains one of the most fondly recalled films of the thirties; and almost two decades later it was still a box-office magnet as *An Affair to Remember*, remade by McCarey with Cary Grant and Deborah Kerr.

In the movies' greatest year, *Love Affair* was one of the works nominated by the Motion Picture Academy as best picture. There were several other nominations, including Miss Dunne's performance and the supporting stint by the venerable Maria Ouspenskaya, formerly of Stanislavsky's legendary Moscow Art Theater. Nevertheless, *Love Affair* was swamped by *Gone With the Wind* in almost every competitive category. That Boyer's account did not earn a nomination elicited some surprise within the film community, but was also taken as an indication that he now was merely discharging an excellence that had come to be expected of him.

The Boyer projection in *Love Affair* was shaded altogether differently from any role that had preceded it, yet it may be viewed as the prototype for his subsequent "typical" portrayals. His Michel Marnet was a fellow both amused and bemused, but in an understated way. By conscious design, Boyer was becoming a more subtle and economical actor. His voice quality and accent were responsible for his international fame and they remained more than incidental to his status as a matinée idol; but he was now a more powerful physical actor, if an incomparably delicate one. With a half-smile that was ever more characteristic of him, and with "eye performance" that perhaps was equaled only by Spencer Tracy in that era, Boyer conveyed enormous understanding while also revealing his own affirmative view of the world. Yet *Love Affair* did not so much enhance his reputation as certify his drawing power, which to a few skeptics had remained unresolved. At least for the women who attended the movies in America and around the world, this was the very pinnacle of Boyer's popularity.

His later judgment was that to have followed *Love Affair* with *When Tomorrow Comes* was a mistake for both himself and Irene Dunne. Their next picture was not enough like *Love Affair*, which disappointed some moviegoers; yet it was *too much* like it to avoid comparison. It must have seemed a good idea at the time. There was a decisive clamor by the distaff audience to get the stars of *Love Affair* together again as quickly as possible.

Boyer had not expected to be involved again so soon on the screen with Miss Dunne. From *Love Affair* she went immediately to Paramount for a picture with Fred MacMurray, while Boyer anticipated a summer in Paris. He expected to make another film there with André Daven and Marc Allégret, his producer and director for *Orage;* but when that project got delayed, he elected to remain in Hollywood and line up something else. He might yet have taken the long-delayed *Good Girls Go to Paris,* which Columbia was finally getting into production, but his interest waned when Jean Arthur was no longer available—she and Cary Grant were involved in the high adventure of *Only Angels Have Wings* for Howard Hawks. At about this time the announcement that Boyer would costar with Warner Brothers' ascendant Bette Davis in *All This and Heaven Too* was major industry news, but the shooting schedule for that lavish project was off in the future. This was also when Boyer was supposedly "set" for David Selznick's *Intermezzo,* and it may have been Irene Dunne's persuasiveness that made Boyer unavailable for the picture that would introduce Ingrid Bergman to American audiences.

Miss Dunne owed Universal a picture; and in the immediate wake of the *Love Affair* smash hit, that company's story department produced a subject that with some modification could accommodate a Dunne-Boyer reunion. The story was a James M. Cain "original," actually a paraphrase of his *Serenade* novel that in 1939 rated as unfilmable. Dwight Taylor, the writer son of actress Laurette Taylor, devised a laundered screenplay that rendered Cain's story almost unrecognizable, but in which Irene Dunne and Charles Boyer were very recognizable indeed, as characters obviously patterned after their *Love Affair* models. Years later Boyer would reflect that the musician in *When Tomorrow Comes* and the painter of *Love Affair* were "really the very same fellow," and that even in 1939 he had been reluctant to accept a part so similar. He did so with an eye on the box office, and because Universal was willing to match his RKO fee for *Love Affair*—believed to be one hundred thousand dollars, a ceiling figure for that period.

It was also big news when the encore picture was put before the cameras by John M. Stahl, who had directed Irene Dunne's memorable *Back Street* seven years earlier. The first scenes were shot in the late spring while *Love Affair* was still in wide circulation. Reporters clamored all over the Universal set to profile the well-liked "new team," and a common expectation at the time was that Boyer and Dunne would make many pictures together, emulating the professional habit of, say, William Powell and Myrna Loy.

Again, the costars got on very well together. Taking exception to a remark about Boyer's well-known "coldness," Irene Dunne said "Charles really had a rare and genuine warmth, like a fire that starts slowly. He was the kind of log that was difficult to ignite, but then would burn so beautifully."

The shooting schedule was as harmonious as *Love Affair* had been, if rather a contrast. Instead of their changing it on a daily basis, the finished script was honored by director and players, and they always knew exactly where the story was headed. This time Miss Dunne played a waitress, but a waitress as bright as she was refined—one could easily suspect her of being underemployed, except that this was still the Great Depression. Stepping right out of *Love Affair* into the restaurant where she works was the Boyer figure, now a renowned concert pianist. They fell in love in a humorous atmosphere that again suggested the earlier picture, but without the same nimbleness of wit. The script provided a convenient storm and ensuing flood, plus a nice church in which they could take refuge and fall deeply, unmistakably in love, but without yielding to natural passion. Again following the *Love Affair* blueprint, the story took a sudden somber shift, casting soap bubbles upon those flood waters. It was revealed that the musician had a wife who only occasionally would lapse out of her chronic insanity—as when she confronted the love-struck waitress on the sly and said she wouldn't give up her husband. The really striking departure of *When Tomorrow Comes* from *Love Affair* was that it did not make the concession of a "happy" ending. When Dunne and Boyer meet for a farewell dinner, they agree to defer their dreams until a tomorrow they both realize will never come.

Other than the immediate critical consensus that the encore picture was not quite in the same class with *Love Affair*, it was well-received and well-attended and was Universal's most successful 1939 release, outgrossing even Deanna Durbin's *First Love*. It was an exquisitely made love story with excellence in all its "production values," and unlike *Love Affair* it did manage to pick up an Academy Award—for Bernard Brown's sound recording. The reputation of *When Tomorrow Comes* has also risen over the passing decades. It is particularly admired by proponents of the *auteur* theory of film criticism, who see it as typical of John Stahl at his best level. Citing it as a successful follow-up to *Love Affair*, England's Leslie Halliwell notes that *When Tomorrow Comes* is "full of clichés but impeccably set and acted, the stuff Hollywood dreams were made of."

Yet five years would pass before Boyer made his only other screen appearance opposite Irene Dunne. Despite the favorable commercial result for *When Tomorrow Comes*, there was evidence to suggest that their continued teamwork would not be in the best interests of Boyer's career. The trouble was that both Dunne and Boyer appealed to the same audience. Although she had a general popularity, Irene's support came primarily from women moviegoers—the same ones who had lost their collective heart to Boyer. It was noted that while the audience for *When Tomorrow Comes* had been only slightly smaller than the one that endorsed *Love Affair*, it had a markedly different mix. The McCarey film had charmed patrons of every age, among both sexes; but the Stahl picture, adored by female moviegoers, was only grimly tolerated by a smaller percentage of male adults and was disliked by most children.

It had also become apparent that many American men who liked their Tracys and Gables and Coopers and Cagneys plainly did *not* like Hollywood's foremost Frenchman. To their mind, he was somehow sissified by his accent, and they may also have resented a renowned screen lover whose continental manner they could not hope to emulate. Boyer read the signs and concluded that continued appearances opposite Irene Dunne in calculated "women's pictures" might produce an even more fragmented audience. So they agreed to quit for a time, while they were still ahead. Miss Dunne proceeded to make two pictures in a row with Cary Grant.

Before any of that had been resolved, the Boyers forsook their customary rail travel and flew to New York for the first time in August of 1939, where they took in the World's Fair.

Then, following personal appearances by the actor in connection with the Broadway opening of *When Tomorrow Comes*, Charles and Pat sailed for Europe.

Upon their return to the United States, six months later, Boyer brought an altogether different set of priorities. In a world once again engulfed by war, he had a new mission to which the acting profession was distinctly secondary.

9

That Charles Boyer was a visionary and prophet of international politics was certified by the grim events of history. In both France and America, he had grasped the reality of the Nazi terror when most people either underrated Adolf Hitler or considered him a joke.

Boyer deplored the Austrian *Anschluss* and Hitler's subsequent deception at Munich over the Czechoslovakian "settlement." He never doubted that Hitler's Germany was committed to unlimited territorial conquest. In Hollywood, Boyer gained early identity with an anti-isolationist element that was regularly accused of "war-mongering."

He might have been a more vocal protester but for the inhibition stemming from his status as an alien. Although he and Pat had made application for U.S. citizenship years earlier, they had not followed through. Yet Boyer was involved in the genesis of one of the American screen's first and most articulate anti-Nazi statements.

When he was filming *History Is Made at Night,* Boyer passed on to director Frank Borzage a new novel, Erich Maria Remarque's *Three Comrades.* Remarque, author of the celebrated pacifist novel *All Quiet on the Western Front,* had left Germany to become an outspoken critic of the Nazi regime. He lived in Paris and began a friendly acquaintance with Boyer there when the actor was filming *Mayerling* and Remarque was writing *Three Comrades.* Frank Borzage had made what in reality was the American screen's first anti-Nazi film in 1934, very early in the Hitler era: *Little Man, What Now?* from Hans Fallada's novel. And when Borzage joined M-G-M as a contract director, he persuaded the company to obtain screen rights for *Three Comrades*, which he eventually directed.

The *Three Comrades* screenwriter was none other than F. Scott Fitzgerald, who at that time had worked into Pat's "English set" through his liaison with columnist Sheilah Graham, herself a Briton. It is feasible that Fitzgerald's critical stance toward the Nazis sharpened in the Boyers' living room, which increasingly was a setting for international political debate among both Charles's and Pat's countrymen. At least philosophically, Boyer was also involved in an even more controversial Hollywood screen venture of that era, encouraging his friend Anatole Litvak's production of *Confessions of a Nazi Spy.*

The Boyers had much thoughtful discussion of what they would do if war should break out in Europe, which seemed ever more likely. It was also likely that any armed conflict with Germany would involve France and Great Britain first, whether or not the United States got involved later on. Their home countries, grasping the folly of the Munich appeasement, were allied with an official resolve to take action against any additional land-grabbing that Hitler might pursue. Charles and Pat were prepared for separation if war should will it, and each recognized a duty to return to one's own homeland in such a crisis.

That was not what they had in mind, however, when they sailed for Europe in August of 1939. They anticipated a sentimental journey—reunion with old friends in familiar settings still blessed by peace. Charles even hoped to pay a return visit to Figeac, where he had not been since leaving there more than twenty years earlier. His mother was again residing in Figeac, where she was once more a widow after having remarried only recently.

Boyer's professional reason for the trip was the Daven-Allégret production of *Le Corsaire,* to be filmed both in Paris and at an Atlantic location near Brest—a period costume spectacle, a love story more in the manner of *Mayerling* than of the more recent *Orage,* a contemporary subject. Boyer hoped to follow the film commitment with a return to the Paris stage, expecting to accept a long-standing invitation from Henry Bernstein for a limited-engagement revival of the antic hit, *Melo.* To accomplish all that would be a challenge, for Boyer was due back in Hollywood in November to begin *All This and Heaven Too.*

When the Boyers sailed out of New York Harbor, the world was at peace, however uneasily. The Second World War actually commenced on the very day of their arrival in France—September 1, 1939, when Germany attacked Poland. The Boyers encountered a French public excitedly on the brink of war. The formal declaration of war against Germany came from both France and Great Britain on September 3. The Boyers heard the declaration over radio in a Nice hotel room in the company of André Daven, who had met their ship.

While Boyer filmed some studio interiors for *Le Corsaire* in Paris, the German military machine pulverized Poland in less than a month. France merely watched, while also belatedly making its own preparations for combat. The first days of the war saw the closing of German and Italian border stations, while speculation rose over how and where the French might get into the war. Before that had been determined, the filming of *Le Corsaire* was abandoned only shortly after it had commenced. Allégret's production crewmen were deserting to join the Army, and ability to complete the ambitious project now seemed risky in any event.

Twenty-five years earlier, the French people had expected to dispose of their German adversaries within a few weeks. That earlier cruel lesson, coupled with a fair appreciation of Germany's military muscle, produced a more cautious attitude. Yet, however falsely, the French felt secure. Along their German border they were protected by the awesome Maginot Line, whose fortifications extended northward from Switzerland to the border junction of France, Belgium, and Luxembourg—believed to be the most formidable line of defense in modern history. Confident that the Germans would not attempt a penetration of the Maginot Line, the French and

British anticipated a German assault into France from the North, through Belgium. Allied troops began massing there; and throughout France, men left their workaday jobs to enter military service and begin training for another awful adventure.

Late in September, Boyer put his wife on a plane to London, where she was to await his further instructions. Then, at age forty, he joined the French Army. Boyer's reason for this action, other than patriotic impulse, was to remain unclear. André Daven believed that Boyer joined the Army expecting to be placed in a responsible position appropriate to someone of his attainments, but that he became "a victim of army bureaucracy and incompetence," probably through an errant shuffling of papers and military orders. Following his induction, Boyer was detached to a training unit near Lyon to learn military communications. A few weeks later, with the rank of second-class private, he was assigned to the 37th Artillery, to perform switchboard duties at one of the Maginot Line's southern fortifications.

Perhaps Boyer still harbored feelings of guilt for having failed to serve his country during World War I. Whatever his rationale for joining the French Army, it was a personal decision and a very private action, clandestine in nature. The French people did not immediately know that their internationalized movie idol was in the military service of his home country. The French Army was itself slow to recognize that its body now included so illustrious a personage at the lowest rank. Nor was anyone in Hollywood aware of this development—from the Boyers' friends, to the actor's agent, and to the people at Warner Brothers who were undertaking the preproduction activity for *All This and Heaven Too*. Had Boyer been on the regular contract list of a Hollywood studio, his movements surely would have been tracked and his soldier status detected much earlier.

Boyer and his wife stayed in touch with regular letters and occasional telephone calls. He may have asked Pat to keep his situation secret, pending further developments. Boyer in later years had very little to say about his eleven-week career as a private soldier, and discouraged interviewers from pursuing the subject.

Anatole Litvak was probably the first person in the filmland to hear from Boyer directly, through a letter received several weeks after it was written. Boyer regretted that because of the war and his switchboard duty, he would not be able to appear in *All This and Heaven Too*. But before Litvak informed anyone at the Warner studio that Boyer was not available, it had been confirmed that Boyer had joined the French Army and—more important to the Hollywood interests—was being mustered out.

Later there was speculation that persons in the power structure of the American motion picture industry conspired to have Boyer released from French military service. The actor insisted that he knew of no such intervention, although his return to Hollywood was definitely in the interests of the Franco-American alliance. Boyer was reported to have been pulled off his duty station by an emissary for France's Premier Édouard Daladier, whose appeasement of Hitler at Munich had provoked Boyer's loathing. Through his intermediary, Daladier urged Boyer to return to America, where he could be of singular and invaluable benefit to France's cause.

Boyer's tenure as a common soldier ended in early December. He remained in France only a few days, but in that time he met two men who would emerge as heroes for his patriotic impulses: Paul Reynaud, then the minister of finance, soon to be premier of the collapsing Third Republic; and Colonel—later General—Charles de Gaulle, whose pleading for military preparedness had been rebuffed by the Daladier government in earlier years. More than Daladier, these were the men Boyer hoped to honor in his newly emerging role as France's goodwill ambassador to the American people.

He met Pat in Lisbon. They booked sea passage for America, and were briefly in New York before returning to the film colony by air. They arrived just in time to spend the Yuletide in their own home. Pat and Charles hastily trimmed a Christmas tree but passed the holiday quietly, alone together in the Beverly Hills mansion that was temporarily without house servants.

The Boyers were subdued, unable to catch the community's euphoria in the aftermath of the *Gone With the Wind* opening at the Carthay Circle Theatre. Boyer noted that the picture people generally attached more importance to that event than to the far-off war they were not yet ready to acknowledge.

On New Year's Day the Charles Feldmans gave the Boyers a small reception, attended by a few of Pat's and Charles's more intimate friends. David Niven, who might otherwise have been there, had already departed the Hollywood scene for British military service. As an occasion more muted than festive, the Feldmans' party emulated the Boyers themselves, and Charles most especially.

It was his nature to be the least jovial person in any crowd. Now, with his thoughts preoccupied by events in Europe, his gloom was exceeded only by his determination to serve his country—or to serve *both* of them.

*   *   *

All This and Heaven Too had commenced shooting without him, before the Christmas holidays. Boyer joined the company in the first week of 1940 and found himself involved in the most elaborate production of his career.

A memorandum from production chief Jack L. Warner to all departments specified that in all internal studio correspondence, reference to *All This and Heaven Too* should be made only by its initials—*ATAHT*. This suggested a blatant imitation of David Selznick's epochal *Gone With the Wind* procedure, wherein *GWTW* became the most important initials of Selznick's private and public correspondence, and then in all of movieland journalism. The three surviving Warner brothers, but Jack especially, were painfully jealous of Metro-Goldwyn-Mayer for having obtained the distribution of Selznick's independently produced epic, after the Warner company had zealously courted that function.

In 1937 Jack Warner proposed an arrangement to Selznick that would make his studio the distributor of *Gone With the Wind*. The four leading roles were all to be played by Warner contract stars at no expense to Selznick—Bette Davis as

Scarlett O'Hara, Errol Flynn as Rhett Butler, Leslie Howard as Ashley Wilkes, and Olivia deHavilland as Melanie Hamilton. At the time the deal was suggested, Bette Davis had not yet joined the superstar ranks but the extent of her talent was hardly in dispute. Along with her fellow thoroughbred and exact contemporary Katharine Hepburn, Miss Davis actively sought the Scarlett O'Hara role; and careful interpretation of Selznick's often contradictory memoranda indicates that the producer was not really opposed to using her in the "role of the century." He may have been less favorably disposed toward Errol Flynn, as was Davis herself—he was the part of the Warner package she never approved. Finally, though, Selznick rejected the Warner proposal because of an ever-shriller public demand that Clark Gable play Rhett Butler. Selznick and Gable disliked one another on personal terms, but the producer felt compelled to engage "The King" as his Rhett Butler; and to accomplish that he was forced to give the *GWTW* distribution to Metro-Goldwyn-Mayer, the price extracted by his then father-in-law, the stubborn Louis B. Mayer, who ran M-G-M.

Bette Davis continued to campaign for the Scarlett plum, even after Warner Brothers appeared to give her as a consolation prize another Southern-belle role—in *Jezebel.* It was a great success for her, as solemnized by her Academy Award as best actress in 1938; but it also wrecked her chances of playing Scarlett O'Hara. Selznick was furious that Warner Brothers, having previously refused to purchase the *Jezebel* play that had starred Tallulah Bankhead on Broadway, made the belated purchase only after the better known but similarly constituted *Gone With the Wind* project became the dominant filmland topic of the age. Selznick also believed—possibly correctly—that Jack Warner would not lend Bette Davis for a picture to be distributed by M-G-M. Nevertheless, Selznick finally obtained both Leslie Howard and Olivia deHavilland on loan from Warner Brothers, as an ironic legacy of the original Warner proposal.

So troubled was the production history of *Gone With the Wind* that many industrial pundits foresaw a disaster. Instead, *GWTW* in December of 1939 became, surely, the most

rapturously embraced movie of all time. The unqualified triumph fired the jealous Warner interests into a spirit of challenge. All the betting was that *GWTW* couldn't be surpassed
or even approached, but Warner Brothers would try; and *All
This and Heaven Too* was the clearly designated subject for
contention.

It was also based on a novel of comparable girth; and if
Rachel Field's novel sold less phenomenally than Margaret
Mitchell's story of the Old South, *All This and Heaven Too*
indeed was the work that finally supplanted *Gone With the
Wind* in the lead position on the sales chart, after the latter's
gaudy two-year residence there. It was also a comparable
subject for trappings of scenery and costumes, if not for action spectacle. *All This and Heaven Too* was similarly set in a
period of castles and carriages. Instead of a plantation mansion, there would be an imposing manor house befitting the
French aristocracy. But where *GWTW* was entirely a work of
fiction well-grounded in history, *ATAHT* was offered as a
"true" story, wherein author Field recreated her own grandmother in the role that Bette Davis would play. It was the
story of unrequited love between a governess and the French
nobleman father of her charges; and in 1940, the combination
of Bette Davis and Charles Boyer indeed suggested a venture
for exceptional prestige.

In pictures for almost a decade after apprenticeship on the
stage, Miss Davis had endured dozens of humdrum assignments in lackluster films that could only have been powerfully
frustrating for an actress of her ability and ambition. She first
attracted major attention in 1934, when John Cromwell borrowed her from Warner Brothers to play Mildred Rogers opposite Leslie Howard's Philip Carey in the RKO version of
Maugham's *Of Human Bondage*. Even after her devastating
projection of Mildred announced an actress of great force and
skill, her Warner employers were inclined to consign her to
pulp vehicles. She rebelled, seeking a new career for herself
in English films, but Warner Brothers in a famous court case
successfully retained her contract service. Thereafter, however, they treated her rather more respectfully; and with
Jezebel, the great Davis vehicles began. In 1939 alone, she ap-

peared in four films that were each trumpeted in turn as an Event. First there was *Dark Victory* and her definitive neurotic portrayal. Then she was Paul Muni's nominal costar, but had no scenes with him, in *Juarez;* and Muni's title role had less footage and less interest than the Maximilian-Carlota story involving Brian Aherne (who stole the notices) with Miss Davis. *The Old Maid* was more properly a Davis vehicle, although Miriam Hopkins as costar sparred with her effectively, and it also registered a considerable hit. When Miss Davis closed out the year as Elizabeth to the Essex of Errol Flynn, she was poised at a level of artistic recognition unprecedented for a screen actress to that time.

As "big" as were these entries in the 1939 inventory, her first project for 1940 was designed to be even bigger.

Although denied the adornment of Technicolor because of its dubious appropriateness for a somber story, *All This and Heaven Too* would be accorded an all-stops-out production, sparing no expense. At an estimated final cost of $2,500,000, it was cheaper than *Gone With the Wind* by about a million dollars; yet among all Warner Brothers pictures of the prewar period, only the lavish Max Reinhardt–William Dieterle production of *A Midsummer Night's Dream* was more expensive. Studio publicists made capital of sixty-seven interior sets being built and furnished for *All This and Heaven Too,* surpassing the fifty-three for *Gone With the Wind* and otherwise believed a record for any studio production. The publicists were kept busy reporting on every aspect of *ATAHT,* but their most marketable copy involved the teaming of the two illustrious stars.

In the early reckoning *All This and Heaven Too* was calculated for four stars, another likely emulation of David Selznick's Civil War epic. For the role of Boyer's shrewish wife, director Anatole Litvak had a tentative plan to cast his own spouse, Miriam Hopkins. Litvak said "The Duchess de Praslin is a heartless and venomous bitch. Miriam will be perfect." The second male lead, as the young Reverend Field, was assigned to the pallid Jeffrey Lynn, who once had been rejected by Selznick as an Ashley Wilkes candidate, but who had been officially if shakily "elevated" to stardom by Warner Brothers.

Lynn had an earnest expectation of star billing in *All This and Heaven Too* because it was considered obligatory for an actress of Miss Hopkins's standing, and his part was as large as hers. Finally Lynn retained the minister role but had his billing reduced when Miss Hopkins withdrew or was withdrawn from the picture, after the Litvaks' marriage predictably crumbled. Another star-level actress was sought for the duchess role, but at Boyer's suggestion it was given to Barbara O'Neil, who had portrayed his demented wife in *When Tomorrow Comes* and had also played Vivien Leigh's mother in *Gone With the Wind,* although she was barely past thirty. Although a respected actress, Miss O'Neil was not a familiar name or face to most moviegoers, so *All This and Heaven Too* would have to be sold to the public on the strength and novelty of the Davis-Boyer teaming.

Having made pictures with Colbert, Hepburn, Dietrich, Arthur, and Dunne, Boyer was not attempting something new in appearing opposite a formidable distaff personality. Yet the teaming with Davis suggested the stature of his famous outing with Garbo, because Davis was not accustomed to costars of Boyer's caliber. Early in her career she had made pictures with such varied but esteemed actors as George Arliss, Spencer Tracy, and William Powell; and while progressing to her lofty pedestal she had teamed with Leslie Howard, Paul Muni, James Cagney, and Edward G. Robinson. But in her major emergence she was more likely to be squired by a leading man she could easily dominate, most often George Brent. In *All This and Heaven Too* she was paired for very nearly the first time with an actor whose rise paralleled her own, on almost an identical timetable. Boyer and Davis were brought together at what was approximately the highwater mark for both of their careers.

Along with her new reputation as the screen's dominant actress, Bette Davis was acquiring identity as a hard-to-please star who was particularly rough on her leading men. The two pictures she had made with Errol Flynn may have ignited the legend of the difficult Davis, and in later years she had occasional titanic clashes with such costars as Robert Montgomery and Alec Guinness. Her coexistence with Boyer, however, was more peaceful than might have been predicted. It was also uncommonly respectful. Toward the end of shooting *ATAHT*, Miss Davis in a press conference maintained that "Of all the fine actors I have appeared with on the screen, Charles Boyer is the greatest." Boyer also had kind words for Miss Davis, and it was through no failing on her part that their picture became a distinctly unsatisfactory experience for him.

All This and Heaven Too was filmed in the early months of 1940, when Boyer was still distracted by international events, and quite depressed by them. It was the Nazis' year. While Boyer was occupied with principal photography for the ambitious Warner project, Hitler was conquering his smaller eastern neighbors and plotting the invasion of France. Denmark was virtually defenseless and easily overrun; the Netherlands buckled after a five-day blitzkrieg; the conquest of Norway was assured for the Nazis after Anglo-French forces were driven from the fjords; gritty little Luxembourg fell, and in Belgium the Allied forces fought gamely without real hope of withstanding the German assault.

During the early shooting period Boyer kept a radio in his studio dressing room and at every break listened for an update on the grim news from Europe. Then, when Anatole Litvak openly noted Boyer's extreme nervousness on the set, the actor said "Yes, the war news is destroying my ability to concentrate. The radio will have to go." More than merely removing the radio, Boyer politely forbade any discussion of the European war news in his presence. In his mania for concentration, he left the war at home when he left in the early morning for the studio shooting call; and on his return to Beverly Hills in the mid-afternoon, he would be briefed by Pat on the day's events in and around France. Although usually exhausted from the filming ordeal, Boyer would spend the evenings maintaining his contacts abroad—through letters, wireless messages, and expensive, often incoherent, transatlantic telephone calls. Pat shared his concern, which amounted to real grief; the British and French were vulnerable allies, and the Nazi bombing of London and other major British cities had begun.

In later years Boyer could remark that his extreme unhappiness during this period was quite appropriate for his role as the Duc de Praslin in *All This and Heaven Too.* He was a morose fellow, this duke, and no doubt with ample reason. Even when Boyer summoned his maximum powers of concentration, he found himself groping to understand a nobleman who would finally be driven to murder his cruel wife. Not even the greatest actor of Bette Davis's experience could believe that he had penetrated the psyche of the ducal character, or justified the man's drastic action, which was motivated, surely, by his love for a governess. Boyer decided belatedly that he had no particular liking for his role or for the picture itself.

It was characteristic of Boyer to be under great tension while acting, but this was never so evident as during the filming of *All This and Heaven Too.* Twice a studio physician was summoned to the set to find the actor suffering from nervous fatigue, and on one occasion his temperature had risen to 105 degrees. He lost ten pounds during the shooting schedule—an amount that might not have altered the appearance of a more robust man but made Boyer gaunt at just less than 140 pounds.

Other than for intense private rehearsals with Bette Davis, Boyer was a loner at the Warner Brothers studio in Burbank, taking long, solitary walks in a trance of concentration, seeking just the right nuances for lines already committed to memory. Players in the large supporting cast generally remained strangers to him. Walter Hampden, a leading American stage actor who had a fairly prominent part in *All This and Heaven Too,* said "I hardly knew Charles Boyer when the production commenced, and knew him not one whit better when it was over." Lunchers in the commissary never saw him; the light snacks he ordered were delivered to his dressing room where he dined in solitude while working into the mood appropriate for his next scene. To the other players he could only have seemed cold, remote, unfriendly; but Boyer preferred being distressed alone. He made an exception of the child actress Virginia Weidler, who in the screenplay was the most prominent of the duke's several children, and had a special relationship with her father. He allowed little Miss

Weidler to teach him the game of gin rummy that had become a movieland fad; and he prevailed upon his stand-in, Fig Newton, to find for Virginia a puppy version of Newton's own dog that she liked so much—the pooch named Casbah.

An elaborate party at the studio honored the completion of shooting in April, but Boyer made several returns for additional takes in the weeks that followed. When the first edited print was screened at the studio, Boyer did not view it because he was out of the country on what amounted to international business. So thoroughly did the mounting world conflict command his attention that he seemed only remotely aware of the ultimate failure of *All This and Heaven Too*.

As failures go, it was certainly an honorable one. Previewed in June at three-hour length, it was released in July with running time reduced to 144 minutes, and still it seemed much too long to many viewers. The reviews were almost entirely favorable, but generally were more respectful than enthusiastic. To call it a flop would do it a disservice, but *All This and Heaven Too* was a major disappointment mainly for having been shrilly oversold by its producers. Its failure to create a considerable stir on a national scale was a bitter disappointment to Jack L. Warner, who had himself designated as coproducer with Hal B. Wallis; and it was to be Warner's only formal credit as a producer until *My Fair Lady* almost a quarter-century later.

Although Casey Robinson's adaptation was carefully faithful, readers of the novel were dismayed by the movie's heavy-going narrative, unrelieved by the lightness that had been inhabited in Rachel Field's descriptive prose. Finally *All This and Heaven Too* was done in by its unrelenting gloom. Could such a picture have fair expectation of widespread popularity? It went into direct "roadshow" competition with *Gone With the Wind*, playing major cities on a reserved-seat basis, and got soundly trounced. Eventually it turned a nice profit but was never the box-office phenomenon that had been anticipated, and its appeal was restricted to female moviegoers. Once again Boyer was in a soap-operatic "woman's picture" that male patrons despised.

If for Bette Davis it was another "triumph" in a chain of

such, she clearly surpassed it with her next picture—*The Letter*, which on all counts earned the praise and popular endorsement that Jack Warner had coveted for *ATAHT*. The Davis performance was properly applauded, but the delicate consensus was that Boyer, with perhaps the more difficult and demanding role, had more than held his own with her, as Bette Davis costars were not accustomed to do. Within the film community there was casual assumption that the Academy would honor both stars with nominations, and Boyer was given a fair chance of winning the Oscar. In the New York Film Critics balloting he was runner-up to *The Great Dictator*, who was Charlie Chaplin, and who then refused the award. Boyer, though, was denied an Academy Award nomination, and Bette Davis was cited not for their picture together but for *The Letter*. The best-picture nomination for *ATAHT* came to be regarded as an industrial concession to Jack Warner, and the picture's only other major nomination was the volatile supporting performance by Barbara O'Neil, who dropped out of pictures soon afterward.

In the decidedly uneven career of Anatole Litvak, *All This and Heaven Too* became a neutral entry, neither plus nor minus. Years later, Litvak could articulate his own grievance: "The picture was overproduced. You couldn't see the actors for the candelabra, and the whole thing became a victory for matter over mind. Bette Davis was the world's most expensively costumed governess. I'll tell you what was wrong with the picture. *Gone With the Wind* was wrong with it. If it hadn't been for the one picture, the other might have been managed nicely on a more modest scale. Somehow, though, Charles's performance transcended the curse of overproduction. He was easily the best actor I ever directed, although in the three pictures we made I didn't direct him once—he was his own creative artist. Possibly *All This and Heaven Too* was the best work he ever did. It was a much more complex performance, certainly, than for *Mayerling* or for *Tovarich*. It also shows that the great performances are not given by contented actors. Charles was a happy fellow in the other pictures we made, but in *All This and Heaven Too* he was surely the least contented man with whom I've ever worked."

Boyer's discontent was such that he took a six-month leave from film work, and launched an altogether new career for himself.

❄ ❄ ❄

In costume as the Duc de Praslin, Boyer was doing retakes at the Warner studio in May of 1940 when Winston Churchill succeeded Neville Chamberlain as Prime Minister of a beleaguered Great Britain. It was a dark hour for the Anglo-French alliance, and only a matter of days until Belgium would be lost to the Nazi invaders. More retakes were slated, but Boyer begged off; he felt miserably inert, so far removed from the desperate events that possessed him. He and Pat flew immediately to New York and then on to London. They were in England when the British completed the evacuation of Dunkirk in early June, leaving France vulnerable to the German onslaught.

In the days that followed, Mussolini's Italy joined Nazi Germany in the war against France and Great Britain, and Boyer sensed the imminent collapse of the French nation. When the Nazis entered Paris on June 14, he was working feverishly to assist friends seeking refuge in England. He arranged his mother's evacuation that same day, meeting her in Lisbon after her flight from Nice. Within the next few weeks, before and after France's capitulation to Germany on June 22, Boyer made several flights to Lisbon in an official capacity for the British Government, to obtain security for French refugees. Jean Renoir and Jean Gabin were among those whose escape Boyer aided. Another was the Jewish Henry Bernstein.

Boyer was in London for Charles de Gaulle's arrival as the self-appointed leader of the Free French. Boyer himself recorded De Gaulle's famous patriotic address on the London radio, to rally the groggy French and encourage the Resistance against the Nazi conquerors. He also recorded the speech in English for broadcast in the United States. Friends even before their meeting in London, Boyer and De Gaulle forged a finer kinship in the crisis, and the actor found himself important if unofficial functionary of the Provisional Government of the French Republic.

In August the Boyers fled the bomb shelters of London and returned to America, each with the confidence of a clearly defined job to perform. Pat was already involved in British war assistance, and in Hollywood would be a central figure in the local Bundles for Britain drive. Boyer himself founded the French War Relief Committee, along with Henry Bernstein, who accompanied Charles and Pat from London to New York. Bernstein soon became the most audible voice of French patriotism on the East Coast and worked doggedly to assist the escape of Jews from France. On the West Coast, Boyer was a quieter patriot but no less effective.

In the fall of 1940, Charles Boyer founded the French Research Foundation in Hollywood. It was an idea that had percolated within him for several years: to gather together and preserve documents pertaining to France and its people. Boyer had long been easily aggravated by Hollywood's careless and consistent misrepresentation of France and the French people in its feature films. Now he sought to establish a research center that could enable more honest and authentic depictions. While that was to remain the primary stated function of the French Research Foundation, its dominant activity became the documentation of the French involvement in World War II, both during the conflict and for years after France's liberation and the restoration of peace. Boyer was himself the foundation's first employee, and in a consciously businesslike arrangement afforded himself a modest salary as a researchist. Soon he hired an assistant, then withdrew from active library science, for which he was ill-prepared, and eventually hired a staff of three full-time researchists whose labors he supervised. And he took himself off salary.

To many in Hollywood, Boyer was a tightwad, someone who in the cliché of exaggeration "still had the first dollar he made as an actor." Those closer to him could cite his generosity whenever he understood the *need* of money he could provide. The French Research Foundation evolved into Boyer's own private philanthropy. Although eventually it received funding from many agencies including the postwar French Government, he remained its primary benefactor. Over the dozen or so years of the foundation's major documenting effort, Boyer was estimated to have contributed more than two million dollars of his own money.

For more than a year after establishing the French Research Foundation, Boyer capitalized on the United States' diminishing but still-official "neutrality" and used the foundation effectively as an agency for spiriting French citizens out of Nazi-occupied Europe under legal cover. His efforts enabled Julien Duvivier to leave France and relocate in Hollywood. Boyer also assisted in the rather more surreptitious escape from France of André Daven, who also eventually made wartime settlement in the U.S. film colony. Boyer soon found himself in the vortex of a new filmland community of French exiles that included such old, good friends as Victor Francen and Marcel Dalio.

Michèle Morgan, the lovely French actress who had been intimidated by the Boyer presence when they made *Orage,* was another beneficiary of Boyer's diplomacy in the period before the U.S. entry into World War II. He prevailed upon his agent and ever-closer friend Charles Feldman to see what might be engineered for Mlle. Morgan in Hollywood. Feldman, whose Famous Artists agency was a rising power in the movie industry, negotiated an uncommonly lucrative contract for Michèle Morgan at RKO. She arrived in Hollywood expecting to play in Orson Welles's *Journey into Fear.* Instead, after an extended period of waiting around, she made the stridently anti-Nazi *Joan of Paris* opposite another refugee, the Austrian Paul Henreid. It could not be said that her brief Hollywood career was any kind of success, but in the early postwar years she emerged as perhaps the most honored and popular leading actress of the French cinema, without the stigma of suspected collaboration that was upon Arletty, Danielle Darrieux, and many other actresses who continued to film in France during the German Occupation.

Boyer, who might have welcomed relief from his obligations to a succession of American screen queens, had certainly expected to film in Hollywood with Michèle Morgan. With Jean Renoir and writer Dudley Nichols he planned a Resistance drama that seemed appropriate for both himself and Morgan, as her follow-up to *Joan of Paris.* The property was

This Land Is Mine and Renoir eventually made it, but without Boyer and without Mlle. Morgan. When Charles Laughton "replaced" Boyer, he brought with him as costar the gorgeous, flame-haired Maureen O'Hara, who earlier had been his protégée in England, and whose American screen debut had been as Esmeralda to his *Hunchback of Notre Dame* for RKO. That left Michèle Morgan out in the cold.

Boyer never actually rejected *This Land Is Mine*, because, finally, it was not offered to him. The RKO studio, earlier the producer of his smash-hit *Love Affair*, decided that in view of recent developments, Boyer was too expensive an actor. He would not reduce his fee, and they refused to meet it.

IO

From *Private Worlds* in 1935 to *All This and Heaven Too* five years later, Charles Boyer could pick and choose. As a free-lance actor he regularly considered, rejected, and accepted offers from all the producing firms. Some films might never have been made had he not indicated his interest. Along with Ronald Colman, Cary Grant, Irene Dunne, Fredric March, and the few others who managed their own careers, Boyer had power in a way that screen players hadn't had earlier. If he was less than a leading draw with the mass audience, he was solid enough at the box office; and that, coupled with his accruing prestige, kept the studios' interest. His fee escalated smartly, leveled for a time at one hundred thousand dollars, and was comfortably above that for *All This and Heaven Too*. Then there was an economic retrenchment in the film industry; and suddenly, Boyer was looking for offers and finding none.

He was not written off as "box-office poison" as were some other high-wattage stars a few years earlier, but he was too costly for the new economics. While 1939 had marked Hollywood's zenith, it was also the last year for an industrial system based on a worldwide market. In the discipline of their system, the major studios alone had conspired to make 365 films annually, one for every day of the year. Foreign revenue was vital to the studios' formula for profit. But the system sustained its first serious injury in 1939 when Benito Mussolini banned the showing of American motion pictures throughout Italy. Adolf Hitler and Joseph Goebbels had prohibited the screening of American films in Nazi Germany some years earlier and the U.S. film industry made adjustment; but the loss of the Italian market was only the first in a rapid succession of blows as the German conquest of Europe removed a significant source of revenue from the Hollywood enterprise. With the fall of France to the Nazis, this had a vital bearing on Charles Boyer's status as a high-salaried free-lance performer. Even if Boyer had failed to penetrate the *Motion Picture Herald's* widely publicized annual lists of top moneymaking stars, that was a strictly domestic accounting and Boyer's pictures always did very well in their French bookings. Without that market, Boyer became less desirable to American producers, if no less respected.

It could also be noted that feature film production was reduced significantly in Hollywood from 1940, and the wartime norm for a major studio was twenty to thirty pictures annually, against forty to sixty only a few years earlier. Certainly there were far fewer major-scope productions such as had regularly enlisted Charles Boyer as an actor. With fewer properties to accommodate their own contract stars, the studios could shun an expensive outsider. There were occasional overtures for Boyer to reduce his fee, but on Charles Feldman's advice and his own intuition, the actor refused to do that. Persuaded at last that he could retain his customary fee only by signing a multi-picture contract, Boyer reached an agreement with Universal Pictures.

It was a non-exclusive contract and rather an odd one. Professing that he had always been interested in the business end of film production, Boyer agreed to *produce* up to nine pictures in a nine-year period, and to appear in a minimum of four of them. He could, however, trade any of his producer commitments for such Universal acting assignments as he may be inclined to accept. He could not be made to appear in any project which he did not approve, and as an actor for Universal he would have script, director, and costar approval. Perhaps the oddest thing was his choice of Universal, a company that usually dispensed undistinguished program films and only a handful of major features annually. It was logical that Boyer could not have obtained a similar arrangement with one of the more ostentatious companies; besides which, money talked for Boyer, and the Universal offer was a bundle of it.

Six months after completing *All This and Heaven Too,* Boyer returned to work in a Universal picture that he did not produce. This was *Back Street,* the first of three Boyer films released in 1941. It was a remake of the Fannie Hurst story that had been a big hit for Irene Dunne in 1932, but for Boyer it now suggested a comedown. It was carefully produced as a period piece on a major scale, and Boyer was accorded first billing; but *Back Street* was shaped (or reshaped) as a vehicle for his costar.

She was Margaret Sullavan, a splendid actress to whom such adjectives as "fey" and "enchanting" were often applied, not without reason. It was widely believed that she could have had one of the great screen careers if she had had sufficient enthusiasm for one, but her strong preference was the stage. Her 1933 bow in Universal's *Only Yesterday* caused almost as much stir in Hollywood as Katharine Hepburn's the year before, and she also quickly emulated Miss Hepburn in being "difficult." She was the only player of real consequence nurtured by Universal during the movies' first talking decade, Deanna Durbin apart.

Margaret Sullavan had been briefly married first to Henry Fonda, then to William Wyler, her director for the beguiling *The Good Fairy;* and when she filmed with Boyer she was married to Leland Hayward, a leading agent but more famous later as a Broadway producer. After marrying Hayward she had abruptly quit the movies, scored a Broadway hit in *Stage Door,* but was lured back to Hollywood by M-G-M. A later court ruling obligated her to Universal for two more pictures. The company owned no new properties that interested her, so a remake was suggested. She screened several Universal items that rated as golden oldies of the early talking period, and selected *Back Street,* the one about a woman growing old while being faithful to a married man. Her stipulation was that Charles Boyer had to be the leading man, and to get him she relinquished the top billing that had been the custom of her Universal pictures. Boyer accepted the assignment as the best thing available, and because he greatly admired Miss Sullavan's work.

Indeed, *Back Street,* despite its datedness, emerged a decent enough picture, and is one of the few instances of a remake comparing favorably with its original. For Margaret Sullavan, the actress with the peculiar and affecting catch in her husky voice, it meant another set of fine notices. Boyer's work also came in for high praise, and it hardly mattered that his was the subordinate role. He said "When in doubt, be in a hit," and *Back Street* was quite popular in its second incarnation. It indicated a promising start in American films for its English-bred director, but Robert Stevenson gained his primary identity much later as director of some fantasy-trimmed farces for Walt Disney.

Boyer had been warned that working with Margaret Sullavan would try both his nerves and his patience. They must have gotten on well, though, for at some point during the *Back Street* filming they agreed to make another picture together, to complete Sullavan's obligation to Universal. By Boyer's own account, "I mentioned to Maggie that I was about to drown in all the tears my pictures were causing, and I would like to do a comedy just for a nice change. They had been trying to talk her into making a farce that she thought had possibilities, but she chose *Back Street* instead. However, she would agree to make the other picture if I would be in it, and everything was settled so easily."

But not so soon. Boyer and Sullavan might have gone directly from *Back Street* into the farce that came to be called *Appointment for Love,* but for the intervention of what he believed was the best role he'd been offered since Napoleon. Ketti Frings, a sometime ghostwriter for the movie fan magazines, had written a novel about a French refugee who uses marriage as a ruse for getting into the United States from Mexico. This was *Hold Back the Dawn,* which in its Charles Brackett–Billy Wilder screen adaptation for Paramount bristled with good sardonic dialogue and defined its protagonist more as a rogue than a hero. The part seemed to have consciously been written for Boyer to play, even as shaded less sympathetically than the general line of his characterizations.

Soon afterward the writing team of Brackett and Wilder became producer and director, respectively, of their own pictures; but the director of *Hold Back the Dawn* was Mitchell Leisen from Paramount's front rank, and the project earnestly courted prestige. Unlike Boyer's recent run of set-bound photoplays, the new picture was shot mostly on locations—some of them quite gamy, as along the Mexico-California border, largely the scene depicted. Pat had a general rule never to haunt the shooting set of any of her husband's pictures, but on this occasion she briefly joined him on location for the adventure of it. Her presence even touched off some mild filmland gossip that she was "worried" about Charles, who for *Hold Back the Dawn* was accommodated with not one but two leading ladies, both of them extremely pretty and both considerably younger than he. Pat heard the talk and made light of it, but reasoned that if Charles *were* of a mind to play around, he could hardly do better than Olivia deHavilland and Paulette Goddard, neither of whom was married at the time.

Well, not exactly. Paulette Goddard was not quite divorced from Charlie Chaplin, whose marriage of several years' duration had been a poorly kept secret right up to their separation, following their joint appearance in *The Great Dictator*— Chaplin's belated debut as a talking actor. Miss Goddard was being built up by Paramount and was a newly certified star, already quite popular. She was older by several years than Olivia deHavilland who, although only twenty-five, was the screen veteran on comparative terms. Miss deHavilland had been in pictures for half a dozen years and had been a leading lady from the word go. Warner Brothers latched onto her to play Hermia in the film of *A Midsummer Night's Dream*, after her favorable accounting of the role in Max Reinhardt's famous production staged in the Hollywood Bowl. Still, Olivia had not quite attained an autonomous stardom, being most often used as window dressing for Errol Flynn's costume adventures. Her emergence as a major actress began with *Gone With the Wind*, and her portrayal of Melanie transformed a sticky-sweet second-lead heroine into an admirable human being. Now she was fighting for better roles, and *Hold Back the Dawn* was a coup. On loan from Warner Brothers to Paramount, she proceeded almost to take the picture away from Charles Boyer.

Boyer was the dominant presence throughout the film, alternating his scenes with the Misses Goddard and deHavilland who were seldom collected in the same frame. The Boyer performance at times bordered on the extraordinary, as he conveyed through facial nuance his character's changing disposition toward life and love. As the immigrant Georges, who is in love with the Anita character played by Paulette Goddard, but is stranded with her south of the border, he charms the American schoolteacher Emmy Brown into marrying him, for safe passage into California. Once there, of course, he'll abandon her and again take up with Anita; except it won't work out that way—not when Emmy Brown is the gentle Olivia deHavilland. Boyer was powerfully attracted to *Hold Back the Dawn* because, after his series of coat-holding stints for the screen's most glittery ladies, it gave him the kind of strong focal role he hadn't had since *Algiers*. Making the picture was an entirely gratifying experience for him, and a bonus was that he persuaded the Paramount folk to give Victor Francen a start in American films with a strong character role. He may not have been exactly jealous of Olivia deHavilland, but he was certainly surprised when she stole all the notices. That was because the depth and subtlety of her playing was still something of a revelation, Melanie Hamilton notwithstanding. Olivia delivered the unexpected, and there was no longer an element of surprise in Boyer's excellence. The surprise would have been his failure to attain it.

Hold Back the Dawn received an Academy Award nomination as best picture for 1941—the third year in a row that Boyer had appeared in a picture so honored, without securing a nomination of his own. Once again a "sure thing" Oscar nomination was denied him, although Olivia deHavilland obtained candidacy as best actress. (She lost to her younger sister, Joan Fontaine.) More important to Boyer was the evidence of his having carried a picture that was very nearly a smash hit. *Hold Back the Dawn* entertained the moviegoing body proper, not just the clubwomen and the prim librarians who never missed a Boyer picture. Yet perhaps more indelibly than any picture since *Algiers,* the Paramount entry revived and recertified the Great Lover designation he wished to avoid or transcend. For both the implications of combustible sexuality in his scenes with Goddard, and his artful if bogus seduction of deHavilland, the Boyer of *Hold Back the Dawn* impressed vividly as a one-of-a-kind charmer.

The dominant mood of *Hold Back the Dawn* was melodrama, and that made a return to comedy as desirable for Boyer as it was overdue. So he kept his *Appointment for Love* with Margaret Sullavan, and they had a delightful time shooting all of it in just four weeks. (As a contrast, *All This and Heaven Too* kept Boyer occupied nearly five months.) If it was the least important title of both Boyer's and Sullavan's big-star periods, it was nevertheless politely applauded by critics as a pleasing trifle, and it managed a neat little profit at the box office. In one of those incomparably obscure pieces of trivia that are mined in the filmland on random occasions, it was revealed that on Pearl Harbor Sunday, more Americans saw *Appointment for Love* than any other picture. No doubt most who saw it forgot all about it soon afterward, but it provided entertainment for the moment—a screwball romp about two doctors who were married to one another yet could seldom get together for a connubial rendezvous because of their professional responsibilities.

Given a choice from among such medium-priced directors as were available at Universal or through a studio loan, Margaret Sullavan insisted on the journeyman William A. Seiter, who had guided some of the Deanna Durbin pictures, and had also directed Sullavan and ex-husband Fonda in *The Moon's Our Home.* That was a Walter Wanger production and Boyer recalled meeting Bill Seiter but had no opinion of him as a director. Miss Sullavan said "Oh, but he's a wonderful person for comedy," and Boyer rubber-stamped her choice; and she may have been right.

Although never a "name" director, there is fair evidence that Bill Seiter was an able craftsman, and there has been a recent mild effort among film critics to upgrade his accomplishment. William Everson in *American Silent Film* makes a good case for Seiter's visual mastery, especially of comedy, before the movies could talk. He was a prolific director over a thirty-five-year period into the mid-fifties, and thoroughly routine credits dominate his ledger; but the indication is that he was always as good as his material. Seiter pictures weren't rushed, but they never dragged, and the lighter exercises of which *Appointment for Love* is representative always show good spirit.

Boyer was amused by an exchange with Seiter that occurred shortly after shooting commenced, and recalled it often in unidentical versions. The gist of it is that Seiter after taking a scene between Boyer and actor Eugene Pallette yelled, "Hey, Charlie, you just said that line as if you really believed it." Boyer proudly replied that he always tried to believe everything he played. Seiter said "Well, that's wrong. The essence of farce is disbelief, and this isn't high comedy, it's farce. Here we have some very tentative dialogue that sure won't be funny if it's played straight. In a farce you have to be suspicious of every syllable." From that point Boyer enjoyed constructing a performance that was *suspicious* of every word, every sound, every thing. Perhaps his happiest moment occurred not long afterward when Bill Seiter said "Now, come on, Charlie, what's all this great lover crap, anyway? You're a born light comedian!"

Born or made, the light comedian was also tired. After his return from Europe he had made three pictures with hardly a chance to catch his breath between assignments. Through most of 1941 he was concurrently involved with the Free French, and maintaining regular contact with the Resistance. He was never without a cigarette, and now was smoking an incredible six packs a day. He worked himself into a state of visible physical exhaustion, and palpitations following a large Thanksgiving meal caused some anxiety that he'd sustained a mild heart attack. X rays proved negative, but an attack loomed as likely if he didn't pursue a more reasonable physical discipline. He was immediately ordered to reduce his smoking at least by half.

He had worked too hard, and at forty-two Boyer knew it was time to slow down. He would heed the warning and take a year's vacation. After that, his discipline would be never to work more than half the time as a screen actor. After each completed project he would submit himself to a long rest, and a picture a year would be his limit. Or maybe two.

But he kept on smoking.

❉ ❉ ❉

He really did take a long holiday that amounted to almost a year away from the movie cameras. It wasn't all play, though. Boyer became a regular participant in "Voice of America" propaganda broadcasts. He narrated *The Heart of a Nation*, a documentary film about the French Resistance. He broadcast *Hold Back the Dawn* in French for the Office of War Information, and then enlisted the legion of French actors exiled in Hollywood in the transcribing of other screen dramas for broadcast in Paris.

He also moved the French Research Foundation into larger, sleek offices in a building he bought on La Cienega Boulevard. The fully staffed office stepped up its documentation of the war and particularly of the efforts of the Resistance.

Following the lead of his countryman Jean Renoir, Boyer became a U.S. citizen without renouncing his French citizenship. Both he and Pat were naturalized on February 13, 1942. He said they had agreed to wait until the United States had joined the Allies in the war against the Axis powers.

Yet there was a lot of play. The Boyers resumed the habitual travel by rail that they both enjoyed, and visited many American cities for the first time. Sometimes they were accompanied by the actor's mother, who had joined them in Hollywood. Pat and her mother-in-law had a relationship that was more formally polite than friendly, and Louise Boyer was her house guest only briefly before taking her own apartment in Hollywood.

Tennis was a regular activity for the Boyers now, and they also took up skiing in Sun Valley. Charles was no match for his wife, who was the superior athlete in every respect. Nevertheless, they did everything together.

The Boyers appeared to be about the most stable couple in a filmland where any degree of marital stability rated as novelty. They saw their friends through divorces and remarriages, but they stayed together; indeed, they were seldom apart. Their eighth wedding anniversary in 1942 could as easily have been their twentieth. They were thoroughly adjusted to one another, and even their spats had a mocking playfulness.

Rumors of Charles's possible dalliance with Paulette Goddard died so quickly as to confirm their lack of foundation. There were hardly any other rumors, and Pat said their life might be more interesting if someone could think up a few. She insisted that she trusted her husband absolutely. She could also add cutely that she was forever fighting off would-be seducers with her fingernails and wits, but no one was starting any rumors about *her*.

Pat told Hedda Hopper, though, that she wouldn't mind if Charles never made another movie. She enjoyed having more of his time, and besides, "we really don't need any more money." Yet she was finally glad when he got back in front of the cameras, because Charles began to get irritable after any long absence from acting.

His return was capricious. Boyer's good friend Julien Duvivier cajoled him into appearing in one of the American screen's occasional aberrations—the portmanteau picture that was *Tales of Manhattan*. But if it was atypical of Hollywood, it was entirely typical of the great French director whose exile in Hollywood it punctuated.

In France, Duvivier had made the episodic film into his own fashion, most notably in *Un Carnet de Bal*, whose success brought him to Hollywood for a first brief stay to direct *The Great Waltz*. As a political refugee he initiated his second Hollywood career with *Lydia*, a showcase for Merle Oberon that was a recognizable facsimile of *Un Carnet de Bal*. Now Duvivier was onto a project that had actually been the brainstorm of Ben Hecht, himself one of the writers of the compartmentalized screenplay. *Tales of Manhattan* was a punning title, as it involved a tuxedo—a dress coat with tails. After the model of Paramount's antic *If I Had a Million*, the new project linked several unrelated stories by a common device—in this case, the dress coat that passes through several owners before finding its destiny as a tattered scarecrow in a black sharecropper's field.

Duvivier's inspiration was to assemble an all-star cast that would compare favorably with the legendary *Grand Hotel* and even outnumber it. Boyer accepted the assignment at a negotiated small fee, as all the *Tales of Manhattan* stars did, not because he liked his role, but because he could not refuse a good friend who clearly sought a favor; and he wished to help Duvivier get solidly established in a Hollywood that had considered *Lydia* a classy failure. Besides, nothing better had turned up.

With the United States now in the war, the European Resistance dramas that might have beckoned Boyer were being deprogrammed in the studios in favor of dramas about America's fighting men. Few parts were available for an actor of Boyer's definition—interpreted by many producers as his *limitation.* There was also a new wave of escapist comedies, but Boyer's nimble work in *Appointment for Love* had not touched off an explosion of offers. The most interesting possibility that had been dangled for him was *Her Cardboard Lover* at M-G-M. If for no other reason, it interested him because it could enable him to put a check by the name of Norma Shearer in the scorecard of the great ladies he had squired on the screen. But he read the script and found this particular lover to be hopelessly cardboard indeed; so he backed away from the picture that ended the Shearer career with a whimper.

In *Tales of Manhattan* he could put a check by the name of Rita Hayworth, a popular "new" star after years of B-picture drudgery. They were the principals of the opening sequence, with Thomas Mitchell as Hayworth's jealous husband who shoots Boyer as a suspected cuckolder—not killing Rita's lover, but putting a nice hole in the tuxedo. Later the coat is worn by Charles Laughton, ripping while he conducts a symphonic performance; and then Edward G. Robinson wears it to a college reunion, seeking to disguise his failure. There was also a misfiring sequence with Ginger Rogers and Henry Fonda, and cut from the release print was an episode built around W. C. Fields—ostensibly because it was *too funny*.

Tales of Manhattan was uneven in the certain tradition of all episode pictures, but Duvivier imparted to it a consistent rhythm and style—at least until the concluding shantytown sequence that was later denounced by Paul Robeson, one of its players. Today the final episode can only be viewed with embarrassment, if it is viewed at all: *Tales of Manhattan* has never been revived and has obtained few bookings on television—justifiable for a picture of arguable merit at best. No matter—the gimmick worked. *Tales of Manhattan* was a substantial wartime hit, playing to large audiences that generally seemed to enjoy it. Its display ads also had the effect of giving Charles Boyer more eminence than he could have demanded, as he appeared to command billing over several of the screen's more illustrious stars. There was no clear indication that the star players were billed in the order of their appearance in the film.

Had *Tales of Manhattan* not been successful, Boyer and Duvivier might never have made *Flesh and Fantasy*—which some in the industry later contended *should* have been left unmade. In 1942 they were not able to persuade Darryl Zanuck, for whose 20th Century–Fox company *Tales of Manhattan* was made, of the feasibility of *Flesh and Fantasy*. The star-laden *Tales* was Boyer's first picture for a 20th Century–Fox that bore scant resemblance to the Fox Films enterprise for which both Charles and Pat had played their first leading roles in America. Now Zanuck rebuffed the notion of a follow-up episode film with supernatural trimmings, citing the well-known law of diminishing returns; but Zanuck nurtured a friendship with the actor whom he had coveted in earlier years, and Boyer did not come away empty-handed. He coaxed Zanuck into taking on André Daven as a 20th Century–Fox producer. The Davens had joined Hollywood's mushrooming French colony, and for an extended period were house guests of the Boyers.

To serve proof that his producer contract with Universal was not a rumor, Boyer decided to produce *Flesh and Fantasy* himself, with Duvivier as director. He put different writers to work on a four-part omnibus picture, then tabled the matter to accept a full-length role in what promised to be a picture of consequence, returning him to Warner Brothers.

The Constant Nymph was a steadily popular English novel that had served as a British talkie with Brian Aherne and Canada's Victoria Hopper. Warner Brothers purchased subsequent screen rights, intending it as a showcase for Geraldine Fitzgerald when there was some thought of building her as a studio rival to Bette Davis. The property languished until someone saw it as eminently suitable for the emerging Joan Fontaine. As the newest Oscar winner—nominally for *Suspicion,* but in deferred payment for *Rebecca*—Olivia deHavilland's younger sister was the toast of Hollywood, however briefly. She had been a lackluster RKO chattel until David Selznick stunned the film world by giving her the frightened-bird heroine in the movie adaptation of Daphne du Maurier's famous novel, *Rebecca.* No longer under contract, Fontaine was wanted by every company but selected her roles carefully, with a picture-a-year rhythm. When Warner Brothers dangled *The Constant Nymph,* she grabbed it, for the child-woman Tessa was the dream of any young actress.

The role of the older composer whom Tessa secretly loves, and with whom she shares a deep spiritual bond, was offered around to variably distinguished male stars from Fredric March to Robert Taylor, once it was established that no ranking star of British origin was available. Director Edmund Goulding made bids for both Robert Donat and Leslie Howard, but neither could be pried away from the British war effort. (Had Howard taken the role, he might not have been killed some months later, when the Nazis shot down the plane in which he was a passenger, and which they believed carried Winston Churchill.) No major actor desired to play second fiddle to Miss Fontaine, but there was the thought that a bundle of money might encourage Charles Boyer, who often appeared to have a corner on Hollywood's musician roles anyway. No matter that he was nobody's Englishman; he could speak in his own agreeable French accent and there would be no mention in the screenplay of the chap's national origin. Boyer accepted the part with a guarantee of first billing, and for a suspected sum of $150,000.

Boyer admired both the Margaret Kennedy novel and the earlier film wherein, ironically, his role was played by the same Brian Aherne who was still Joan Fontaine's husband when the second *Constant Nymph* was made. He also liked certain aspects of the drama Edmund Goulding was mounting, its good rustic atmosphere contrasting smartly with music-salon elegance. What he did not like was his role as Louis, who was credited in other characters' dialogue with qualities of depth and sensitivity that were not facets of the role as written, and were difficult for him to express. Boyer decided that the composer was a stick-figure out of radio soap opera, manipulated entirely by women. Early in the story he marries a young woman who was humorless and severe as Alexis Smith played her, making his professed love for her all the more dubious while the mortally ill Tessa pines in the background.

As a mid-1943 release *The Constant Nymph* was well liked by both the press and the paying patrons, without attaining the major recognition that had been forecast for it. Boyer seemed to have assessed the issue accurately. His role and Alexis Smith's were impediments, besides which such fine actors as Charles Coburn and Peter Lorre were wasted. Once again, though, Boyer had set up an effective display by an actress. Joan Fontaine made very nearly the most of her splendid role, and was rewarded with her third Academy Award nomination in four years. It was also her last one, as the Fontaine career followed a generally downward trajectory from that high point.

If *The Constant Nymph* was a successful picture that Boyer disliked, *Flesh and Fantasy* was an acknowledged flop in the industry that he liked very much. The stories, unrelated but for the common element of supernatural phenomena, were narrated by Robert Benchley in the flashback custom of Duvivier's French films, from the original setting of a gentlemen's club. As filmed, there were four stories, each running to half an hour; but against Boyer's wishes the studio heads later eliminated one of the segments to reduce the overall length. Excised was the vignette featuring the least prominent players in the cast—Alan Curtis and Gloria Jean from the Universal contract list. Quixotically, Universal then expanded the footage of the deleted component under another director, altered it for a happy ending, and released it as an hour-long B picture called *Destiny*, which became a surprise hit, a "sleeper." The subsequent experience of *Flesh and Fantasy* may have caused them to wish they'd done the same with the other segments.

Boyer's initial plan was not to appear in his own first personally produced picture, but he changed his mind in the interest of the box office, to give the strange film a reasonable all-star aura, enlisting Barbara Stanwyck for his own sequence, expert veterans Edward G. Robinson and Thomas Mitchell for another (Oscar Wilde's "Lord Arthur Savile's Crime," the most successful of the vignettes), and the younger Betty Field and Robert Cummings for the one story that was not resolved tragically.

Critics liked the picture more than did its audiences, which tended to be small ones. But the critics didn't like it enough. They were not impressed by the Boyer-Stanwyck chapter about a trapeze performer who foresees his own death, and the general reaction provoked a cynicism uncharacteristic of Boyer. He said "If the dialogue had been spoken in French or some other foreign language, the American critics would have called it a work of art."

When it was finally shown in France after the war, critical opinion was divided but some did hail it as a Duvivier masterwork. *Flesh and Fantasy* was also a kind of working model for the British-made *Dead of Night* that was a subject for world acclaim when produced only a few years later.

Echoing filmdom's generally favorable appraisal of Barbara Stanwyck's consummate professionalism, Boyer called her the American screen actress least likely ever to give a poor performance. To friends he also confided that he was more nearly satisfied with his *Flesh and Fantasy* account than with anything he'd done since *Hold Back the Dawn*.

Boyer's grievance was not so much with the critics or even the unresponsive audience, as with Universal Pictures. He believed the company lost faith in the picture, after having lacked sufficient faith in the first place, and had just thrown it away, without careful promotion and with no effort to obtain choice bookings. *Flesh and Fantasy* did not really lose money, as was freely reported; but while the wartime box offices were booming, its profit was only microscopic. The experience caused Boyer to lose his speculative interest in producing; and when he and Universal's Martin Mayer were unable to make their union more blissful, the Boyer contract with Universal was dissolved by mutual consent. Boyer's association with Julien Duvivier was also at its end, although they remained friends for many years, in both America and France. After *Flesh and Fantasy,* Duvivier made only one other American picture—*The Impostor,* also for Universal. Jean Gabin played the title role that was first offered to Boyer. It was another failure, even more so than Gabin's only other American picture during his forced exile, *Moontide.*

The rupture at Universal also delivered Boyer from a decidedly weak picture he had apparently agreed to star in, although no announcement to that effect had been given. Boyer's interest in *The Climax* may have been prodded by its screenwriter Lynn Starling, whose *Private Worlds* had put Boyer into Hollywood orbit. *The Climax* was designed as a melodrama in an operatic setting to serve the soprano Susanna Foster, whose career failed to ignite despite Universal's best effort. Perhaps sensing a need to begin a transition into character parts, Boyer was attracted to a sinister and decidedly unromantic role that would have been a departure for him. Indeed, it was finally played by none other than Boris Karloff.

Boyer later reasoned that *The Climax* could have finished him in American pictures, as the assignment that might have pre-empted *Gaslight.*

✻   ✻   ✻

Hollywood's Academy Awards ceremony began as a sedate little hotel dinner in 1928, when the Academy was new and its membership quite small. It gained importance as the Oscars, as the awards were soon called, quickly commanded the national fascination; but it was still an intramural dinner in 1943, long before there was any thought of the ceremony's eventual degeneration into a preening telecast for the nation to behold.

The Boyers attended the function dutifully with annual regularity. If Charles was not himself a nominee, one of his pictures would inevitably be involved in the awards competition. Not until 1942, when *Tales of Manhattan* was his only credit did he absent himself from the actual balloting. Yet when the 1942 awards were presented the following March, he was involved. It wasn't a competitive thing, but Charles Boyer got his Oscar. The Academy's governors elected to present the actor with a special award "for his progressive cultural achievement in establishing the French Research Foundation in Los Angeles." That he would receive the award was known in advance, so he prepared and memorized an acceptance speech. In that era, rather than reciting a litany of thank-yous to their co-workers, the Oscar winners delivered rather formal addresses. Boyer spoke for three minutes, then fretted about having been too verbose. Not long afterward, Greer Garson accepted her statuette for *Mrs. Miniver* and talked for forty minutes.

Boyer took great pride in his special award, which for several years was displayed in the French Research Foundation library. He said that receiving the award was the best thing that had happened to him in Hollywood.

If he really meant that, he would probably have changed his mind before the year was over. He even wondered if his and Pat's euphoria on that occasion might not have caused them to conceive a child.

11

❧❧❧❧❧❧❧❧❧❧

In the spring of 1943, while her husband was occupied with
the only motion picture he ever produced personally, Pat Paterson Boyer became subject to mild attacks of dizziness. She
told no one about the "spells" that grew more frequent, and
she especially wouldn't tell Charles who, she said, "wanted to
call a doctor every time I cleared my throat."

She was exceptionally healthy, without susceptibility even
to seasonal head colds. She scorned all medicines, more consciously after her friendship with Jeanette MacDonald made
Pat interested in some of the principles of Christian Science.
She teased Charles for his hypochondria; all the pills and
ointments and nasal sprays in their medicine chest were *his*.
In one respect, though, she was not a physical paragon. She
had never been "regular"; otherwise she might have suspected
the nature of her condition much sooner. Even when she
scheduled a doctor's appointment without telling Charles, she
doubted what she had begun to hope.

It became a favorite joke: when she informed Charles that
she was three months pregnant, the news stunned him just as
in the movies, and he said, "But this is impossible!"

It had begun to *seem* impossible. In her memoirs that were
so affectionate, even worshipful, toward Boyer, Ingrid Bergman said that Charles and Pat "for at least ten years had been
trying for a baby." That was slightly longer than the Boyers
had known each other, but was an innocent error not far from

the truth. The full effort had been made to produce the baby they both wanted. Pat dropped hints of having more than once miscarried early in the first years of their marriage. She probably concluded that if conception were possible, carrying to delivery was not. She reasoned, though, that "it's not something you have to stop trying just because you've given up."

On several occasions they had considered adopting a baby, and were thinking about it again, just before the revelation of Pat's pregnancy put Charles into a happy nervous spin. No husband could have been more attentive. He engaged a personal nurse over Pat's protest that she didn't need one, then wouldn't allow the nurse to give Pat any assistance he could provide personally. Pat accepted the doctor's word that she was past the point of likely miscarriage and in fine shape otherwise, but Charles's worrying could not be soothed. This was real drama and high adventure, altogether a novel experience for him—more so than for Pat whose sisters, at least, had become mothers.

With *Flesh and Fantasy* completed and his association with Universal Pictures soon to be severed, Boyer put the activity of motion pictures entirely out of his mind and became his wife's faithful shadow. Other than to make a brief daily visit to his French Research Foundation offices, he was in Pat's constant attendance. He accompanied her on her appointed visits with the obstetrician, and to the Beverly Hills shops where she selected her maternity frocks.

Alone by themselves, they played a lot of gin rummy and also took to reading plays aloud together, acting all the parts. If they were occupied with the reading of separate books, he was still by her side. Yet Pat adapted herself to pregnancy more easily than her husband did. He was in a chronic nervous state, impatient for the baby to arrive once he had been assured that one was coming.

Pat said it was a good thing for both of them that *Gaslight* materialized for him. First he intended not even to consider another film project until after the baby's arrival. But the *Gaslight* package proved irresistible to him—for its Victorian melodrama that furnished him a challenging villain role, and for the prospect of Ingrid Bergman as costar. He expected to complete the picture before the baby's arrival, calculated at about Christmas Day.

Just before principal photography for *Gaslight* had been completed, the baby turned the tables on them by arriving two weeks early. Boyer had expected to be with his wife at the time of delivery, but was at the M-G-M studio in Culver City, endeavoring to complete an assignment in a prestige picture. He was taken by surprise. A phone call to the studio informed Boyer that his wife was about to deliver. The event occurred before he could get to the hospital.

Michael Charles Boyer was born December 9, 1943. A robust baby weighing in just under nine pounds, he had black hair at birth but was very fair-skinned, appearing "very French" and suggesting a resemblance to his father that would be more pronounced in childhood.

Pat, who gave birth to the Boyers' only child at age thirty-three, followed an easy and comfortable pregnancy with a difficult and lengthy delivery. Internal complications followed the birth. The Boyers soon accepted the likelihood that there would be no more children—without disappointment because, as Pat said, "Michael is the finished product."

Ingrid Bergman, who recalled that during the filming of *Gaslight* Boyer was always rushing to the phone to call home and check on his wife, wrote of the actor's euphoric return to the movie set: "He had a son! Champagne—everybody had to have champagne! More champagne and Charles's tears falling into every glass. You'd think no one in the world had ever had a son before."

* * *

A squabble over billing almost caused *Gaslight* to be canceled, or to be made available to other players. It was an M-G-M project employing starring players on loan, and the Boyer-Bergman combination was largely engineered by Charles Feldman, who represented them both.

Bergman was under contract to David Selznick, who personally had produced only her American debut vehicle, *Intermezzo*, but who provided adroit management of her career. Inconclusively at first but then with fabulous success, he loaned her to other companies for a series of newsworthy projects that put the Swedish import into the American top-star class. At the beginning of 1943 she was on the screen in the marvelously entertaining *Casablanca* opposite Humphrey Bogart, and was filming Hemingway's *For Whom the Bell Tolls* with Gary Cooper. By the time that ambitious work played its first reserved-seat engagements in July, she and Cooper had already completed another big one together—*Saratoga Trunk*, whose release would be withheld for two years.

Although *For Whom the Bell Tolls* was something of a movie monstrosity, Miss Bergman's showing as Maria made her the most topical of film players, and the actress most coveted by all the studios. Aware of that, David Selznick demanded that Bergman be given the lead billing in *Gaslight*, otherwise she would be withdrawn from the assignment. Boyer refused to yield the billing and was supported on the point by Feldman. Their contention was that since Boyer had been a star in American films considerably longer than Miss Bergman and was accustomed to top billing where she was not, taking billing beneath her would be read to suggest that he was slipping. Boyer was contracted for *Gaslight* with his billing guaranteed before Miss Bergman was signed, and Selznick's refusal to compromise led insiders to predict that M-G-M's Greer Garson would play the beleaguered wife. But Ingrid Bergman desperately wanted *Gaslight*, and also wanted Boyer, and didn't care about the billing. She pleaded with Selznick, who was placated by producer Arthur Hornblow's offer to upgrade a subordinate role as a third star part for Joseph Cotten to play. Cotten was also under contract to Selznick, and being groomed as a romantic star—concurrently shooting *Since You Went Away* which Selznick wrote as well as produced. To have Miss Bergman positioned between Boyer and Cotten in the display ads merely retained a favored practice of sexual symmetry in matters of billing.

Gaslight was a recycled screen title for *Angel Street*, Patrick Hamilton's period stage thriller, which was a long-run hit in both London and New York. It was first filmed in England by Thorold Dickinson, and his *Gaslight* with Anton Walbrook and Diana Wynyard was and is regarded as a minor masterpiece; the Boyers saw it in London in 1940, before M-G-M secured the property for a film of its own. Before putting its own *Gaslight* into production, M-G-M committed one of the most barbarous acts in the history of world cinema, acquiring the negative of the English film and then having it destroyed, to assure exclusive worldwide distribution of their own product. (Despite M-G-M's action also to seize every existing print, the English *Gaslight* survives, and a print was exhibited in New York many years later as *Angel Street*.)

Throughout his career Boyer had been selecting his screen subjects from an abundance of story treatments and finished scripts and occasionally from half-baked notions—but always other people's ideas. Later, in a retrospective assessment of his career, he believed he hadn't been aggressive enough, hadn't gone after some really good parts he might have played. Even Napoleon had been served to him on a platter. But he went after *Gaslight,* as soon as M-G-M announced its intention of producing an elaborate film with George Cukor as director. He was determined to play the wily Gregory Anton, who charms an impressionable and love-struck young woman into marriage to get at her fortune and her jewels, then proceeds cleverly to begin driving her into insanity. Although it is virtually the only display of rank villainy in the inventory of his big-star period, it is the performance that for many people represents the quintessential Boyer: a rogue of such polished persuasion that he can charm an audience already onto his diabolical design. If subtlety is the hallmark of Boyer's dramatic art, then *Gaslight* exemplifies it, and not only in his scenes with Bergman. Consider the scene wherein Gregory, alone, discovers by accident the jewels he has quietly been seeking with Javert-like doggedness: it might have provided an eye-popping display for a lesser actor, but it revealed Boyer's power for understatement.

For *Gaslight* to retain the allure and impact of its stage model, it had to remain essentially a claustrophobic theater piece. Boyer recognized George Cukor as precisely the right director for it. Boyer preferred theatrical directors such as John Cromwell and Philip Moeller who placed drama above cinema and had something of an actor's perspective, but

Cukor was the most exacting dramatic director he had worked with in an American film. It made for a rewarding experience. Cukor committed each scene to thorough and intense rehearsal before putting the cameras on it. Ingrid Bergman was as serious-minded about acting as Boyer was, and the stars engaged in give and take with a compatible director whose judgment and dramatic intuition they both admired. Miss Bergman, echoing Bette Davis and others who played with him, also believed that "Charles Boyer was the most intelligent actor I ever worked with, and one of the very nicest." *Gaslight* seems to have been a gratifying experience for everyone concerned.

Today the M-G-M version appears overproduced, a characteristic it shares with Boyer's other melodramatic period piece, *All This and Heaven Too*. But in 1944 it was counted an unqualified triumph all around. Retakes were ordered in January following a studio screening, and Boyer was pried away from his wife and infant son just long enough to accomplish what was believed needed in the way of finishing touches. It was released in May and probably would have been a sure bet commercially even without the extravagant reviews. To people throughout America, *Gaslight* was "the new Ingrid Bergman picture."

Her star was still rising, and *Gaslight* kept it on an upward trajectory. She had just missed taking an Oscar for *For Whom the Bell Tolls*, which was still being shown; but *Casablanca*, her other 1943 release, was the Academy-honored best picture. *Gaslight* was the event that solemnized her, and the thought that it would deliver her an Academy Award started early. Boyer was philosophical about being thoroughly eclipsed by his costar's blaze. He was happy to be in a hit, and was satisfied with his own performance to a degree not characteristic of him. Although his role was equal in size to Bergman's, it was another instance of a screen story projected from the point of view of the woman as protagonist. *Gaslight* easily transcended the stigma of the "woman's picture," but Boyer expected again to be bypassed for the Oscar competition while the lady got all the attention. He had about decided that his specific function in the Academy's scheme of things was artfully to set up other actresses for nomination—his experience with the Misses Dunne, Davis, deHavilland, and Fontaine. But when the nominees were revealed early the next year, Boyer was one of the contending actors.

Through a freak development, he also was given an excellent chance to win. The great popular hit of 1944 was Leo McCarey's *Going My Way*, wherein Barry Fitzgerald in a role almost as large as Bing Crosby's gave an endearing performance that somehow got nominated twice—both as a supporting player and as a lead. With Crosby also nominated, there was conjecture that a split of ballots for the two *Going My Way* actors might work decisively to Boyer's benefit. The other nominated actors, Cary Grant and Alexander Knox, represented films that had disappointed at the box office. Nevertheless, Boyer again was a loser. Some powerful lobbying by Paramount may have coaxed the voters into going for a straight *Going My Way* ticket, as both Crosby and Fitzgerald were winners in the separate categories. Boyer later revealed that he did not vote in the 1944 contest. He said that in 1937 he had voted for his own performance as Napoleon, hoping to win; and that in 1938 he of course wanted to win for *Algiers* but did not deserve to, and knew he wouldn't anyway, so had voted for Leslie Howard's Henry Higgins in *Pygmalion*. Of the 1944 balloting he said he could not vote against himself, but in good conscience also could not vote against Barry Fitzgerald. He added, though, "Pat still votes every year, and I expect she voted for me this time, although she doesn't tell me."

Ingrid Bergman won her first Oscar for *Gaslight*, which lost recognition as best picture to *Going My Way*, but was again a winner for black-and-white art direction. For her very first screen role the teen-aged Angela Lansbury was a supporting nominee, as the cockney housemaid with whom Boyer dallies. Most who remember *Gaslight* recall Miss Lansbury's stint, but have forgotten that Joseph Cotten was even in it. As the film's third star, Cotten enacted a Scotland Yard investigator into the strange doings on Angel Street, functionally the "hero." It was rather a typical exposure for an actor who gave splendid performances in many major films of the forties,

without creating a lasting impression—the screen's good serious actor most easily forgotten.

That Boyer was not to be forgotten or otherwise shunted
aside was assured. If his misadventures with Universal Pictures had created a tentative impression that he was on a
downslide, *Gaslight* restored him to the Hollywood pantheon.
With Gable, Stewart, Fonda, Montgomery, Power, and other
established movie heroes in wartime military service, Boyer
was one of the few actors in Hollywood who could qualify for
the new vogue designation of superstar.

*   *   *

Shortly after obtaining American citizenship, the Boyers
registered to vote in California, both as Democrats. Then they
canceled one another in the 1942 gubernatorial election.
Boyer voted for the Democratic incumbent, Culbert Olsen,
who lost in his reelection bid to the state attorney general,
Earl Warren, who was Pat's choice. In subsequent state elec-
tions Boyer also voted for Warren as governor, and came to
regard Warren as a great American statesman, particularly
during his later tenure as Chief Justice of the U. S. Supreme
Court. But in 1944 Earl Warren was running mate for
Thomas E. Dewey's presidential candidacy, and had the support of neither of the Boyers.

Boyer campaigned actively for the Democrats' Roosevelt-
Truman ticket in 1944 and became permanently identified
with Hollywood's liberal community. Boyer's older friend, the
French-but-American-born Adolphe Menjou, was one of the
film colony's leading supporters of the Dewey candidacy.
Menjou had an abiding loathing for Franklin D. Roosevelt,
whom Boyer had enshrined as a political hero even before
making personal acquaintance with the nation's thirty-second
President. In the spring of 1944 Boyer was in Washington to
give an address for the French Research Foundation, and to
meet the press in connection with the opening of *Gaslight* in
the nation's capital. Pat remained in Beverly Hills with the
baby but later wished she'd made the trip as Charles had
wished. In Washington, he accepted an invitation to dine in
the White House—not because of his support of FDR's bid

for a fourth term, but for his continued activity in the "Voice of America" broadcasts. President and actor had a moment of private conversation, with Roosevelt remarking on Boyer's memorable portrayal of Napoleon, and both men expressing hope for the ultimate liberation of France by the Allies. After his return to Hollywood, Boyer assured Adolphe Menjou that "President Roosevelt sends you his very best personal regards." In 1944 they could be good friends on opposite sides of the political fence; only a few years later it would be much more difficult.

Boyer kept close watch on all the war developments, especially in the European aspect; and from his own intuition and the texts of his "Voice of America" broadcasts, he sensed when the Allied invasion of France was imminent. In the Italian campaign, Rome fell to the Allies on June 5; and when President Roosevelt addressed the nation over radio that evening, ostensibly to commemorate the event, Boyer interpreted the speech with its concluding prayer as a subliminal message. André Daven, a dinner guest at the Boyer home that evening, would recall that after Roosevelt's speech Boyer sprang to his feet and exclaimed, "It is about to happen, I know it!" The Allies landed on the coast of Normandy the next morning. It was D-Day; the liberation had begun.

During the eleven ensuing months to V-E day on May 8, 1945, Boyer made only one picture—*Together Again,* filmed briskly over nine weeks in the 1944 summer. The rest of his time was given to affairs of the Free French. He gave a series of patriotic speeches "sponsored" by his French Research Foundation. He wrote his own speeches, and collaborated with Jean Benoit-Lévy in the writing of a dramatic oral pageant called *Liberté, Égalité, Fraternité* that Boyer recorded as an album for the Decca company. He played Danton, Lafayette, Victor Hugo, and other heroes in the tribute to French democracy.

Paris was liberated on August 25, and most of southern France—including Boyer's home town of Figeac—was redeemed by the Allies within the next few weeks. Boyer established contact with Georges Adam, leader of the French underground press, to expand the vital documentation of the war. This was a busy, exciting time for him. He was in touch regularly with the aged Henry Bernstein in New York, still directing the program of the French War Relief Committee.

With peace restored to Europe after the German surrender in May but with the Pacific war against Japan continuing, Boyer in the summer of 1945 addressed a New York *Herald Tribune* forum on world affairs:

"I know very little about politics. But I know that while victory may have been gained at all costs, a true peace must be based on justice and on the triumph of moral and spiritual values. It is not sufficient to repeat that we are fighting to save civilization. We must see to it that our children will never again take their liberties for granted only long enough to be asked once more to die to defend them."

* * *

While Boyer was at M-G-M for *Gaslight,* he found his good friend Irene Dunne filming on another set. Louis B. Mayer, who was scheming to add Miss Dunne to his gaudy contract list as a strategic replacement for the retired Norma Shearer, had presented her with two of his company's more imposing wartime ventures. Following the popular *A Guy Named Joe* with Spencer Tracy, she was involved with an especially pampered project, *The White Cliffs of Dover*. Despite such bait, Mayer couldn't get Irene to agree to a contract. She treasured her independence as much as Boyer treasured his. They could also agree that it was time for them to make another picture together.

It wasn't only their idea. Although they hadn't filmed together for five years, in 1944 a national body of women's clubs named Irene Dunne and Charles Boyer as their favorite movie team. Columbia's mercurial, profane Harry Cohn picked up the item, and got a reunion project going while both *Gaslight* and *The White Cliffs of Dover* were luring large audiences. A story property that had been prepared as a likely Jean Arthur vehicle was dusted off and given a succession of temporary titles until they decided just to call it *Together Again,* since getting Dunne and Boyer together again was the name of the game.

Both stars were in a mood for comedy after their respective heavy duties, and Columbia specialized in smooth, slick comedies that also made unpretentiousness a virtue. *Together Again* was smooth and slick, but a little behind the times. It was a thirties screwball affair made about half a dozen years too late. Indeed, it bore a disturbing resemblance to Irene Dunne's own antic *Theodora Goes Wild*, made at the same studio. In that picture she had been a prim small-town librarian who wrote a spicy bestseller and went to the big city and found Melvyn Douglas. In *Together Again* Irene was a demure widow and small-town mayor who went to the big city and found Charles Boyer.

There weren't enough good one-liners and the complication of the proper lady getting arrested in a police raid already was shopworn. Boyer played an artist who in his first scene mistook the lady mayor for a model arriving to pose. His first line was "Take off your clothes, please"—a case of a picture's best laugh coming too early. Some good humor was generated by Boyer's late inspiration to identify the scandalized woman as P. Borat Sosa, from the label on a bottle of spirits they had been sharing. Irene masqueraded as P. Borat Sosa for much of the distance, and it was really *her* picture. Despite Boyer's effortless excellence in her shadow, the stint might have suggested a comedown for him, but for one thing: it was a substantial box-office hit. Finally it was a neutral entry for both stars, doing harm to neither of them, but quickly forgotten by fans who kept on remembering *Love Affair*.

Boyer approved of Columbia's expeditious, no-nonsense production regimen, but he didn't have an easy time on the set between takes. *Together Again* was shot during the height of the presidential campaign, and there was a chronic political argument between Boyer and the great character actor Charles Coburn, who had the picture's key supporting role as Miss Dunne's father. Coburn was an ardent and articulate Republican, as also were Irene Dunne and the *Together Again* director, Charles Vidor. They ganged up on Boyer who obstinately held his ground. Although seldom given to such frivolity, Boyer sent Charles Coburn a telegram of condolence when Roosevelt easily defeated Dewey. Toward the end of the shooting schedule Boyer and Coburn had managed to agree on something: they both believed that "The Star-Spangled Banner" was an atrocious piece of music for a national anthem, and Boyer signed a petition drawn up by Coburn, asking Congress to replace it with "America the Beautiful."

The movies proved a fountain of youth for Charles Coburn, who came to Hollywood from Broadway in his sixties and etched scores of notable characterizations, working steadily in films for more than two decades. He told Boyer that "acting for the movies requires no great effort if you're just naturally good." Boyer could conclude that *he* wasn't naturally good, because acting for the cameras still filled him with a tension that left him physically drained—even when the chore was so modest a comedy as *Together Again.* Upon its completion he resolved to stay off the screen a full year, and very nearly kept his pledge.

He rejected the RKO offer of *Experiment Perilous* as an imitation of *Gaslight,* in which his intended sinister role was subordinate to the lady in distress played by Hedy Lamarr. He also sent regrets to Ernst Lubitsch who sought to team him with Tallulah Bankhead in *A Royal Scandal,* the bonbon about Catherine the Great. In a dry period two or three years earlier, he might have taken either offer as a fair opportunity. But in 1945 he could be more selective, and was also distracted by the world scene and variously involved in the rehabilitation efforts for France.

When movie work reclaimed him at last, the war in Europe had just ended and Boyer's strongest impulse was to visit France; but Jack Warner prevailed on him to stay in town a while longer to be Graham Greene's *Confidential Agent.* There was a sudden urgency to make a film of a literary property that had languished for several years on the Warner Brothers shelf. The anti-Fascist novel published in 1939 was purchased for Paul Muni, but seemed destined for Edward G. Robinson after Muni and Warner Brothers agreed on a professional divorce. Humphrey Bogart had been a more recent prospect to play the Spanish Loyalist in the peril of international skullduggery, but in 1945 Charles Boyer was made to seem indispensable to the project.

Herman Shumlin, the Broadway producer engaged to direct *Confidential Agent,* insisted that no other actor would be a fair substitute for Boyer. That was ironic, for Boyer might have made the film of Lillian Hellman's *Watch on the Rhine,* as most in the Warner fold would have preferred, but for Shumlin's insistence on Paul Lukas, who had appeared in the play. Lukas was a surprise Oscar winner for having thoroughly dominated Miss Bette Davis, but Boyer bore no grudge for either Lukas or Shumlin. He regarded the Hungarian Lukas as more appropriate than himself for the German refugee of *Watch on the Rhine.* Boyer remained unreconciled to the Hollywood dogma that a foreign accent is *any* foreign accent. He hadn't really wanted to do the Hellman piece, although he *would* have; and he didn't really wish to play the weary Spaniard of *Confidential Agent,* but of course he did.

Yet the factor for the hurry-up attitude in making the picture was a thick-browed, feline creature named Lauren Bacall. In the spring of 1945 she was easily the hottest of the newer screen personalities, coming off a sensational debut in *To Have and Have Not.* She was "The Look"—a fashion model discovered by the wife of Howard Hawks. Nineteen-year-old Lauren Bacall appeared opposite Humphrey Bogart in William Faulkner's diabolically transmogrified screenplay of the Hemingway novel, with Hawks directing. In an incomparably throaty voice, she told Bogart that "All you have to do is whistle." Bogie more than whistled; he took Lauren Bacall for his fourth wife as quickly as he could be free of his third. Yet the union endured gloriously for a dozen years before Bogart's death.

Before they were married, and before *To Have and Have Not* was released, Bogart and Bacall were teamed again by Hawks in *The Big Sleep*—also written by Faulkner, adapting Raymond Chandler. But in the wake of the emphatic response to Bacall's fussed-over debut, the Warner folk elected to defer release of *The Big Sleep* until she had screen exposure opposite a leading male star other than Bogart. Somehow they perceived *Confidential Agent* as the property most suited to her; and Lauren Bacall found herself teamed with another actor of Bogart's precise age, by name of Charles Boyer.

It was a miscalculation fatal to the design of Graham Greene's grim political fable. Still not yet twenty-one when she filmed *Confidential Agent* in which supposedly she enacted an Englishwoman, Miss Bacall was painfully out of her element, and she knew it as well as anyone.

"God, I was so miserable making that picture," she recalled many years later. "The critics chopped me to pieces and I hated them all, but they were right. Hawks gave me valuable guidance in the pictures we made with Bogie, but I had no guidance whatever in *Confidential Agent,* and the critics all said I ruined the picture."

The film was an ordeal for Boyer as well. He did not clash openly with director Shumlin, but was frustrated that the director had no clear conception of Boyer's fat part, and no stylistic viewpoint toward the melodrama. Some imposing character players were involved—Peter Lorre, George Coulouris, Katina Paxinou, and Boyer's estimable friend Victor Francen—but there was unevenness in the acting, allowing some unnecessarily stagey accounts. *Confidential Agent* was the second and last picture directed by Herman Shumlin who, according to Pauline Kael, "showed little evidence that he'd learned anything about the medium."

Those reviewers who were so hard on Lauren Bacall weren't terribly impressed by other aspects of the picture, but history's judgment is that *Confidential Agent* wasn't so bad after all. Graham Greene has rated it as the best of many screen treatments of his various works. He particularly liked Boyer's performance as the harassed and disillusioned agent, which remains the best thing in the film. But it was a flop. Shot in the waning months of World War II and completed just before V-J Day, *Confidential Agent* was a release of the new peacetime, in one of the healthiest hours for movie receipts. Yet the picture coupling a respected veteran star with a volatile young siren could not find a large audience, or stimulate a small one.

Fortunately for Lauren Bacall, Warner Brothers could bring *The Big Sleep* out of storage as a very positive exposure for her; and fortunately for Boyer, there was *Cluny Brown.*

Despite his announced determination always to take a long vacation between film assignments, he went from *Confidential Agent* to *Cluny Brown* almost without a break. He frankly did not trust *Confidential Agent;* and anticipating its bleak reception, felt a need to get into a good picture as soon as possible. If for no other reason, he might have accepted *Cluny Brown* as a favor to his wife, for Margery Sharp was Pat's favorite English novelist, and the Boyers had read the satirical story of a saucy girl's passion for plumbing—alone together, in bed. Still, Boyer's primary delight in taking the assignment was simply that it was a Lubitsch picture.

Ernst Lubitsch was the screen's undisputed master of sophisticated comedy, an incomparably witty pictorialist, and the guide for the great Chevalier vehicles of the early talking period. It was through Chevalier that Lubitsch and Boyer became friends who often thought and talked of someday doing a picture together. The mediocre *A Royal Scandal* had tempted Boyer only because Lubitsch was involved, even though Lubitsch merely produced that picture after withdrawing as director in favor of Otto Preminger. The combination of Lubitsch and a delightful if frothy script nudged Boyer to accept *Cluny Brown,* although, as implied by its title, the focus was on the principal actress. Yet Boyer was set up for something more colorful than straight-man service, and won yet another dispute over top billing from David Selznick —who, although not yet married to the lady in question, was managing Jennifer Jones's career and had loaned her to 20th Century–Fox to be Lubitsch's Cluny.

She had won the 1943 Oscar for *The Song of Bernadette,* but the Selznick hard sell of Jennifer Jones to the American people still lacked conclusive result in 1945. Miss Jones had been viewed in two other major films—*Since You Went Away* (written by Selznick as well as produced by him) and *Love Letters*—and had been politely praised for both; emulating Lauren Bacall and *The Big Sleep,* Miss Jones had completed another picture that would not be released until well after

Cluny Brown had come and gone. That was Selznick's own production of *Duel in the Sun,* calculated to secure for her the position of Most Important Star for the dawning postwar period. After that gaudy western spectacle there would be others almost as big—*Portrait of Jennie, We Were Strangers, Madame Bovary,* the Dreiser *Carrie*—of which none, however, performed well at the box office. Jennifer Jones never really made a public impression. The delayed conclusion was that while Jennifer Jones was a careful and intelligent actress, she lacked the spark of personality. Yet *Cluny Brown* almost belies that judgment.

They all had a happy time turning Margery Sharp's gentle spoof of English aristocracy into a movie. Lubitsch assembled a cast of enjoyable veteran players whose cumulative skill could be assessed as incredible—C. Aubrey Smith, the Reginalds (Owen and Gardiner), Una O'Connor, Florence Bates, Sara Allgood, and especially the adenoidal Richard Haydn, who stole scene after scene. Boyer, as Hollywood's man of all nations, was this time a refugee from Czechoslovakia in England's immediate prewar period—an impoverished refugee to be sure, but ever so debonair: a parasite but an unreconstructed free spirit, in kinship with Cluny and her wrenches. Boyer more than held his own. As certain as he had been of the *Confidential Agent* debacle, he was as confident that the Lubitsch picture would be a warmly embraced giddy success. He and Pat attended the sneak preview in Westwood Village and absorbed the chuckling, sometimes roaring approval of the large audience. Later, though, he would say that was the only time that *Cluny Brown* played to a packed house.

It was no flop, surely. Reviews were almost entirely favorable, but usually fell short of being raves. The receipts were disappointing for being no better than ordinary. Turning a routine profit after its expected word-of-mouth boost never occurred, *Cluny Brown* failed to create a distinct general impression—unusual for any picture made by Lubitsch.

Why did such a charmer among the 1946 film titles fall so far below its commercial expectation? There were possible answers. The movies' domestic patronage, which had risen steadily during the war years did its turnaround in 1946, setting its downward course even before the advent of mass-marketed television sets. Movie fashions were changing, and even M-G-M was made to concede that not enough people cared if "Gable's back and Garson's got him." Even such a picture as Frank Capra's *It's a Wonderful Life*—an acknowledged classic decades later—was a financial disappointment at the time of its release. Ernst Lubitsch himself expressed the view that *Cluny Brown* was rather too sophisticated in its time and place, with its farce element compromised by too much richness of satire. The box-office performance was also read by some observers in the industry as an early indication that Jennifer Jones had not secured a large following.

Boyer knew that something was wrong, and his conclusion was that the something was himself. He had heard no recent gossip that he had grown too old for his accustomed romantic rituals on the screen, but he expected to hear it soon. He *was* hearing, again, that he was overpriced. The Warner Brothers accounting for 1945 revealed that Boyer was the studio's highest-salaried employee that year, drawing $207,500—more for one failed movie than regular Warner contract players made in a year of working steadily in several pictures. Presumably the 20th Century–Fox stipend to Boyer for *Cluny Brown* was comparable.

He considered the situation. In his last two pictures he had partnered actresses at least twenty years younger than himself. It had to stop. His disposition was to reject any and all offers to reprise his standard impression of the "great lovair." Now he was aching to make a transition into character roles, following the lead of Fredric March and Spencer Tracy. It was the most logical means of assuring for himself a long-range professional future. The postwar screen already was beginning to spill over with players returned from military service—not only the previously well-established Gables, Stewarts, and Fondas, but able younger actors such as William Holden, Van Heflin, and Glenn Ford, all seeking their own firmer footing. That stardom's highest echelon already was in a transitional state was evident, as some of Boyer's splendid costars were slipping toward retirement or were otherwise leaving the screen—Irene Dunne, Jean Arthur, Claudette Colbert, and Margaret Sullavan within the next few years; and Garbo was already gone.

Boyer was tired himself, and again desirous of an extended leave from picture-making. But pressure was being exerted upon him to make the *Arch of Triumph* picture that he believed he wanted no part of. So to get away from the people who were hounding him, he went to France.

12

❊❊❊❊❊❊❊❊❊❊

Having waited until age forty-four to attain fatherhood, Charles Boyer found that its novelty did not wear off easily. The advent of Michael Boyer broke the rhythm and altered the discipline of his father's well-ordered day.

Hours that previously were given to reading now found Boyer at play with his agreeable young son. Pat, who resisted the temptation to smother Michael with love, could only scold her husband for *not* resisting. She said she was sometimes embarrassed over Charles making such an absolute fool of himself in his attentions to Michael.

It was Michael, not Michel. During Pat's pregnancy they decided that the baby—girl or boy—would have an American name and would learn French only as a second language. Only Louise Boyer, the *grandmère,* would persist in calling him Michel, besides addressing him only in her native language after refusing to learn even the rudiments of English. The grandmother saw the boy infrequently during his first two years and then hardly at all, as she returned to France immediately after the end of the war in Europe.

During the boy's first months, Boyer was a stay-at-home between film assignments, in constant attention to Michael's needs despite the regular presence of nursemaids. Later, when engaged in a film or at work in his office at the French Research Foundation, Boyer made daily phone calls home to ask "Is Michael all right?" He worried that the boy might have some affliction that had gone undetected. Assured that Michael indeed was all right, Boyer worried that his son was such a healthy baby; why wasn't he getting sick like a normal infant? Michael seemed immune from even the most common ailments of infancy, nor did he appear to require much attention, although he always had it. Negotiating a playroom floor cluttered with every kind of toy, the baby Michael had no particular need of them. He entertained himself without a dependence on props, or even on people; but he took to people. Michael was a social and exuberant baby, and most of the Boyers' friends believed he inherited his mother's personality.

On Michael's first and second birthdays his parents hosted celebrations for him that were attended by the young progeny of some picture people and of other Boyer friends. Michael evidenced an actor's love of the limelight, but maintained a rather odd indifference to other children. Even among strangers, he appeared clearly to prefer the company of adults. It was also established in theory that Michael favored men over women, although he seemed to have an aversion to bald men.

In 1945 Charles Boyer, who had been almost completely bald for several years, underwent a simple but exorbitant scalp treatment to effect a hair transplant. His "everyday toupee" installed for permanence was a modest patch of thin dark strands, resolved in a receded widow's peak. It was a subtle difference that might escape someone who saw Boyer only infrequently, but it created a noticeably younger demeanor. In earlier years when Boyer could be observed on the screen in a wide variety of toupees and wigs, he had worn no hairpiece in public. Now his vanity was suspect, but Boyer's motive in taking this measure was his son. Perhaps harboring a dim memory of his own father, he said "A boy does not wish to believe that some nice old man is his father." Thenceforth, Charles Boyer would never be entirely bald, and he trusted that Michael was reassured by the illusion of his father's youthfulness.

While Michael was still a toddler, separate and distinct relationships were established with each of his parents. Pat was his playmate, and laughter was the certain issue of their time together. Charles was Michael's teacher. However companionable they were, he used all of their activity as occasion for instruction. Very soon it was evident that Michael adored his mother and admired his father.

In the time Michael spent with both his parents, a third relationship developed. They were a company of adventurers, and he was merely the junior partner. They were destined to become fellow travelers around the world. In 1946, before he was three years old, Michael for the first of many times accompanied his parents to Paris.

❋ ❋ ❋

Charles Boyer had first beheld the magical city of Paris less than two months after the end of the First World War. It had a boisterous carnival atmosphere then, as it exulted in victory and peace. Twenty-seven years later he expected to find something of the same spirit. He returned to the City of Light in the summer of 1946, having been away more than six years. Instead, he found a metropolis that was almost morose, despite the noisy revelry of the first postwar wave of tourists, most of them American.

Paris was as shimmeringly beautiful as ever, or more so; Boyer said that to appreciate its grandeur, one had to return to it after experiencing other world capitals perhaps thought to be as charming. Paris miraculously had been spared such devastation as had been absorbed by London and Berlin—a benefit of France's early capitulation to the Nazis. While German cities began clearing away their bomb rubble, and while French cities west of Paris contended with debris from the Allied invasion, Paris was barely blemished by the war; yet it was scarred both psychologically and emotionally from the melodrama that collected all the French people during the German Occupation. Boyer sensed that a spasm of national paranoia had thrown France into political chaos. Charles de Gaulle, the leader of the Free French who was acclaimed France's savior upon his tumultuous return to Paris, already had resigned as President of the Provisional Government; and political stability would be denied France until the aging De Gaulle's return to power fully a dozen years later.

The discomfiting issue was of resistance versus collaboration during the Occupation. In the immediate postwar period, most in Paris and indeed in all of France were filled either with mistrust or the fear of it. Although the Resistance has been romanticized into one of the glories of modern French history, it involved only a small percentage of French citizens, whose continuing war against their German conquerors was pursued at great risk and the sacrifice of many lives. At the other extreme were the undoubted collaborators whose accommodation to the Nazis included their infiltration of, and informing on, the *résistants.* Those most easily marked as traitors after the liberation were the *miliciens*—the French Militia that had served the Nazis as a constabulary force. Caught in a position no less embarrassing were the French girls who had given German soldiers their own accommodation, glaringly testified to by illegitimate babies. These "horizontal collaborators" were paraded through the jeering throngs, their heads shaved and their foreheads smeared with swastikas.

Caught somewhere between the clear examples of resistance and collaboration were the French millions who merely eked out their daily existence during the Occupation, when taking no side was the safest course. But in the aftermath of liberation it became increasingly difficult to determine the point that separated cooperation from active collaboration. This problem nagged at France in every walk of life, but there was the customary exaggerated attention to the performing arts.

French theatrical activity was reduced but by no means eliminated during the Occupation, but the French cinema to all outward appearance was barely compromised. There were fewer productions but they were well patronized by French moviegoers temporarily deprived of the always popular American product, and who were generally unaware of the degree of control exercised by the Nazis upon the French filmmakers. It was the militant view of Henry Bernstein that anyone who had worked in French motion pictures under the Nazis was a collaborator, pure and simple. Boyer disagreed vigorously:

"If a baker in France sells loaves of bread in his shop, and

German soldiers buy some of his loaves, is he a collaborator? He must make his living, and he cannot afford to have his shop closed by the Nazis. Actors also must eat, as must directors and writers and costume seamstresses."

Boyer, who had encouraged the Resistance in many propaganda broadcasts, now became perhaps the most powerful voice of postwar conciliation for France's performing arts. If the Nazis on occasion had used French films for their own means, Boyer could cite examples of audacious French patriotism filtered through them—most notably Jacques Prévert's screenplay for *Les Visiteurs du Soir*, bravely conveying an anti-Nazi statement allegorically. Prévert and director Marcel Carné also collaborated on an unargued masterpiece of world cinema during the Occupation—*Les Enfants du Paradis*. While receiving rapturous embrace by American moviegoers after the war, its leading players were being variably defamed in France: Jean-Louis Barrault, who was the mime Debureau, and who was actor-director for the Comédie-Française throughout the war; Boyer's longtime friend Pierre Brasseur, as the actor Lemaître; and most especially Arletty, who enacted Garance in the Carné film, and who was jailed as a collaborator for having had a love affair with a German officer.

Sacha Guitry, a friend to Boyer and the son of the legendary Lucien Guitry, also was briefly imprisoned for having been too friendly with the Vichy government of Marshal Philippe Pétain and Pierre Laval. Boyer, in an early test of the French Research Foundation as a political influence, helped Guitry obtain release and eventual exoneration. He also assisted in the rehabilitation of his *Mayerling* costar, Danielle Darrieux, whose execution had at one time been ordered by the Resistance. Mlle. Darrieux was the most prominent of the French film personalities who had been exploited by the Nazis for propaganda purposes.

Then there was the disturbing case of Maurice Chevalier. The Nazis had made capital of the Gay Boulevardier singing in Paris before mixed French and German audiences, but that could be said of almost every Parisian entertainer during the Occupation. Charles Boyer was astonished in 1942 to find Chevalier listed among other prominent Frenchmen as a collaborator, in an issue of *Life*. A photograph of Chevalier had been circulated by the Nazis as evidence of him entertaining German troops. In reality, Chevalier had entertained French prisoners of war, in the same camp wherein he had been interned as a prisoner of the Germans in World War I. Boyer and Chevalier met in Paris in 1946 after having not seen one another for nearly a decade. Chevalier appeared broken in spirit, and Boyer took it upon himself to restore Chevalier to the affection of both the French and American peoples. Chevalier later said that of all the people who stood by him during that bleak period, Boyer gave the most decisive support.

In the fall the Boyers left Michael in Paris for two weeks with a governess and his paternal grandmother, and went south to the inaugural Cannes Film Festival, accompanied by Maurice Chevalier. The festival at Cannes had originally been planned as an event for the 1939 autumn, which Boyer had expected to attend, just before the outbreak of war forced its cancellation and put Boyer himself briefly in army uniform. The 1946 festival was really the first postwar convention of international film artists, and Boyer was an articulate panelist in a program examining the postwar industrial adjustment. He cited Chevalier as a victim of a grave injustice caused by hysteria. Boyer also remarked that such artists as Renoir, Clair, Duvivier, Gabin, and Michèle Morgan who had joined him in Hollywood (and whose escapes from France he had even assisted) were not qualified to judge the actions of those who remained at home to endure the Nazi tyranny.

At the Cannes festival Boyer was also reunited with Pierre Blanchar, the friend from his earliest days in Paris and the conservatory. Blanchar and Michèle Morgan, in her first film since returning to France, were the stars of *La Symphonie Pastorale*, Jean Delannoy's winner of the festival's grand prize. Impressed that Blanchar had retained his stardom while moving gradually into character roles, and impressed also by the merits of André Gide's tragic story as a film subject, Boyer briefly had a notion of purchasing the American rights to produce his own starring vehicle. Boyer and Gide already were well-acquainted and the author was receptive to the idea, but Boyer decided against the purchase when *La*

Hold Back the Dawn (1941). With Olivia deHavilland in the wedding scene of a critical and popular success.

Appointment for Love (1941). A pleasing trifle with Margaret Sullavan, his costar in the wistful *Back Street* earlier that year.

The Constant Nymph (1943). A romantic drama resolved tragically, with Joan Fontaine as Boyer's adoring young friend.

Flesh and Fantasy (1943). With Barbara Stanwyck in one segment of a supernatural omnibus produced by Boyer himself.

Gaslight (1944). Melodrama with high production gloss, as Boyer squires Ingrid Bergman in her Oscar-winning role.

Confidential Agent (1945). Boyer and Lauren Bacall in a sinister Graham Greene mood.

Cluny Brown (1946). Boyer in a mostly endearing Lubitsch picture with Reginald Gardiner and Jennifer Jones.

The Happy Time (1952). Boyer as head of a French-Canadian household in the 1920s, with Marsha Hunt and Bobby Driscoll.

Around the World in 80 Days (1956). Boyer as one of the "cameo" players in Mike Todd's Academy-honored picture show, here with Cantinflas.

Fanny (1961). Raymond Bussières, Salvatore Baccaloni, Maurice Chevalier, and Charles Boyer celebrate Old Home Week in Marseille.

Barefoot in the Park (1967). An atypically raffish Boyer projection, with Jane Fonda in Neil Simon's box-office bell-ringer.

Stavisky (1974). The Boyer valedictory, with Jean-Paul Belmondo in the title role.

Symphonie Pastorale was given a wide American distribution after its triumph on the French Riviera.

At the banquet that brought the Cannes festival to a close, Boyer received an ovation that may have been surpassed only by the one accorded Maurice Chevalier. Soon afterward, Chevalier made a triumphant screen return in René Clair's *La Silence est d'Or;* and in 1947 he brought his one-man show to New York, where its sensational first performance was applauded by an audience that included Mr. and Mrs. Charles Boyer.

*   *   *

In 1946 Enterprise Pictures was founded by David Lewis and Charles Einfeld with formidable financial backing by David Loew. It was the most ambitious independent production company conceived in the early postwar period, and Boyer was favorably acquainted with its founders. Lewis had been Irving Thalberg's assistant at M-G-M, and then was Hal Wallis's associate producer at Warner Brothers—for Boyer's *All This and Heaven Too* among other imposing projects. Einfeld was also a Warner graduate, having headed its promotion department. He became president of Enterprise, most of whose pictures would be produced by Lewis as vicepresident. Both men had close ties to Erich Maria Remarque, and their acquisition of his *Arch of Triumph*—an international bestseller of the moment—made the film community take notice. Then, to make the Enterprise launching even more spectacular, they played Hollywood's favorite game of deception. They told Ingrid Bergman that they had Charles Boyer, and told Boyer they had Bergman, before they had either. It worked, and they got both.

Within three years since filming *Gaslight* with Boyer, Ingrid Bergman had attained a level of achievement comparable to Bette Davis's half a dozen years earlier. She had appeared in the Selznick-Hitchcock *Spellbound* with the new Gregory Peck; and with veteran stars Gary Cooper and Bing Crosby in, respectively, *Saratoga Trunk* and *The Bells of St. Mary's*. All were robust hits in their day, as her next one also would be in its late 1946 release—*Notorious*, another good Hitchcock, with Cary Grant and Claude Rains. Maxwell Anderson now was writing a play for her, about Joan of Arc. There was time to make another picture before reporting to Broadway, and she chose *Arch of Triumph*, or was talked into it:

"I really didn't want to do it and I told them so, but they persevered, and there was Charles Boyer in it and Charles Laughton, so I decided it was ridiculous not to do it."

Boyer had reservations of his own, but in this instance it was not because the female role was bigger or supposedly stronger. The prostitute role of Joan Madou in the Remarque story suggested a daring departure for Bergman, but the leading male role of Ravic—a German refugee strongly suggesting Remarque himself—was of at least equal importance. No one other than Boyer had been mentioned for it, and film folk who had been whispering that Boyer was a has-been were astonished that he would resist a major opportunity. Yet Boyer was telling David Lewis, "I am a Frenchman. For me to play a German, that would be ridiculous. And for me to play a *good* German, that would be impossible—I would not know how to begin to act such a part."

Only after Remarque's death would Boyer reveal that he had hated the novel in the first place. He admired the novelist's earlier work, from *All Quiet on the Western Front* to *Three Comrades* and the less familiar *Flotsam,* which he believed was Remarque's masterpiece and was filmed as *So Ends Our Night,* with Fredric March, Margaret Sullavan, and the very young Glenn Ford. Boyer also had a solid intellectual friendship with Remarque, who later married one of his *Hold Back the Dawn* costars, Paulette Goddard. Finally it was Remarque's offer to eliminate specific reference to Ravic's nationality and render him "a European of indeterminate origin" that coaxed Boyer to accept a role he didn't like, in a story he didn't trust.

Boyer insisted that he wasn't a holdout to obtain more money, although *Arch of Triumph* probably yielded his highest-ever base salary as an actor. Beyond that, Charles Feldman worked a deal with Enterprise to cut both of his illustrious clients in on the picture's anticipated high profits. The arrangement called for equal salary for both stars, but it surprised no one that Bergman now would command top billing. Boyer's rationale for accepting echoed Bergman's. Everyone was telling him it couldn't miss.

So the Boyers left the festival scene at Cannes, returned to Paris to collect their son and some art they had bought there, and went back to Hollywood and the picture Charles had tried to flee.

Set in Paris just before the war, *Arch of Triumph* was a gloomy anti-Nazi thesis drama about a refugee doctor obsessed with finding and killing the gestapo official responsible for torturing his wife to death. He has a bittersweet love affair with an embittered café singer and sometime streetwalker. She fills him with new hope but it is vanquished by her death, which closes the picture. Only a few years later, any American film company would have journeyed to Paris to make the picture. *Arch of Triumph* was shot mostly in Hollywood, relying on stock footage for its suggestions of Paris in 1939.

The production became an example of mismanagement such as would be more prevalent in the postwar period than in the prewar era of stronger studio control and less power wielded by the crafts unions. Committed to a twelve-week schedule, it stretched to twenty weeks and was not finished when Ingrid Bergman left to begin rehearsals for Maxwell Anderson's *Joan of Lorraine*. There was a rush to get all of Bergman's scenes shot, after which Boyer remained on the set for additional scenes with some of America's more accomplished actors.

The director was Lewis Milestone, who in 1930 had also made Remarque's *All Quiet on the Western Front,* the first American talking picture with a claim of greatness. Milestone had been a Hollywood link to Broadway's fabled Group Theater of the thirties, and employed several of its members in *Arch of Triumph*—J. Edward Bromberg, Ruth Nelson, Art Smith, Roman Bohnen. The cast also offered the distinguished Charles Laughton in virtually his first supporting role in an American film. Another leading character actor, Louis Calhern, played the Nazi tormentor. It certainly looked like an important picture, and they all endured a dispirited shooting ordeal, hoping for the best. Charles Laughton called it "a tragedy relieved by heavy doses of gloom and good honest tedium."

Director Milestone was also co-adapter with Harry Brown, and during the production grind they kept expanding a screenplay that surely needed trimming. Milestone had made strong pictures before and would do so again, but with *Arch of Triumph* he was gambling, hoping that from a staggering amount of footage, an excellent dramatic film might be salvaged. He must have made an honest effort, for *Arch of Triumph* was edited and re-edited throughout 1947.

Ingrid Bergman had made a break from David Selznick, who had nurtured her career so skillfully. *Arch of Triumph* was the first picture she made as an independent artist, and very early on she confided to Boyer that "I am afraid I may have made a terrible mistake." Boyer said "I believe we both have, but now we must make the best of it." When his last scene had been shot, he sensed not only the picture's failure, but his own failure in a role that made no sense to him other than to seem contradictory. So in early 1947 he went to New York, where he would see Ingrid Bergman on the stage as a Swedish Maid of Orléans, and also try to find a play for himself.

The Boyers took over a large suite in the Hotel Pierre, which would become an alternate address for them in a developing pattern of more and longer visits to Manhattan. By day, their attentions were mostly to museums and art galleries, but with ample allowance for shopping; the advent of Christian Dior's "New Look" gave Pat an excuse to acquire a complete new wardrobe. Their evenings were given to the theater, in a season that included Eugene O'Neill's *The Iceman Cometh*. Subtly and politely, Charles Boyer also advertised himself as an actor agreeable to a good Broadway drama, or even a comedy.

During years given exclusively to the screen, he had kept insisting that he was primarily a stage actor. That his absence from the theater had stretched so long was due in part, he believed, to the Second World War; he had intended to resume his stage career in Paris rather than New York. In his recent trip to Paris he had discussed a new play with his friend Marcel Achard, and later got the idea of doing it on

Broadway, in English. S. N. Behrman, with whom Boyer had become acquainted during one of the dramatist's screenwriting jaunts to Hollywood, received Boyer's account of the play Achard was writing, and must have been charmed. Behrman later adapted it as *I Know My Love*, but not for Boyer; the Lunts played it, and it earned an odd measure of fame as the play Holden Caulfield sees in J. D. Salinger's *The Catcher in the Rye*.

Behrman was one of the founding playwright-producers of the Playwrights' Company, and that organization was interested in developing something specifically for Boyer. Behrman was himself destined to write a play for him, but that was far in the future. The Theatre Guild also was interested, and also unable to offer an appropriate property. He very nearly accepted *The Big Two*—one of the first anti-Communist plays of the fermenting Cold War—but backed away on a "literary judgment," thus canceling an opportunity to act on the stage with Claire Trevor, whose screen work he rated very highly. His judgment was sound; *The Big Two* was a quick failure. His discarded role was inherited by the Dutch actor Philip Dorn, who at that time qualified as another Hollywood "name," if one less substantial than Boyer. The search for a play was abandoned altogether when Boyer was summoned to the West Coast for some *Arch of Triumph* retakes.

The script was heavier by several grams; he shot a new scene with actor Stephan Bekassy, and then endeavored to forget all about a picture he had grown to despise. He buried himself in his office at the French Research Foundation where he proceeded to reject other picture overtures—*My Own True Love* from Paramount; *A Kiss in the Dark* from Warner Brothers—which indicated that just being in *Arch of Triumph* had made him desirable once more. The office was also the contact point for agents and brokers in Boyer's various investments, but he also retained a serious commitment to the research foundation. Indeed, it was a busy time, as the staff met the prodigious task of documenting World War II with new material arriving from Europe almost on a daily basis. The research library also had attained some direct importance for the film community. *The Song of Bernadette, The Razor's*

Edge, and other pertinent films had their preproduction research accomplished there, leading to the partial fulfillment of Boyer's quest for more accurate representation of French subject matter in American films.

Increasingly, though, Boyer went to the office not to work or to supervise others working, but to have time just to himself. He did most of his reading there. Fatherhood had made it difficult for him to read at home, as he was too easily distracted by Michael. The office was also a place to do nothing at all. This was a troubled time for him and he often sat alone at his desk, lost in thought that wouldn't be shared; and even Pat knew that a part of him had to remain secret.

He also usually lunched alone at Ernest's, a favorite French restaurant only a few doors away from the research foundation on La Cienega. In the evening he dined out often, always with Pat and often with added company, but lunch was a solitary affair—a habit begun at the studios in his need for concentration, but then carried on away from the shooting scenes. He had a private table at Ernest's, obscured from the general view, and only rarely lunched with someone else. On one such occasion the someone else was Aldous Huxley, and it was another case of a famous author pleading Boyer into a film against the actor's own instincts. But at least he did not dislike the Huxley story.

It was *The Gioconda Smile,* which Huxley had written both as a short story and play early in his career—the grim tale of an innocent man convicted as a wife-murderer. The deed actually was committed by a jealous woman whom he had loved earlier but had discarded. So it was a would-be *Gaslight* in reverse, in modern dress, but Boyer accepted it after squirming through the first screening of *Arch of Triumph*—at 224 minutes of running time, it was longer than *Gone With the Wind* by three minutes. Certain that it couldn't be saved, Boyer reasoned that *The Gioconda Smile* couldn't be as bad and might be quite good with Zoltan Korda directing; and he wanted to have another picture ready to follow *Arch of Triumph* and improve upon it. His acceptance of the bid brought the project into being for Universal Pictures. Aldous Huxley did his own screen adaptation, with title changed to

Mortal Coils, the name of the story volume in which *The Gioconda Smile* had been collected.

Made with routine efficiency in the 1947 summer, the picture shot as *Mortal Coils* was again retitled, this time pulpishly, as *A Woman's Vengeance.* So labeled, it went into its first-run engagements late in the year while the editors remained confounded by *Arch of Triumph.* They were cutting and cutting, while the likelihood of a turkey was gossiped throughout the filmland. Nevertheless, Louella Parsons reported its producers' regret that *Arch of Triumph* could not be released in time to qualify for the 1947 Academy Awards.

As Universal's Christmas release, *A Woman's Vengeance* obtained decent enough reviews. There was perfunctory high praise for Boyer's first solo starring role since *Algiers,* and for Jessica Tandy, who was the vengeful woman. The Universal promotion effort failed to capitalize on Miss Tandy's having just opened on Broadway as Blanche du Bois in Tennessee Williams's tantalizing *A Streetcar Named Desire,* opposite the sensational young Marlon Brando. That might have given the box office a little nudge, although a big nudge was needed. *A Woman's Vengeance* just died. Well made it may have been, but it wasn't a picture for people to *like.* It came in a time of industrial panic, amid stunning evidence of a diminishing national movie audience even before television was a competitive influence. Boyer's Universal picture was limping through its second-run engagements in February, when *Arch of Triumph* opened on both coasts.

Asked if cutting the release print to 120 minutes had hurt or helped *Arch of Triumph,* Charles Boyer told Los Angeles *Times* journalist Edwin Schallert in confidence that "It has improved it considerably. It was terrible for four hours, but now it is only terrible for two hours." That it was terrible was more than consensus; it was a universal judgment. It hardly mattered that critics who were rough on Ingrid Bergman were rather sparing of Charles Boyer; the picture was a mess —dull and plodding and also confusing, but not even interesting to people who understood what was going on. The most fortunate person involved with *Arch of Triumph* figured to be actress Ruth Warrick, who had the female role second in importance to Bergman's, which was deposited in its entirety on the cutting-room floor.

Boyer's profit-sharing status was irrelevant. The picture was a box-office disaster virtually without precedent, for its five-million-dollar cost made it the most expensive American film since the silent *Ben-Hur,* and it might have been Hollywood's all-time loser but for satisfactory business in its European bookings. It was more than the enterprise called Enterprise could withstand. *Arch of Triumph* left the company bankrupt, ironically, after it had started so promisingly. Although the Bergman-Boyer extravagance was the first picture put into production by Enterprise, it was the company's third release and the first to lose money. It was preceded by *The Other Love,* a Barbara Stanwyck vehicle from another Erich Maria Remarque novel that had been purchased in a package with *Arch of Triumph.* Then John Garfield attached his own production company to Enterprise and made the much admired, highly profitable *Body and Soul* with Robert Rossen directing. Another strong Garfield film, *Force of Evil,* was in production under the Enterprise wing when the company folded, as was also *No Minor Vices,* another Lewis Milestone picture, this one with Dana Andrews, Lilli Palmer, and a possible "successor" to Boyer, the young Louis Jourdan. *Force of Evil* and *No Minor Vices* were both taken over by M-G-M for distribution, and Enterprise Pictures was no more.

* * *

As if professional difficulties hadn't made his life miserable enough, Boyer was shaken up in an automobile accident and briefly hospitalized, with two cracked ribs. At the wheel as he and Pat went home from a dinner party given by pianist Arthur Rubinstein, he struck another moving car from behind. Pat, who had fallen asleep beside him, was not hurt. No charges were filed against Boyer after an investigation revealed that the car he hit on a dark street had no lights of its own.

Boyer had taken wine with his dinner and a cognac afterward, which was customary for him. Only rarely was he even tipsy, and both he and Pat insisted this was not one of those occasions. Inevitably they intercepted the filmland rumor that

Charles Boyer had been drunk, and he decided to get out of town.

In the spring of 1948 he again went to Paris, determined not to mention *Arch of Triumph* to anyone there. The three Boyers flew to New York and then to London, after covering their furniture and putting their valuable paintings into storage; they expected to be gone awhile. After seeing some of the new London plays, Charles went on to Paris while Pat stayed in England to show off the four-year-old Michael to various relatives.

As in his previous visit, Boyer's arrival in Paris was big news. If Hollywood thought he was slipping, France still regarded him as the world's foremost international star. His stay in Paris was brief, and literary fellowship was its primary accomplishment. Boyer was photographed with Joseph Kessel, Marcel Achard, and his newer literary hero, Albert Camus; and with the great existentialist philosopher and dramatist Jean-Paul Sartre. His specific reason for being in Paris was to discuss the prospect of appearing on Broadway in an English translation of Sartre's drama, *Les Mains Sales*. At that point Sartre was entirely encouraging.

Boyer also was attentive to his aged mother, who had resettled in Paris. She had been robust only a few years earlier, in Hollywood during the war. Now she was painfully frail but full of spirit. At her urging they made a sentimental journey to Figeac, to which he had never returned since leaving there almost three decades earlier. Figeac surely would have given him a parade had his visit been forewarned. Charles and his mother motored down from Paris in a Bentley that drew more attention than he did when they drove into the village, since no one recognized the driver.

His mother did manage to summon the mayor and a few of her old friends, who were mostly strangers to her son. However, Boyer was delighted to find Philippe Gambon, the closest friend of his teen years, with whom he had been entirely out of touch since then. Gambon was practicing law in Figeac. He and Boyer tried awkwardly to summon remembrance of old times as they dined with the actor's mother, but most of their conversation finally centered on Greta Garbo. Along with Gambon and the mayor, Boyer and his mother were photographed at Charles's birthplace, where he was also photographed alone—on the balcony outside the room in which he was born, over a luggage store where the bicycle shop had been almost half a century earlier.

Figeac was exactly as he remembered it, yet he felt a stranger's discomfort in that lovely river village. He prevailed upon his mother for them to leave before word of his presence spread throughout the village and swamped him with ceremony. The return drive to Paris appeared to have exhausted Louise Boyer, who was more emotional than was her custom when Charles flew back to London. The next time he would see her would be at her funeral.

* * *

Holding his son up to the rail to behold the glistening, choppy water, Charles Boyer said "I hope Michael remembers this. He may never do it again."

On pure impulse, the Boyers canceled their airline reservations and sailed for America on the *Queen Mary*—their last of several leisurely ocean voyages, and the only one they took after the war. Whether or not Michael would remember it, he certainly enjoyed it.

In New York the Boyers again checked into the Hotel Pierre, and Charles accepted the leading role in the Sartre play. Its title was changed to *Red Gloves* for the presentation in English, after having been called *Dirty Hands,* the more literal translation of *Les Mains Sales*. That Boyer was coming to Broadway was the most newsworthy casting item for the 1948–49 season, causing excitement similar to that stirred a few years earlier by Spencer Tracy's stage appearance in Robert E. Sherwood's *The Rugged Path*. The play built a large sale before its Broadway opening, reaffirming that a prestigious film star—even one in decline at the cinema box office—was a powerhouse draw on the live stage.

Boyer undertook the role of Hoederer, a high official in Russia's Communist party, with great enthusiasm, out of his admiration for Sartre's play—a tragedy shaded by abundant ironic humor. During the tryout tour his confidence was shaken—if not in the play, then in the shapers of its Broadway version, which began to show some alarming departures from Sartre's original text. It wasn't merely a matter of translation; Boyer could see that often the basic meaning of a line or scene was being changed. This was the Broadway practice of out-of-town rewriting by committee, to make the play "work." It had already worked for Boyer, and surely for Jean-Paul Sartre who quickly caught on to what was happening, denouncing the play after its Broadway opening, and disowning authorship of it.

Boyer found himself in an untenable position. Sartre's wish was that he withdraw from the production. As a professional actor with a keen sense of duty to honor his contract, Boyer could not find a legitimate basis for withdrawing. He did consider it. He agreed that the changed emphasis had damaged Sartre's play as a philosophical statement. He had been initially attracted to *Les Mains Sales* as a subtle, moving picture of individual conscience struggling against authoritarianism. Boyer could not disagree that in its transmutation as *Red Gloves* the play had become what Sartre said it now was— "a common, vulgar melodrama with an anti-Communist bias."

There had been no political bias in the original text. Boyer agreed with Sartre that it was not a political drama at all; it could as easily involve persons living in a democracy. Boyer played a man marked for assassination because his progressive ideas are opposed by the Party's reactionary inner circle. The appointed assassin, however, falls under the spell of his intended victim, recognizing Hoederer as a man whose courage and compassion are the equal of his wisdom and intellectual brilliance. Yet Hugo shoots Hoederer when he wrongly suspects him of trying to steal his wife. The final irony is Hoederer's deification by the Party as a glorious martyr.

The objects of Sartre's wrath were the play's dynamic woman producer, Jean Dalrymple, and the writer Daniel Taradash. On personal terms Boyer liked both of them, and would reason later that he should have been less passive about the changes and more protective of Sartre's meaning. But anti-Communist statements were a fashion of the Cold War, and it was obligatory in 1948 to project Communism in an unfavorable light at every opportunity, and to work "red" into a title wherever possible.

By withdrawing from the play at considerable professional

risk, Boyer also could have closed *Red Gloves*. It was a commercial success because he was in it. Another actor might
have been found to play Hoederer, but not one with Boyer's
ticket-selling capability. This was gratifying for him, and his
spirits were also buoyed by his personal notices. The Broadway critics were not hostile to *Red Gloves*. Some reviews
were rather favorable, no one panned the play, and the dominant mood of indifference implied the critics' accord with
Sartre's own assessment. But the actor Boyer collected a uniform set of raves.

Notice was barely taken that John Dall and Joan Tetzel, established young stage players, both with some screen experience, acted roles almost as large as Boyer's. *Red Gloves*
ceased to be "the Sartre play" and evolved into "the Boyer
play"; he was its reason to be, and to see. The word generally
applied to his performance was *great*. Pleased as he was by
the endorsement, Boyer insisted that his greatest thrill was
merely in being back in the theater. He would even make so
rash a statement that he would probably *never* make another
motion picture. And right away, he began the search for another stage property.

He said "The stage is more stimulating. You have a chance
to work on your part until you do it the best possible way.
You speak the lines night after night, month in and out, and
eventually you say them the way that expresses their full content. In films you say them only once or twice and rarely penetrate beneath the surface of their psychological implications."

Ingrid Bergman in her memoirs recalled seeing *Red Gloves*
in New York:

"I was in the theater and there were two women sitting
behind me and as soon as he came on they started, 'Good
God, is *that* Charles Boyer? So small! And that stomach! And
he's nearly bald.' And after a few seconds of this I turned
around and said 'Just wait. Just wait until he starts to act.' And
they waited. And he acted. He acted like he always did with
such magic, he held the audience in his hand . . ."

13

❀❀❀❀❀❀❀❀❀❀❀

Charles Boyer was jealous of his wife for having once met Bernard Shaw and even pulled his whiskers. Intending no disrespect toward William Shakespeare, Boyer believed that GBS was the greatest playwright in the history of the world; or, if not that, the one whose works were most suited to the Boyer taste.

Boyer was a thinking man, and Shaw was a one-man festival of ideas, a thinking actor's thinking dramatist. And to those who might suggest that for all his wit, George Bernard Shaw lacked the power of poetry, Boyer could say "Then you do not know *Don Juan in Hell.*"

Beginning in 1950, Boyer was occupied with an extraordinary stage presentation of *Don Juan in Hell* intermittently for four years. Many of his friends, and others who did not know him, regarded Boyer's rendering of the title role the highest achievement of his career as an actor, either on stage or screen.

There has been some confusion over how the project got started. Agnes Moorehead maintained that she was the instigator, after a few guests at somebody's filmland party fought boredom by retiring to a den to read a play, settling on the *Don Juan in Hell* interlude of Shaw's *Man and Superman.* Cedric Hardwicke, a knighted Briton long established in Hollywood as a polished and often smoothly villainous character actor, read the part of the Devil. Agnes Moorehead was

Ana, the only female role; and the other actors were both strangers to her, whose names she chose not to remember because they were both so terrible, especially the one who read the dominant role of Don Juan. Moorehead and Hardwicke decided it was worth doing again under more agreeable circumstances, and both Charleses—Boyer and Laughton—were brought together socially with them to read the spellbinding dramatic sequence.

Charles Laughton insisted that he and Boyer had begun talking about *Don Juan in Hell,* and the possibility of their doing it, some years earlier than that—between takes for *Arch of Triumph.* Boyer, a person of generally excellent memory, was unable to recall such a conversation, or an original summons from Miss Moorehead and Sir Cedric. All that he could verify was that a young theatrical producer named Paul Gregory had brought them all together, and that Gregory had determined the style of the presentation.

In any event, Hardwicke yielded the Devil role to Laughton and took for himself the fourth role of Ana's father, whose afterlife in Heaven is as miserable as is Don Juan's consignment to Hell—where Ana, however, is quite blissful. The odd casting seemed to be Boyer as Don Juan—a French pariah in illustrious Anglo-American company. Boyer himself suggested that he might never have met the competition had *Don Juan in Hell* been conventionally staged, inviting a clash of physical acting styles. Paul Gregory's plan was to eschew sets, costumes, other aspects of stagecraft, and even physical movement, and to present the work as a dramatic reading. It wasn't divine inspiration; *Don Juan in Hell* had been similarly performed before and often, but not by players of such renown, and never before in America.

The "production" was first presented in New York in 1951, an offering by The First Drama Quartette, as the four actors were collectively saluted. Boyer, Laughton, and Hardwicke came on in black-tie tuxedos, and Miss Moorehead in a chiffon gown, also crowned with a jeweled tiara that represented a substantial portion of the production cost, actor salaries apart. There were four reading stands, each supporting an oversized playscript.

That was it, and the nearly unanimous opinion was that that was enough. A mere reading? The four actors acted up a storm, but with their voices only. And such voices! Laughton and Hardwicke had distinctive rich voices, and Hardwicke especially was a paragon of English diction. Miss Moorehead, the American member, possessed a refined, crisp speech that ideally complemented her brittle vocal quality. Boyer astonished listeners with the clarity of his English, to its most subtle intonations. He demonstrated an ability almost to banish his native accent on demand, while delivering enough to retain his inimitability. That all four voices were beguiling and also complementary and even harmonious was important. *Don Juan* became what John Cromwell had said of *History Is Made at Night*—a musical composition for human voices, but for four voices rather than only two.

Although it is only the distended third act of Shaw's original four-act design of *Man and Superman,* the philosophically elevated *Don Juan in Hell* almost always is excised from conventional productions of a play that without it remains an achievement on Shaw's best high-comedy level. It is in *Man and Superman* that the playwright finds a pure forum for his ideas. Don Juan's conflict is the choice between a pleasure-seeking existence and service for the betterment of the human race. It is to the Devil's despair that Don Juan cannot be compromised to Hell, even with his beloved Ana there. In Boyer's trust, Don Juan attained the status of an authentic hero for dramatic literature.

Reviewers and audiences seldom made qualitative comparisons of the members of The First Drama Quartette, generally rating each as superb. Yet more than the others, Boyer was the revelation, the focal character and dominant presence without whose excellence the presentation surely would have foundered. Boyer loved acclaim—can an actor not?—but he maintained his characteristic modesty, confident that Charles Laughton was representing him ably. Laughton said, "It's a pity that Bernard Shaw didn't see and hear Charles Boyer as Don Juan. Shaw of all people knew how rare is the true intellectual actor. Boyer is that, besides which he is a considerable artist in other respects. I would call him a genius—yes, a genius who belongs on the stage."

The First Drama Quartette took *Don Juan in Hell* on an extended national tour after the New York engagement; and in 1952, after a holiday, they took it to the British Isles. They were unable to play London when John Clements exercised priority for his production of the complete *Man and Superman,* but they brought it to the West End on a later junket. There was also a second national tour, and the four actors got together at irregular intervals for special performances. The *Don Juan in Hell* saga surmounted a formidable logistical problem, inasmuch as the four actors all were in steady demand for other assignments, usually in film roles. Altogether they presented *Don Juan in Hell* more than seven hundred times, and on the very last occasion Boyer said, "It's still getting better."

❋　❋　❋

Boyer may have been serious about never making another film, but there were more of them to come—about thirty all told, over two more busy decades. But the years of major stardom were behind him, at least on the American screen. To some extent it was his own choice. After the debacle of *Arch of Triumph,* he renewed his determination to become a character actor, and stuck to the plan. Thereafter he continued to command star billing but in subordinate roles, and most often in company with players of a younger generation. He remained an always welcome familiar face, especially to older moviegoers whose number, however, was steadily decreasing.

The four films he made during the four years of his fitful involvement with *Don Juan in Hell* illustrated his altered status in the Hollywood firmament. In one he was a supporting player with star billing; in another he was the only star, but the picture was accorded only a minor release; to another that was a piece of junk, he contributed a minor stint just for the money; and he led the cast of the other, which was a major production but not a commercial success. And then he left Hollywood once more.

The First Legion was a play about some priests at a desert mission who are confronted by a possible miracle—actually an allegory with political implications, written by Emmet Lavery. The playwright was a Boyer neighbor, whose bid for a California congressional seat the actor had supported. The Democrat Lavery always lost in politics, and sometimes when he sought to translate his liberal views into dramatic art. *The Magnificent Yankee,* Lavery's play in which Louis Calhern brilliantly impersonated Justice Oliver Wendell Holmes on both stage and screen, was a fair success; but *The First Legion* was a failure in both incarnations—all talk and little action, despite director Douglas Sirk's adventurous camera. Boyer was assisted by such able actors as Walter Hampden, Leo G. Carroll, William Demarest, and Taylor Holmes, who collectively couldn't incite a box-office stampede; and the obligatory girl—Barbara Rush—was then new and unknown. Produced by a small independent company, *The First Legion* obtained few bookings, and fewer important ones.

Boyer's other film released in 1951 should have been of more consequence, and he was eager to do it, even with a secondary role. *The Thirteenth Letter* was an odd venture for 20th Century–Fox: a remake of Henri-Georges Clouzot's *Le Corbeau* that had been made in France under the Nazi Occupation, then was used in German-edited version as anti-French propaganda for its harsh criticism of French provincial life. Clouzot was scandalized and in the early postwar period was denied work in French films, but on reappraisal *Le Corbeau* was hailed as a near-masterpiece. It couldn't be called *The Raven* as an American product because audiences would suspect it as a Poe subject, so it was *The Thirteenth Letter*—now about a French-Canadian village gripped by terror after a siege of poison-pen letters. Boyer was billed between Linda Darnell and Michael Rennie, its leading players, and that he gave the film's best performance might still be a negative judgment. The picture was not a patch on its French model—a lackluster entry in the directorial canon of Otto Preminger, with whom Boyer maintained a civil but cold relationship. If *The Thirteenth Letter* created an impression, it was one of audience shock over Boyer's appearance. Suddenly he looked tired and old—not an accomplishment of makeup, for he was not made up at all, other than having grown a beard for his role. David Shipman noted that "When he returned to the screen it was as a character actor—his toupee abandoned, gleefully attacking any elderly part which came his way. *The Thirteenth Letter* also found him bearded, and some of the magic undoubtedly had gone."

The magic was entirely gone in the picture he made for Paramount in 1951 but was withheld from release for two years because nobody knew what to do with it. It was an action picture set in the Orient, but it lacked efficiency even as hokum. Boyer was a villain, or so it appeared, in support of Alan Ladd and Deborah Kerr, who played a blind girl. Also in the mix was Corinne Calvet, whom Hal Wallis had failed to sell as a French sex goddess despite a lusty effort. The picture went through several temporary titles before going out as *Thunder in the East,* although it bore no kinship with Boyer's much earlier picture by that name—the English transcription of *La Bataille.* The suspicion early in 1953 that Boyer was "through" may have extended also to both Alan Ladd and Deborah Kerr. Ladd's career had become mired in tedium, and Kerr's had never really got going in America, or M-G-M wouldn't have farmed her out for such a dim Paramount prospect. But before the year was over, Deborah Kerr would portray Karen Holmes in *From Here to Eternity,* and Alan Ladd would be *Shane.*

Like both *The Thirteenth Letter* and *Thunder in the East,* the Stanley Kramer production of *The Happy Time* was recorded as a money-loser. But it was a cut above those otherwise dismal entries, and in many respects was a fine film that drew mixed reviews rather than uniformly bad ones. Kramer, a critics' favorite early in his career for such honorable modest entries as *Champion* and *The Men,* in 1951 annexed his autonomous producing unit to Columbia Pictures and proceeded to make a string of medium-budgeted films that earned more respect than revenue. Often the Kramer-produced screen failures had been far more successful as stage properties, as in the cases of *Death of a Salesman* and *The Four-Poster;* and indeed, *The Happy Time* as well. It was Samuel Taylor's play based on Robert Fontaine's stories of middle-class French-Canadian family life early in the century. It was one of Boyer's happiest experiences—working with his countrymen Louis Jourdan and Marcel Dalio, all creating their own carefree atmosphere. Boyer, enacting Claude Dauphin's stage role, was head of a proper family with some raffish edges. His strategic assignment was to give sexual counsel to his adolescent son played by Bobby Driscoll, an engaging child actor who died at thirty from a heart attack induced by drug addiction.

The Happy Time is essentially a French-Canadian paraphrase of Eugene O'Neill's New England-based *Ah, Wilderness,* and perhaps it is as good. Under Richard Fleischer's direction, the film has disarming vitality, and offers Boyer's last star performance in a major American production. He has a nice bemused quality and a gentle warmth, but those were too much the characteristics of the film itself, restricting its audience potential.

The unmistakable flop of *Thunder in the East,* juxtaposed upon the disappointing fate of *The Happy Time,* might well have caused Boyer to leave Hollywood, but for one important reason: he was already gone.

*   *   *

In 1952 Charles Boyer made some significant real estate transactions. First, he sold the house on Alpine Drive, selling also at auction many of its furnishings and even a substantial portion of his art collection, retaining only his and Pat's special favorites. Concurrently, he discharged his researchists at the French Research Foundation, closed its files, and sold the building to Sol Lesser. Some of the Boyers' more cherished belongings were shipped to New York and installed in their permanent suite in the Hotel Pierre. Then Charles and Pat went to France and bought a luxury apartment in Paris.

He said he was leaving the film community for a while for many reasons, most of them logical but also diplomatically stated, concealing other motives.

Selling the house was a natural consequence, he said, of its having become too big. It was no bigger than it had been even before the Boyers had a child, but after the decision to send Michael to a private boarding school it *seemed* larger without him, and hollow-empty.

Pat said "It's a lovely home and it deserves to be lived in. For the past few years Charles and I haven't been there for even half the time, but it still has held us down just because it was there and it was ours. Now we'll be entirely free."

Had Boyer lost interest in the French Research Foundation?

"Certainly not. It has made a wonderful contribution and I take pride in it, but now the work is finished."

The work had continued through Boyer's frequent absence, and through his diminished attention when he was in town. Boyer did appear to lose interest in the research foundation in March of 1950 after being host there for a glittering reception for Paul Reynaud that was attended by all of Hollywood's princes of industry. Reynaud, although consigned by history to De Gaulle's shadow, earned at least equal esteem from Boyer for his heroic if unsuccessful attempt to save France from German occupation in World War II. Almost alone, Reynaud had protested the appeasement of Germany by England and France at Munich. As Prime Minister of France in 1940, he was unwilling to be a party to the armistice with Germany that Pétain and Laval demanded and achieved; and Reynaud was imprisoned by the Nazis throughout the period of war. The reception in Hollywood ten long years later celebrated the French Research Foundation's completion of the World War II documentation. Two years later, when the office was disbanded, Boyer donated the war documentation to the University of California at Los Angeles, and the 15,000-volume general library to the University of Southern California, to assure the continued availability of research material to the film industry and to scholars of every kind.

He said "The French Research Foundation has been my first interest, my driving purpose in southern California. With its work completed, I now feel, well, lost."

The Boyers left Hollywood because they were unhappy with the community itself. It probably had little to do with Boyer's reduced position in the pecking order of American motion picture stardom. They had disaffection for an inbred community that was sanctimonious on the one hand, as in its persecution of Ingrid Bergman, and vindictive to a degree of bewildering cruelty on the other, as in the matter of the political drama that was then choking the film industry.

Miss Bergman's much-publicized indiscretion of 1949, when her love affair with Italian director Roberto Rossellini produced a child out of wedlock while she was still married to Dr. Peter Lindstrom, had the effect of banishing her from American film activity for seven years before she was industrially forgiven for her sins. At almost the same time a young, unestablished screen player very nearly had her contract canceled by 20th Century–Fox for having posed nude for a calendar artist, when she was hungry—Marilyn Monroe, with whom Pat had a budding friendship. Boyer was enraged: "Years ago it was poor Simone Simon. How can these people be so vicious?"

He concluded, though, that moral sin was more nearly tolerable than political sin in the filmland. From the time the House Committee on Un-American Activities went into action in 1947 with its investigation of Communism within the film industry, to its splashy televised inquisition four years later, Boyer was disenchanted with the American West Coast chapter of his profession. "They are all murderers," implicating both the witch-hunting congressmen (who included California's Richard Nixon) and the enforcement of the blacklist by studio heads who, Boyer said, were as cowardly as they were condescending. It was a disgrace for honorable people to be deprived of their professional identity, he said, but it was unthinkable tragedy that it should cost them their lives. J. Edward Bromberg, whom Boyer befriended when they made *Arch of Triumph* together, was a suicide following his blacklisting. So, it was believed, were Philip Loeb, Mady Christians, Canada Lee; and John Garfield's tragic death in 1952 was attributed to the same thing, despair and desperation having driven him to his last and fatal heart attack.

This was a time of newly formed enmities, often among old friends. Boyer had a falling out with Adolphe Menjou, whom he regarded as one of the community's leading inquisitors. Years later they were reconciled when Boyer made the first friendly move; he could forgive, but he could not forget.

Within a few years the Boyers would be back in Hollywood, but never for long stretches, and without an illusion of permanence. They would buy and sell other houses in Beverly Hills—"It's good business," Boyer said—and they would always have a place in the environs of Hollywood that approximated a home. But it was only one of many such. There was also the Paris apartment, and later, a château as well, in the country to the south of the City of Light. In the mid-fifties the Boyers bought a house in London that they occupied only fitfully, leasing it out for long periods. There would also be their summer retreat at Ischia, off the Italian coast south of Naples. A clue that their primary home now would be considered New York was given by the installation of their most prized possessions in the hotel suite—among them Boyer's specified favorites among the paintings they owned, Jean Béraud's "Le Bal Public" and Marie Laurencin's "Deux Femmes."

All of these places were home to Michael. The Boyer son could not feel uprooted by the departure from Beverly Hills, for he was accustomed to moving around the world. When Michael was a teenager, the three Boyers made an around-the-world trip that was concentrated in the Orient, which none of them had visited previously. Later as a threesome they flew to Rio de Janeiro and Montevideo. For the spring of 1966, they had planned a trip to Africa.

❋ ❋ ❋

After a sustained diet of heavy dramatics, Charles Boyer was always easy prey for frivolity. Examination of his screen credits reveals a pattern—usually three or four sober exercises punctuated at some point by a light frolic or an occasional authentic rib-tickler. The same psychology must have been at work in 1953 when he agreed to appear opposite Mary Martin on Broadway in Norman Krasna's *Kind Sir*.

Norman Krasna was a prolific screenwriter, sometime producer, and occasional playwright, always in a lighthearted vein. Well, not always: Krasna's original screen story for *Fury* provided Fritz Lang with an exciting but grim first American film, with its great Spencer Tracy performance. But Krasna's calling card was gaiety. His plays—*Dear Ruth* and *John Loves Mary*, for examples—inevitably were rollicking affairs featur-

ing characters laughing their heads off even while contending
with the necessary complications. Some of his movie scripts
are classics of the screwball genre—the Harlow-Tracy-Loy-
Powell *Libeled Lady;* Carole Lombard's *Hands Across the
Table* and *Mr. and Mrs. Smith;* Jean Arthur's *The Devil and
Miss Jones;* Ginger Rogers's *Bachelor Mother;* Olivia deHavilland's *Princess O'Rourke.* Even with some clunkers among all
the others not mentioned, it would be a good track record.
Boyer trusted it, and it suggested the comical idiom he
believed he needed after the rigorous melodramatics of *Red
Gloves* and the heightened rhetoric of *Don Juan in Hell*—
with which he was again briefly occupied after the *Kind Sir*
episode passed into the record books without having broken
any records.

It wasn't a flop, because stage flops close on the first Saturday night, or not long afterward. *Kind Sir* had a respectable
run of several months, surely due entirely to the stature and
magnetism of its two leading players. But playgoers as well as
critics must have expected more, especially since the director
was Joshua Logan. In that era he was the "most successful
man of the theatre" (according to Brooks Atkinson, and probably others), and he had directed Mary Martin in the epochal
Rodgers-Hammerstein musical *South Pacific.* There was general
agreement that Logan had done all that could be done with
Kind Sir, and that Mary Martin and Charles Boyer (billed in
that order) were superior examples of players making something of nothing. Boyer was given the edge. Mary Martin was
a splendid actress as well as an expert musical comedienne,
but less practiced than Boyer in the traditional drawing-room
style. But *Kind Sir* wasn't bad, because there just wasn't
enough there really to be bad. An actress and a diplomat fall
in love. She wants to get married but he says they can't, because he's already somebody's husband. She finds out he was
lying, out of simple fear of marriage, and they get together.
As simple as that. It hardly seemed more complicated five
years later when Cary Grant did it as a film called *Indiscreet*
with Ingrid Bergman, after her rehabilitation; but it seemed
more substantial, causing Boyer to reflect that few of Krasna's
jewels of screen comedy would have glittered as brightly on a
stage.

Boyer did not look back on *Kind Sir* as a mistake. It did no harm to him professionally, nor did it harm anyone who may have watched it. He said it was fun and also necessary—that any screen actor needs to go on the stage at regular intervals to refine his technique: "I now understand the mistake I made, working in films year after year without the—what is the word?—orientation that the stage can provide. You are shooting a film and the cameras are right there, and people all around. All of it is unreal. It is impossible to achieve total concentration, it is so unreal. On a stage you do not see all those people, you only see the other actors who most often are your collaborators, creating or recreating a realistic situation in a setting that also seems real. You can concentrate on a stage. You can become more real in what you say and do, even if all you are doing is *Kind Sir*."

❀   ❀   ❀

In the 1950s there ceased to be American films and English films and French and German and Italian and Swedish films as they had existed with precise and separate identities since the early development of the medium. Gradually the screen was being internationalized. An American company making a film set in France might shoot in Yugoslavia and Spain. Consider the possibilities.

In 1957 Billy Wilder filmed *Love in the Afternoon* entirely in Paris. A decade earlier the same story would have been shot on Hollywood sound stages, with an occasional stock shot of the Eiffel Tower edited into the print as a geographic reminder to the audience. Yet the Gary Cooper–Audrey Hepburn *Love in the Afternoon* was also the occasion of Maurice Chevalier's trumpeted return to "American" pictures. It became ever more difficult, however, always to know the difference.

Charles Boyer soon reached the point of not knowing the difference in his own continuing activity. In the years ahead he would make French, American, Franco-American, Franco-Italian, Franco-Austrian, and Franco-American-Spanish pictures without losing his balance, always remembering which language he should be speaking in the given scene.

He became a Paris-based motion picture actor, most of whose

"American" screen ventures would be filmed in France or nearby on the European continent. Just occasionally he would make a picture in a Hollywood studio, although he would film many television playlets there. Even when it could no longer be denied that he was a very old man, he was still there, one of the verities of his profession.

Perhaps a few years earlier, his return to French films would have been an event of greater consequence in his native land. By 1953, however, the French had become accustomed to having him again in their midst, and they seemed almost to have forgotten that he had been away. When Boyer reported to Max Ophüls for *Madame de . . .* , the "angle" was not that it was Boyer's first French film in fifteen years, but that he was reunited with the gorgeous Danielle Darrieux, his costar in Anatole Litvak's *Mayerling* of lingering memory, made all of seventeen years earlier. The Ophüls film alone would restore him to the highest echelon of French artists performing in their native land, and soon he would hold affectionate status as the Grand Old Man of the French cinema. But never again would he make a picture that approached the spellbinding *Madame de . . .* in any measure of art or craftsmanship, in any language.

Max Ophüls was one of the world's great creative artists in motion pictures, whose reputation has appreciated steadily since his death at the peak of his powers, at age fifty-five. Ophüls was apprenticed in Germany's UFA films and was acquainted with Charles Boyer in Berlin, barely and briefly. A German Jew, he fled to France immediately upon Hitler's succession to power, becoming a naturalized French citizen—only to be forced again to wander following the Nazi takeover. Eventually he arrived in the United States without definite reputation, nor was it resolved in the postwar films he made in Hollywood. Indifferently received in their time, Ophüls's American films now are rated highly and at least one of them—*Letter from an Unknown Woman*—is a belatedly acknowledged classic. It can now be seen that Ophüls in that work and also in *The Exile, Caught,* and *The Reckless Moment* was refining a personal style that would find mature artistic expression in the four films he completed after his return to France in 1950. *La Ronde* and *Le Plaisir* preceded *Ma-*

dame de . . . and *Lola Montès* followed it, before Ophüls's death in 1955. *Madame de* . . . signaled the pinnacle of Ophüls's art. Andrew Sarris has made claims for *Lola Montès* as *the* greatest film ever made (as he has also very nearly said of *Madame de* . . .), but *Lola Montès* is the less nearly perfect work, wherein Martine Carol's accounting of the title role is no match for the tragic artistry of Danielle Darrieux, Charles Boyer, and Vittorio De Sica in *Madame de* . . .

The Italian De Sica, himself a great movie director but also a splendid actor of technique comparable to Boyer's, was the lover in an aristocratic triangle story. Darrieux was the wife indifferent to her husband, and Boyer was the husband coming gradually to understand his loss. Boyer's sympathetic performance was a triumph of irony and innuendo, but it wasn't his picture. Darrieux was the fulcrum, giving the performance of her life; yet it wasn't her picture, either, or De Sica's. The tragic tale of three people destroyed by love was narrated by a fluid camera with Ophüls's famous penchant for tracking shots as integral to the film's artistic discipline as were the players in their depth and subtlety.

Madame de . . . was an international *succès d'estime,* and in its American engagements was titled *The Earrings of Madame De,* without the ellipsis, in reference to the jewels that are used symbolically throughout the film, as agents of truth. Darrieux pawns the earrings Boyer has given her, only to receive them later as a gift from De Sica . . .

A masterpiece when Boyer needed one; and from such a height, he could only go downhill.

The French slide began with Christian-Jaque's *Nana,* one of the many failed efforts to make a suitable talking film of Emile Zola's famous novel about a Paris whore. Jean Renoir's silent version with his wife Catherine Hessling has not been surpassed by any attempt of the sound era, of which Samuel Goldwyn's try with Anna Sten is the best-known flop. In 1954 it was a vehicle for its director's wife, Martine Carol, of whose performance it must be said that her Lola Montès was better. Nominally her costar, Boyer was merely the most authoritative figure in a large and fussy cast, clearly reduced to a support function.

In his pattern of an annual European film over a period of several years, his 1955 credit would have been Ophüls's *Lola Montès* but for a scheduling conflict. Instead he journeyed to Italy for *La Fortuna di Essere Donna,* as an older man spurned by Sophia Loren, who was taller than he. De Sica appeared in that one also, as did the young Marcello Mastroianni, and the picture—shown in America as *Lucky to Be a Woman*—was one of the ones that sent Sophia Loren to Hollywood, although it was lackluster and had three interesting men acting rings around her.

It had been casually assumed for years that any European film with Boyer in its cast could obtain American distribution, but this was not the case of *Paris-Palace Hôtel,* his entry for 1956 and his first film for writer-director Henri Verneuil. Predictably, it was in the *Grand Hotel* mold, and Boyer, just as predictably, was its strongest asset. But every major American city rolled out the welcome mat for *Une Parisienne,* simply because Brigitte Bardot was the hottest thing in French films in 1957. International grosses were impressive, but the subject was a shopworn tale of a love triangle in high circles. The younger man contending for sex-kitten Bardot's favor was Henri Vidal, Michèle Morgan's handsome husband. Boyer was the distinguished older fellow, a part he could now play in his sleep.

Twenty years after making *Orage,* Boyer and Michèle Morgan got together again in 1958 for Verneuil's *Maxime,* an unaccustomed title role for Boyer in this late period. Considering Morgan's status as France's leading actress, and Boyer's assured professionalism, it should have been a stronger film. Woman falls in love with courtly older man until she realizes he is as impoverished as he is polished. The stars were authoritative in a needlessly overlong picture, and scant notice was taken that the legendary, aging Arletty appeared in a very small role. *Maxime* finally got a few U.S. bookings four years later, causing no real stir across the sea.

During this period of sustained filmmaking in Europe, Boyer was not mired on the Continent but was a hemispheric commuter, flying back and forth from Paris to New York several times a year, and sometimes several times a month; or to

California from various new air routes. In the mid-fifties he also made three American films—only one of which, however, was shot in a Hollywood studio.

An echo and a fairly hollow one of Boyer's *Private Worlds* two decades earlier was *The Cobweb,* filmed at M-G-M. The setting was a mental hospital whose doctors had personal difficulties more complicated than those of the inmates. Vincente Minnelli directed a star-swamped project that found Boyer in the company of Richard Widmark and Lauren Bacall as the functional leads, Gloria Grahame of the bit lip in her standard near-trollop impression, and the great Lillian Gish who stole a picture not worth stealing. Perhaps Lauren Bacall thought it superior to *Confidential Agent.* Boyer didn't. He was the head of the hospital, driven to drink by the pressure, in a very classy failure.

He was also in a very classy success: Michael Todd's *Around the World in 80 Days,* filmed around the world in more days than that. The Jules Verne picaresque served Todd as a carnival-coated picture show, for which overrating came easily in 1956. It was the movie that in the grammar of screen acting coined the term "cameo," delivering respectability to a walk-on appearance by a player of high standing. Pleased as Boyer may have been to be finally cast in an Oscar-cited best picture, he was only one of forty-four cameo players weaving their special appearances around David Niven's Phileas Fogg, the Passepartout of Mexican comedian Cantinflas, and newcomer Shirley MacLaine's uncertain hold on Princess Aouda. Some of the cameo players were of dubious luster, but there was an abundance of real stars and veterans who had been that—Ronald Colman, Buster Keaton, Marlene Dietrich, Frank Sinatra, Beatrice Lillie, George Raft. Boyer's stint as a travel agent was brief but enjoyably and broadly played.

Some time later, Cecil B. DeMille talked Boyer into reprising his Napoleon characterization as a cameo appointment for *The Buccaneer,* the story of Jean Lafitte. DeMille had made the story twenty years earlier and it hardly caught fire then, even with Fredric March. The pirate hero for the 1958 remake was Yul Brynner in flowing black wig, and another repeat performance was Charlton Heston's as Andrew Jackson

—a role he played with Susan Hayward in *The President's Lady*, about Rachel Jackson. The elderly DeMille turned the direction of *The Buccaneer* over to actor Anthony Quinn, who at that time was his son-in-law. DeMille was credited only as the producer of a major flop. Boyer deeply regretted having submitted himself to an encore as Bonaparte, fearing that the second appearance might compromise the first timeless performance.

Also in 1958, the Boyers resumed a full-time residence in New York as Charles went into a new play. Leslie Stevens's *The Marriage-Go-Round* had about as much substance as *Kind Sir*, but was a more appealing prospect for playgoers given to nostalgia. This time Boyer's stage mate was Claudette Colbert, to whom he felt indebted for the important early boosts she had given his career. Miss Colbert hadn't made a picture in years, and there was considerable public curiosity over how she might look. She looked terrific, and so did Boyer, corseted and with a new, fuller toupee. They were the most elegant players on Broadway, and possibly the smoothest, if in a trifle. They played a comfortably married couple, rendered less comfortable by the arrival of a young Amazon anxious to conceive a child by the "perfect man" as represented by Boyer—who was several inches shorter than the actress, Julie Newmar.

The attraction of Boyer and Colbert (who alternated first billing in the playbills and display ads) kept the trifle on Broadway more than a year. During its run, Pat Paterson and Charles Boyer celebrated their twenty-fifth wedding anniversary. They had a brief argument over where they should dine. For them it was "the worst spat we've had all year," Pat said.

The play was on vacation break in August of 1959 when Boyer marked another milestone, his sixtieth birthday. Again he was telling reporters he might never make another picture. Again he added a wink, saying that an actor never really retires. But it probably mattered little if he did or didn't film again, and sometimes he must have felt that he was merely going through the motions.

14

❖❖❖❖❖❖❖❖❖❖

Pat was always seeking her island. She was the more adventurous one, and it was a hobby of hers—exploring exotic islands in search of the perfect vacation spot. At different times the Boyers visited a dozen or more islands dotted around the globe, seeking their retreat. Charles came to share his wife's fancy and developed some island pursuits of his own. Once, on a whim, they made a trip to the Isles Dernieres off the Louisiana coast because Boyer had read an intriguing story by Lafcadio Hearn about its nineteenth-century resort, which had been entirely destroyed by a tidal wave. It had only one clear advantage: they were the only people there.

In Ischia, they found what they wanted.

Pat accompanied her husband to Italy when he made the picture with Sophia Loren. They island-hunted in their idle time, and went to Capri like everyone else—a place corrupted by tourism, Boyer believed. They heard about the considerably larger island of Ischia, to the north of Capri and farther off the mainland, at the northern entrance to the Bay of Naples. They found a bustling private world, an island with several ample cities and more than thirty thousand people, of whom many had never been to the mainland. Tourism was a primary trade for the natives, but most of the tourists were Italian; Ischia wasn't an American haunt.

At Ischia they also found enchanting scenery in its craggy mountains and clean beaches; and solitude could also be

attained. They returned to Ischia in the summer of 1956 with
Michael in tow, and bought a villa there. They came again
over ten consecutive summers, often for a month at a time,
sometimes longer, occasionally for a full season. Ischia was
mandatory; Charles would work his professional schedule
around his island communion with Pat and Michael. They all
took up painting there, Michael as well as his parents. Charles
worked in oils, Pat preferred watercolors and tempera, and
Michael liked acrylics.

His parents watched Michael change from boy into man at
their Ischia retreat. He was twelve that first summer, interested only in swimming and surfing. By the next year his upward spurt was visible, and he was noticing the girls. Charles
believed that Ischia was an ideal backdrop for explaining the
mysteries of sex, and he did his duty as father and son drew
closer. Each passing summer would find Michael occupied
with a new girl friend, but Ischia always had to end.

Michael was an athlete by choice, not by natural physical
gift. He had a mild but chronic weight problem, inclined to
take on some fat if not committed to a disciplined diet. He
was stocky, robust, and eventually was taller than his father
by several inches. Michael could also "take" his father in almost any athletic challenge, even before age began to wear
Charles Boyer down and reduce his mobility—as on a tennis
court, where Michael soon only toyed with his father.

Michael Boyer bore a discernible resemblance to his father,
as against no apparent resemblance whatever to his mother.
Like Pat only in personality, Michael was far more exuberant
than his father, and entirely carefree. Charles watched and
waited, looking for Michael's more serious side, seeking a hint
of ambition, a clue about what Michael would choose to do
with his life.

Charles and Pat both expected Michael to become an actor,
or have that urge. They lightly feared it, knowing that few
were chosen for the fame and fortune such as Charles had secured, and knowing that in any event it isn't really an easy
life. Michael fooled them by not wanting to be an actor, and
not wanting to be in the movie business. But television, yes.

Television was the future. Michael at age fifteen knew that he wished to become a producer for television. Furthermore, he knew he *would*.

Boyer thought it odd that his son could be indifferent to both stage and screen, yet so hooked on television. It was the generation gap revealed for him. Michael was in that age group that could not recall a world without television. Watching the home screen had consumed him since early childhood. Television for him was the magic that the movies had spelled for children only a few years older. Indeed, Michael was less impressed by his father's eminence as a stage and screen actor than by his function as one of the producer-stars of "Four Star Playhouse."

Michael insisted that college would only be a waste of time for him. He could get a more valuable education for television production merely by becoming a part of it, right away. He wanted to get to the top sooner rather than later. His father, alarmed by Michael's impatience, promised to give him all the help of which he was capable. And that was a lot.

*   *   *

When television became a force to be reckoned with, most actors and other artists and craftsmen who had been nurtured by the motion picture industry chose to ignore it, hoping that it would go away, or that they could proceed in their accustomed workaday labors without feeling its threat. Gradually they came around, many of them trying tardily to get into the TV game, and finding that the ground floor was already too crowded. But Charles Boyer got in early, when the room was almost empty. Among the picture people who made accommodation for television, he is now seen as a pioneer.

Television sets were first marketed in substantial numbers in the United States in 1947, at first only in the major cities that had viewer access to the programs offered by the few weak stations in early existence. For five years it remained largely experimental. There were gradually more stations with more sophisticated programming, steadily reaching a larger national audience. But 1952 was the turnaround year. Television finally saturated the country, reaching into every isolated valley that hadn't previously been penetrated. And suddenly television was something every family required, much as they had required radio, two decades earlier. And in 1952 there were Dick Powell and Charles Boyer, putting their heads together and starting Four Star Productions.

Boyer gave Powell credit as the true visionary, the one with the original idea; but Powell was at his most visionary when he sought Charles Boyer, a man with whom he was barely acquainted. He knew they had something in common: they were among the richest of the Hollywood stars. Boyer at that point had earned about four million dollars as an actor in American films, but investments had made him far richer than that. And so with Powell: he had toiled for Warner Brothers, the lowest-paying of the major film companies; but he had made his money work.

Powell's career is explained somewhere between remarkable and unaccountable. Originally a crooner in the Busby Berkeley musical extravaganzas for Warner Brothers in the thirties, he was for a time more popular than Bing Crosby, but faded into has-been identity, his cherubic prettiness altogether out of fashion. Miraculously he grimaced that same face into a tough-guy image, and spent his second decade of movie stardom in grainy melodramas, often as a private eye. Then he "got tired of holding my stomach in for the camera" and decided to speculate on the business end of the fledgling television industry. Powell had become a director and producer of feature films as well as an actor, but it was probably as a TV producer that he had the most remarkable career.

Boyer, who indulged his passion for gambling at Monte Carlo, Las Vegas, and other uncommon scenes, elected to gamble on Dick Powell and on television. They sought two other partners to justify the name of Four Star, and their first approach was to Joel McCrea—richer than either of them, from his real estate investments in southern California. McCrea said yes, then no, and Boyer then went after David Niven who made it a three-way partnership. A fourth star was never enlisted, although some years later Tom McDermott joined them as a fourth partner, lured away from an executive position with Benton & Bowles advertising agency. By that time Four Star was solidly established in television production, and the rich were getting richer.

Four Star Productions lost money for three years, then turned a corner for a pattern of increasing annual profits. By 1960 the company's assets were valued at $25 million with annual gross approaching $50 million. TV programming in that era was dominated by half-hour series, and "Four Star Playhouse" was the company's flagship program. The partners rotated as stars of comic and dramatic playlets, and the program proved popular enough to span half a dozen seasons. Powell steadily reduced his own appearances, but guest stars were worked into the rotation, most often Ida Lupino or Rosalind Russell. Boyer and Niven were the workhorses, each appearing in approximately thirty programs during the course of the series. "Four Star Playhouse" and most of the company's other series productions were shot at the old Republic Studios in the San Fernando Valley—as many as five hundred half-hour programs a year, for such series perennials as "Zane Grey Theater," "The Detectives" (Robert Taylor), "The Rifleman," "Michael Shayne," "The Gertrude Berg Show," "The June Allyson Show" (she was Powell's wife), and "Wanted—Dead or Alive."

As an actor for "Four Star Playhouse," Boyer took himself somewhat less seriously than when discharging a role for a feature film or acting on the stage. He didn't work himself into nervousness and high fever for modest entertainments that would disappear forever after a single viewing. He didn't even fret about impersonating national types other than Frenchmen:

"I have only one accent but I use it for Hungarian, Chinese, and Russian roles. American audiences are not particular about their accents, luckily for me. As long as the accent sounds foreign, that is enough. And somehow my accent always manages to sound foreign."

He was not so flippant about all of his acting for television. In one of the earliest ninety-minute "specials" for "Hallmark Playhouse," he costarred with the eminent Katharine Cornell in *There Shall Be No Night*, Robert E. Sherwood's 1940 drama of the Russia-Finland conflict modified to reflect the Hungarian revolution of 1956, retaining its anti-Communist message. The Lunts had appeared in the original for one of their many joint triumphs. Television reviewers who rated *There Shall Be No Night* one of the finest home-screen dramas of that period generally agreed that Boyer's tragic force surpassed Cornell's on this occasion.

Boyer was largely responsible for such movie regulars as Robert Ryan, Jane Powell, Jack Lemmon, and Gig Young getting their feet wet in the waters of TV series acting. Gig Young also became one of "The Rogues"—a Four Star series in which he rotated with Boyer and Niven, regularly solving crimes of an unusual nature. "The Rogues" was a successor to "Four Star Playhouse" after Dick Powell's death in 1963, and in the following year the twenty-year-old Michael Boyer became an associate producer for the program.

Four Star Productions later went public, and both Boyer and Niven withdrew from its operation much wealthier men. Later they could be nostalgic, and they were also entitled to some smug pride. The early betting among the Hollywood gentry had been that the triumvirate of president Powell and vice-presidents Boyer and Niven would never make a go of it: their egos were too gigantic, their temperaments too volatile. Boyer reasoned that they must have solved the problem nicely "just by never getting together." Occasionally they could manage their obligatory annual meeting over lunch, but more often the three partners were scattered around the world and had to manage their meeting by phone. Sometimes two partners were simply unable to find the third, and David Niven remembers that when they did manage an intricate three-way hookup the partners were "like three drunks in a phone booth."

Powell once claimed that he insured Four Star Productions of mental equilibrium by going into partnership with someone who could never be serious (Niven) and someone who could never be anything else (Boyer). Anyway, they never fought, and Niven attributed that to their being actors—"The only voice we pay attention to is our own."

*   *   *

Marcel Pagnol's Marseille trilogy, consisting of *Marius, Fanny,* and *César,* is a treasure of French literature, and all were brought to the French screen in his own and other adaptations in the prewar years. In 1938 M-G-M made a single-film compression of the trilogy as *Port of Seven Seas* with Wallace Beery as César, Maureen O'Sullivan as Fanny, and Frank Morgan as Panisse—a wrongly neglected picture directed beautifully by James Whale. In 1954 David Merrick produced another compression of the trilogy as a Broadway musical called *Fanny* which attained long-run success while remaining a dubious artistic achievement. There was great dissatisfaction with the musical among French purists who resented the portrayals of César and Panisse by actors who were respectively Italian (Ezio Pinza) and German (Walter Slezak). When *Fanny* was turned into a film by Warner Brothers for 1961 release, they tried to get it right.

Although Harold Rome's Broadway score had been popular, they decided to film *Fanny* as a straight comedy-drama without songs, and in Marseille, and with mostly French actors. The big news was that Maurice Chevalier would play Panisse. After the incredible ups and downs of his career and fortunes, Chevalier, although now past seventy, was on a giddy high, once again an international idol after a personal triumph in M-G-M's *Gigi*. Leslie Caron, a French girl who had gone to Hollywood and who was Gigi, would also be Fanny, which figured to enhance her already rising popularity. Subsequent announcement that Charles Boyer would play César failed to obtain similar excited response, although he had not made a film for almost three years.

Every production season yields an ambitious project that is talked about, written about, and watched closely as an event in the making. In the fall of 1960 the conspicuous work in progress was *Fanny*, whose shooting schedule carried into the new year. In the form chart for 1961 it qualified in advance as the year's most important picture.

Reporters found a shooting scene that produced good, gamy copy. There was constant revelry on the production's periphery as several good-fellow Frenchmen rejoiced in one another's company—besides Chevalier and Boyer, there were Victor Francen and Raymond Bussières, not to ignore the irrepressible Georgette Anys playing Fanny's fishwife mother. The favorite angle, though, was the participation of Chevalier and Boyer in the same film, after their forty-year friendship.

Boyer explained that their failure to have played together previously was only logical: "We weren't born to be together because we are so different." Then, periling his credibility, he said "I have always considered myself a character actor, not a handsome lover type." Chevalier put it into a better perspective: "Charles was always the French Valentino. I was the fanciful Casanova."

Their rivalry was very friendly but it *was* a rivalry, a duel of egos. They tried to outdo one another both away from the cameras and before them. Their gleeful tug-of-war gave *Fanny* some vitality that was a critical need of the film. The oft-told tale is of the wanderlusting Marius (played by Germany's youthful Horst Buchholz) going to sea, leaving his pregnant sweetheart, Fanny. Fanny marries the wealthy sail merchant, Panisse, to give her child a home and a name, and Panisse adopts the child, Césario, as his own, giving him a father's love. Marius of course returns, seeking to claim both Fanny and their baby, but is restrained by his father, César, the barkeep who is always the voice of wisdom—telling Marius that "The one who gives the love, *he* is the father."

In 1961 a movie could still be a presold hit, and *Fanny* cashed in on its generous advance publicity, reaping a good financial profit for Warner Brothers. Box-office success often influences industrial Hollywood into overrating a work's artistic merit. *Fanny* did not win an Oscar for best picture, although it was nominated, but lost out to *West Side Story*, whose score wisely was not abandoned. A judgment was also given on the private competition that was a by-product of the production. Maurice Chevalier offered a busy, animated, good-humored characterization, and it was believed to obscure the quiet strength of Boyer's César depiction. At the end of the year when Richard DeNeut, gave his annual forecast of the Oscars, he predicted that Chevalier would emerge best actor. Chevalier wasn't nominated, but Charles Boyer was, for a performance that to some observers was consciously a summing-up of both his skill and his humanity.

*   *   *

Nothing was certain anymore. Although Boyer did not win the Academy Award in his fourth and last official contention, his work in *Fanny* should have redeemed his pedigree for solid roles in pictures of consequence. It did nothing for him. *Fanny* itself was no marvel, until weighed against subsequent Boyer assignments. In France he made a dim film titled *Les Démons de Minuit* for an old, tired director who had lost his touch—Marc Allégret. It was denied distribution in the United States. *Adorable Julia* got American bookings but shouldn't have—a disastrous serving of W. Somerset Maugham's *Theatre*, with Boyer and Lilli Palmer married to themselves and to show business.

In both Paris and Hollywood he was involved in a misguided and dimly advised remake (after forty years!) of Vicente Blasco Ibáñez's *The Four Horsemen of the Apocalypse*, once a ticket to celebrity for Rudolph Valentino. The novel was updated to the Second World War to acquire Nazi villains and French Resistance heroes. Glenn Ford was a miscast Julio, Charles Boyer looked uncomfortable as his father, and the tacky canvas collected Paul Lukas, Ingrid Thulin, Yvette Mimieux, and Paul Henreid.

Then he shot a picture on the Riviera, and had one of the title roles (along with Ricardo Montalban) as long as they called it *The Grand Duke and Mr. Pimm*. Boyer was Pimm, but the title got switched to the ordinary *Love Is a Ball* for Glenn Ford and Hope Lange. Boyer's Pimm was a professional matchmaker on a carousel of lovers changing partners, and some of it worked on a farce level.

It had begun to appear that he would take anything they offered him. Once regarded as possibly the most selective screen actor and the most judicious analyst of a formative screenplay, Boyer now was accepting large parts and small ones, in ambitious works and cheapjack opportunities, without seeming to bother distinguishing between them. Now he said yes if his schedule permitted, and if they made good on the money, which he didn't need anyway; but he had his pride . . .

It was pride that sent him back to Broadway. He still *could* be selective in the matter of plays, and he waited until he got something he could bite into. Ever since his return to the stage in *Red Gloves*, the playscripts hadn't stopped arriving for his consideration. He had rejected a multitude of plays which did or didn't get produced anyway, and those he had accepted—*Kind Sir* and *The Marriage-Go-Round* may have pleased the matinée ladies but hadn't pleased *him*. After another rash of dolorous pictures he was in need of ego sustenance, so he gave close scrutiny to the newest incoming scripts. He didn't find one play he wanted to do, but he found two; and he decided to do both of them, each in its own turn.

From S. N. Behrman came *Lord Pengo*, a characterization masquerading as a play, based on Behrman's studies in the life of Joseph Duveen, whose biographer he was. For years Sam Behrman had known that Boyer shared his fascination for Duveen who, despite being an outrageous character or because of that, exercised enormous influence on changing tastes in art, both in Europe and America. Behrman was acquainted with the art connoisseur-merchant before Duveen's death in 1939, and Boyer had seen Duveen in London without being privileged to converse with him. He knew, though, that while their tastes in art could have coincided, Duveen was the opposite of himself in personality. Duveen was a man of extravagant charm that was out in the open; he was ever the performer. Boyer was never the performer, except professionally, and now he was challenged. He didn't approach *Lord Pengo*, he assaulted the character with color and polish and good physical bearing. At least on personal terms, the half-season engagement as Lord Pengo was his best achievement in the theater since *Don Juan in Hell*.

Lord Pengo in 1963 was followed the next year by Terence Rattigan's *Man and Boy*. Within little more than a year he would portray Rattigan's man in London for his English stage debut, and in Paris where he had not performed in almost twenty years, as well as the New York engagement. *Man and Boy* would not become one of Rattigan's commercial successes even with Boyer's presence, and an exceptionally strong costar in Brian Bedford; but it is rich in theme, an emotionally ambitious drama of a father-son relationship. Although father and son reject one another, each is shattered by the other's rejection. This clarifies their strengths and weaknesses for themselves and for each other, before the deathbed reconciliation.

Boyer felt that *Man and Boy* was the finest play he performed during the postwar period, Bernard Shaw apart. It was a good one for him to go out with. He didn't expect to do additional plays. He was too tired now, and the theater had become exhausting for him.

But in his pride, he said his own son and their developing relationship had been inspirational to him in preparing his role. And there was Michael Boyer, embracing his father in the actor's dressing room on the Broadway opening night, with pride of his own.

❖ ❖ ❖

Now his interviews had a valedictory ring. He was being urged to write his autobiography, but he said he might consider writing a book about acting. He said it had taken a long time, but he was beginning to understand his craft:

"An actor should control his performance, keeping it within a frame. So many others leave the frame and it is like going berserk over the footlights and into the orchestra pit. Let me say, I believe I have learned control. I stay within my own frame emotionally and psychologically."

He was more easygoing than in earlier years, and interviewers became playful with him. They ran a risk of becoming *too* playful, and any revival of the legend of the great bedroom rogue still infuriated him:

"I don't believe I have ever played a seducer or a great lover. I have played Napoleon, I have played professors and diplomats, artists and musicians; I once played a playboy who turns out to be all right; but a seducer, never!"

He could still whiten, could not harness his rage, when they asked him about "come wiz me to zee Casbah."

"I did *not* say that line!"

Yet the great-lover identity could be exploited by his own son. Early in 1965 Charles Boyer made a recording on Valiant Records that sold very well. It was called *Where Does Love Go?* and it was a lover's voice, and the voice of Charles Boyer, as produced by his son, Michael.

*   *   *

Boyer could make pictures quickly now, for many of his assignments were cameos, over and done with at no exhaustion to him. Two cameos followed a star character part in *A Very Special Favor,* a smirky affair that could only be described as a sex comedy. It was competently done but tasteless, and both of its romantic leads—Rock Hudson and Leslie Caron—had hit the downslide.

The cameos were delivered in *How to Steal a Million* and *Is Paris Burning?* The former was a William Wyler picture with disarming players—Audrey Hepburn and Peter O'Toole —but was a disappointment all around, if a very slick one, only affording Boyer a role as drab as it was small.

Is Paris Burning? was a turkey, three hours long, muddled and confused. The story of the liberation of Paris did have some interesting credits—screenplay by Francis Ford Coppola and Gore Vidal, direction by France's René Clément, and a Franco-American star cast.

The Boyers were living once more in Beverly Hills, in a small house now occupied only by Charles and Pat. Pat had stayed at home while Boyer went to Paris to complete the two bit roles in the same trip. The first chore was done, and he had one more scene to film for *Is Paris Burning?* Then he could return to Pat. This was one of the few trips he had made without her, and possibly it would be the last one.

On September 23, 1965, before his scene had been filmed, he was summoned home.

15

When "The Rogues" was canceled as a television series in 1964, its twenty-year-old dialogue director was left without a job. Michael Boyer was expected to rebound, because his famous father had connections and had used them before. But Michael probably heard some of the disrespectful gossip about nepotism, and he could have reasoned that the talk would also reach his father's ears.

Given a production job for which he had neither the training nor other formal qualification, Michael apparently also failed to reveal a pure talent or flair. Apart from his good looks and his acknowledged charm, his most tangible asset was his father. Charles Boyer had become the "great lovair" one more time for the *Where Does Love Go?* recording simply because it was Michael's idea, and he wished Michael would have some others.

Although Michael's position on "The Rogues" production team had quite obviously been "arranged," after the show's termination he said he wanted to make it entirely on his own, without his father's assistance. Boyer respected his son's position but fretted that Michael was being tested by what was virtually his first setback in life.

Michael had always had everything his way, without having to demand it. From the advantage of privileged birth, everything had just come to him. By nature he had been relaxed in his good fortune—a friendly, high-spirited, optimistic young man who easily fell in and out of love.

Michael was a playboy and fitted the label. He wore sharp designer clothes from Paris and Rome and drove sleek, fast cars. He spoke perfect French and could converse in any European language. If those things alone wouldn't impress the girls, he was also handsome enough. But when Michael became an ex-dialogue director, his parents could see that he was distraught, despite his pledge to make his own way. Proud of his father's eminence, Michael was ambitious for recognition at a comparable level, but to make a new start from the bottom only frustrated him. Pat said to her husband "I wish we could do something for our impatient son"; and Charles thought of something.

On Michael's twenty-first birthday his parents presented him with a real surprise—his own two-bedroom apartment in West Los Angeles' luxurious Coldwater Canyon. It was already furnished tastefully, and they had paid the rent for the term of the initial lease. Michael was jubilant, expressing not only gratitude toward his parents, but his determination to accomplish something that would justify their faith in him.

Shortly after Michael left the Boyer home for his own apartment, he was telling his parents that he had a new girl friend, and that this time he was *really* in love. They'd heard it before.

Interviewed in Paris on September 20, 1965, Charles Boyer talked of wanting to help build a new career for his son, possibly in the recording business. He said "Michael is searching. I'm trying to help him find himself."

Three days later the elder Boyer flew from Paris to Los Angeles knowing that his son was dead.

❉   ❉   ❉

Boyer's plane landed at Los Angeles International Airport just before midnight on September 23, still the calendar date of Michael's death. A silent crowd gathered to watch the sixty-six-year-old actor, wearing dark glasses, enter a car to be driven home by a chauffeur.

He was told that Pat had suffered an emotional collapse but was now calm. Pat was coherent when Charles talked with her alone in their house. She already knew the facts, or rather, the suppositions; all the facts probably would never be known.

Boyer absorbed the known particulars.

Michael had begun dating a pretty girl named Marilyn Campbell. Obviously infatuated with her, he had proposed marriage. Michael had told his mother that Miss Campbell had accepted. This was not the first time Michael had carried a romantic relationship that far, and there was no evidence of a ring.

Shortly after midnight in the early Thursday of September 23, a woman's scream that appeared to come from Michael's apartment was heard by a neighbor, who summoned police to the apartment at 1861 Heather Court. Investigators were admitted by Marilyn Campbell, age twenty-two, who took them into the den where Michael lay dead in a sea of blood that was soaking into the carpet.

Also present was John Kirsch, also twenty-two, who by his own information had been Michael Boyer's house guest for two weeks.

Miss Campbell told investigators that she had known Michael for six weeks. They had become engaged, but only moments before the gun was fired she had told Michael that she was going to stop seeing him. According to Miss Campbell "He told me that he was a loser and had always been a loser, and that if he lost me he would kill himself. Then he went into the den."

John Kirsch, who said he had been watching television in another room while Michael and Marilyn were arguing, heard the gunshot and went into the den where he found Miss Campbell hovering over Michael's body, attempting to revive him.

Police noted that the death weapon—a .38 caliber revolver—was resting on a table. Miss Campbell said "I may have picked it up and put it there, but I'm not sure." When Kirsch remarked that Michael was a gun collector and was always playing around with his guns, Miss Campbell remembered that earlier in the evening, Michael had been playing Russian roulette.

Digesting the information, Charles Boyer said he knew of

Michael's gun collection, but doubted that he would ever play Russian roulette. But West Los Angeles police verified that Michael had been known to play Russian roulette before . . .

The possibility of a love triangle also involving Kirsch was explored by investigators, apparently without conclusive result. There was also the matter of why they hadn't called the police after the shot was fired. Suppose the neighbor hadn't called . . .

Michael Charles Boyer was officially recorded a suicide, twelve weeks before his twenty-second birthday. Neither his father nor his mother seemed interested in pressing for the particulars of his death. What mattered to them was that Michael was dead.

In the memorial service he was eulogized as "always friendly and cheerful, with a zest for living." The funeral was attended only by the Boyers and a small number of close friends, including actors Van Heflin and Gig Young.

* * *

They never got over it. That the Boyers could never adjust to the loss of their son was the certain finding of most who knew them.

An actress friend of the Boyers said "Charles adjusted easier than Pat, I think, but you couldn't tell. He appeared to have adjusted, but he wasn't a happy person ever in outward appearance. You couldn't tell that much difference. Pat was devastated, though. Pat, who was always winking and beaming and laughing, and flashing those pretty teeth. Now years could pass and she wouldn't smile."

That both Pat and Charles felt guilty—that each somehow accepted the responsibility for Michael's death—was also a general impression. They had each seemed close to Michael, and the Boyers had kept closeness as a threesome; but both parents were probably plagued by thought of having not been close enough.

Only a few weeks later, the Boyers sold their house and never owned another one in southern California. They would make irregular returns to the movie colony on those rare occasions when Charles filmed there, taking residence in hotels and not mixing socially.

They retired first to their château in the southern reaches of Paris, where they could be more nearly alone to themselves. But apparently it was not agreeable to them; Michael had loved the château. Eventually they sold it, and Boyer also instructed an agent to sell the villa at Ischia. He and Pat never went there again.

Seeking an altogether new environment that offered no troublesome memories, the Boyers took up permanent residence in a lovely but small apartment in Geneva, a city both had always favored. They divested themselves of all their other apartments, houses, and real estate holdings, and discharged all servants other than a part-time housekeeper.

Now they faced the lonely years but faced them together.

✿   ✿   ✿

No one had expected Boyer to continue making movies, but the activity probably offered therapy for his gloom.

Casino Royale, the spoof on all the James Bond movies, was shot around the world, and Boyer's cameo was filmed in Paris. *Casino Royale* was a Charles Feldman production that employed several directors, and Boyer may have taken his small role as a favor to his longtime agent and devoted friend. *Barefoot in the Park* was a robust hit—one of the early Neil Simon screenplays, from his own stage piece, filmed entirely in New York. Robert Redford and Jane Fonda were the attractive newlyweds, Mildred Natwick stole the picture as Jane's cunningly forlorn mother, and Boyer seemed out of his element as the seedy neighbor dodging his creditors while leering at Miss Fonda. *Casino Royale* and *Barefoot in the Park* were released simultaneously in the spring of 1967, and then Boyer was off the screen for two years.

He came back in a moderately successful comedy with Jack Lemmon and Catherine Deneuve—*The April Fools*, shot in New York. Lemmon lives out the tired businessman's fantasy of chucking his dull, uncaring wife and flying away with the most beautiful woman in the world. Still enumerating the movie goddesses of his personal experience, Boyer finally added Myrna Loy to his list; in supporting roles they were a married couple enhancing the general merriment.

Then he was lured into one of the all-time curiosity pieces,

Jean Giraudoux's *The Madwoman of Chaillot* in its movie misfire under two directors and a score of big and little stars grouped around Katharine Hepburn's madwoman. Since the source was a very theatrical masterpiece, the reckoning was that the film would be either a glorious prestige success or a disaster. It was the latter.

Boyer and Robert Taylor, in a last sad credit just before Taylor's death, hit rock bottom in *The Day the Hot Line Got Hot,* one of several international titles for a tasteless political slapstick in which top Russian spy Boyer and top American spy Taylor are top-billed for their ineptitude, although taking small roles in this sleazy project shot in Spain.

Charles Boyer then announced his retirement, "firmly and irrevocably." He made three more pictures, but not just yet.

He was in wretched health now, and there were rumors that he was dying. There could as easily have been rumors that he was dead, for the Boyers dropped out of sight in the early seventies, living in seclusion in Switzerland and maintaining few contacts in Hollywood or even in Paris. During this time Boyer was regularly rejecting medical advice to undergo various surgeries. Excessive smoking over the years had caught up with him at last, and his internal mechanism was full of malfunctioning components.

So it must have approximated inspiration to cast him as a two-hundred-year-old man. Ross Hunter remade Frank Capra's classic *Lost Horizon* and produced a monstrosity with ill-fitting music that was an embarrassment to Columbia Pictures. Boyer played the High Lama who had been rendered so memorably by Sam Jaffe in the Capra picture. Boyer's delicate characterization of the High Lama was rudely served by his voice, which was still too rich and vigorous, but he certainly *looked* old. Just to apply his makeup required three hours. An inside joke was that it took that long to make him young enough, since Charles Boyer was much too old to play the High Lama. Those who saw him without makeup beheld a withered little man, now totally gray. But he was gracious. He gave several interviews while making his last Hollywood film, reprising events of his life and highlights of his career with an aura befitting anybody's lama.

Then Charles Boyer surprised some people. In Alain Resnais's French-made *Stavisky* he seemed almost robust, if in a stately, polished way, and with a gray beard. He could still command a motion picture frame with his sheer presence. *Stavisky*, a complex examination of France's high-dealing "king of the crooks," was a controversial film, not wholly successful, from the director of *Hiroshima, Mon Amour* and *Last Year at Marienbad*. But Boyer was a revelation, dominating a picture that had Jean-Paul Belmondo in its title role. Listen to Pauline Kael, from a generally negative assessment:

"The sole character who has any life is Baron Raoul, and that's because Boyer, at seventy-five, understands that the Baron should be a simple, happy man. And Boyer seems to be laughing at how easy acting has become for him. Boyer's performance is so light—a series of reminiscent gestures—that it makes one suffer a little for Belmondo, who works very hard at a role to which he's unsuited."

Exhibited in New York late in 1974, *Stavisky* earned for Charles Boyer the New York Film Critics Award as the year's best supporting actor. He was not present to accept the award. It was a notable valediction—the summation of more than half a century of an actor's dedication—and it should have been his last picture.

But in Rome in 1976 he made *A Matter of Time* for Vincente Minnelli, with an odd combination of costars—Ingrid Bergman and Liza Minnelli, the director's daughter. Minnelli had been an accomplished director with some imposing credits, but *A Matter of Time* was inept in every respect. It was never shown in France, and did only meager business in its few U.S. engagements. That it could have been Charles Boyer's last picture, which it later proved to be, went unnoticed and unremarked.

✣   ✣   ✣

In the summer of 1977, the Boyers flew to New York, taking only light luggage as they intended to be in the United States only a few days. The purpose of the trip was a medical examination for Charles, who now was suffering from a multitude of chronic ailments. The doctor who commanded Boyer's trust told the actor that he should undergo a prostatectomy as soon as possible. Boyer had begun hearing intermittent complaint from Pat about her feeling below par, and he suggested that she also have a checkup. When he pressed the point she said "Well, all right, but I think this is silly."

In confidence the doctor informed Boyer that his wife had cancer in advanced stages in both liver and colon. Her ailment was incurable, without even the prospect of surgery that might delay the inevitable. Boyer did not flinch. He asked "How long may Pat live?" The doctor said possibly a year, surely no more than that. After a long quiet pause, the actor said "She must never know."

He never told her.

Boyer sought opinions on the best place for Pat to spend her remaining time in greatest comfort. There seemed to be a general agreement that Arizona would allow her more ease and possibly additional time. The Boyers did not return to Switzerland but went to Arizona, and his first deception was to make Pat believe they were going there because of the urgency of *his* condition.

They rented an apartment in Paradise Valley, in the Scottsdale-Phoenix area. Rather than have things sent from Switzerland, Boyer decided that his wife should just buy a lot of new clothes. With Pat he went into the smart shops that abounded in that mecca for sun worshipers, and helped her select bright, gay apparel.

Of course he needed allies, and one of them had to be Pat's doctor. Boyer wanted his wife to have the benefit of every medical attention without having a sense of alarm. The doctor told Charles the truth, and by their design lied to Pat.

The Boyers could enjoy life even as he began to observe daily change in Pat that hinted at her deteriorating condition. Pat loved the hot, dry climate and appeared to thrive in it. She liked the people around her, and they even found some bridge partners.

By February of 1978, when they observed their forty-fourth wedding anniversary at a small party hosted by some of their newer friends, Pat's condition had become visible to others. Her complaints received immediate medical attention, always with the reassurance that her affliction was only temporary. She may have suspected. In May they flew back to Geneva for a few weeks on Charles's sudden whim, because Pat wanted so much to go, and he wanted to grant her every wish. Their travel involved an extended deception enlisting a doctor in Geneva and an exchange of bogus correspondence, as "proof" to Pat that she did not have cancer.

Returning to Scottsdale, they took residence in the large home of Marjorie Everett, who had become a good friend to both Boyers and was one of Charles's confidants. Even when Pat began to sink harrowingly, Boyer and his allies in deception convinced her that she had only a curable case of hepatitis.

Pat had visitors but Boyer confided in them, to keep their visits brief. Most of the time he and his wife were alone together. He read to her—the newspapers, some magazine articles, and even a play or two, as Charles acted all the parts. He read from some books; and when he began reading Dickens's *Martin Chuzzlewit* aloud to her, Pat urged him to read all of it. But it was a big book. He barely got started.

On August 23, after a siege of discomfort, Pat felt uncommonly chipper and said perhaps she was finally beginning to get well. She stayed in bed, but they played some gin rummy. She fell asleep and did not awaken. Pat died at 3 A.M. on August 24 as Charles held her hand.

Boyer said he was confident that everyone would understand his not attending Pat's funeral, for which he had made arrangements long in advance.

Dr. Donald Buffmire, the Boyers' close friend and personal physician, said "Charles never left her side. He was with her constantly, sleeping as little as three hours in twenty-four. He just wanted Pat's days to be as peaceful and calm as possible, without worry."

Now he sought his own calm. While Pat's funeral service was being read in California on August 25, Boyer was sorting out papers, getting their house into very neat order. On the following day he took a fatal overdose of barbiturates, two days before his seventy-ninth birthday.

They buried Charles Boyer in Holy Cross Cemetery in Los

Angeles, beside his wife of forty-four years. In the small group of mourners at graveside was Irene Dunne.

* * *

Friends and professional associates who survived him made appropriate pallbearing testimonials to Charles Boyer and his art. They saluted an artist of consummate dedication and integrity, but it was not remarked that he had ever been "happy." There remains the near-legend of Boyer as a paragon, but one of fixed distance, without humor or contentment.

He had regrets and expressed them often. He fretted that he hadn't tackled the classics, and that for too long he had abandoned the stage altogether—being too much the star and too much the great lover, and less the virtuoso actor. Yet by any reasonable measure he had a life of glorious accomplishment.

Great actor or great lover, he was a most abundant achiever in his profession precisely from the time of his marriage. He became the screen's great lover only after he experienced a great love. He sacrificed his selfishness on the altar of that love, and in the end Charles Boyer was the most selfless of men and lovers.

If his art was compromised, his legacy is stunning for what it is, and it is seductive. Now and in the future, those whose lives are redeemed by the movies will go with Charles Boyer to the Casbah. He won't have to ask.

THE FILMS OF CHARLES BOYER

EUROPEAN FILMS

1. *L'Homme du Large* (1920). Directed by Marcel L'Herbier. (Silent)
2. *Chantelouve* (1921). Directed by Georges Monca. (Silent)
3. *L'Esclave* (1923). Directed by Georges Monca. (Silent)
4. *Le Grillon du Foyer* (1923). Directed by Jean Manoussi. (Silent)
5. *Le Capitaine Fracassé* (1927). Directed by Alberto Cavalcanti. (Silent)
6. *La Ronde Infernale* (1928). Directed by Luitz Morat. (Silent)
7. *La Barcarolle d'Amour* (1929). Directed by Adolf Trotz. (French-language version of German-made *Brand in der Oper*, filmed in Berlin; Boyer's first talking picture.)
8. *Le Procès du Mary Dugan* (1929). Directed by André Chautin. With Françoise Rosay. (French-language version of *The Trial of Mary Dugan*, filmed by M-G-M in Hollywood.)
9. *Revolte dans la Prison* (1930). Directed by Paul Fejos. (French-language version of *The Big House*, filmed by M-G-M in Hollywood.)
10. *Tumultes* (1931). Directed by Adolf Trotz. With Florelle. (French-language version of German-made *Stürme der Leidenschaft*, filmed in Berlin.)
11. *F.P. 1 Ne Répond Plus* (1932). Directed by Karl Hartl. (French-language version of German-made *F.P. 1 Antwortet Nicht*, filmed in Berlin.)
12. *Moi et L'Impératrice* (1933). Directed by Friedrich Hollander. With Lilian Harvey. (French-language version of German-made *Ich und die Kaiserin*, filmed in Berlin.)
13. *The Only Girl* (1933). Directed by Friedrich Hollander. With Lilian Harvey. (English-language version of the above, also filmed in Berlin; titled *Heart Song* for its U.S. release in 1934.)
14. *L'Epervier* (1933). Directed by Marcel L'Herbier. With Natalie Paley.
15. *Le Bonheur* (1933). Directed by Marcel L'Herbier. With Gaby Morlay.

16. *La Bataille* (1933). Directed by Nicolas Farkas. With Annabella.

17. *The Battle* (1934). Directed by Nicolas Farkas. With Merle Oberon and John Loder. (English-language version of the above, filmed in Paris; titled *Thunder in the East* for its U.S. release.)

18. *Liliom* (1934). Directed by Fritz Lang. With Madeleine Ozeray. (Released in the United States in 1935.)

19. *Mayerling* (1936). Directed by Anatole Litvak. With Danielle Darrieux. (Released in the United States in 1937.)

20. *Orage* (1938). Directed by Marc Allégret. With Michèle Morgan. (Sometimes titled *Storm* in U.S. distribution.)

21. *Madame de . . .* (1953). Directed by Max Ophüls. With Danielle Darrieux and Vittorio De Sica. (Released in the United States in 1954 as *The Earrings of Madame De.*)

22. *Nana* (1954). Directed by Christian-Jaque. With Martine Carol. (Released in the United States in 1956.)

23. *La Fortuna di Essere Donna* (1955). Directed by Alessandro Blasetti. With Sophia Loren, Vittorio De Sica, and Marcello Mastroianni. (Released in the United States in 1956 as *Lucky to Be a Woman.*)

24. *Paris-Palace Hôtel* (1956). Directed by Henri Verneuil. With Françoise Arnoul.

25. *Une Parisienne* (1957). Directed by Michel Boisrand. With Brigitte Bardot.

26. *Maxime* (1958). Directed by Henri Verneuil. With Michèle Morgan and Arletty. (Released in the United States in 1962.)

27. *Les Démons de Minuit* (1961). Directed by Marc Allégret and Charles Gerard. With Pascale Audret.

28. *Adorable Julia* (1962). Directed by Alfred Weidenmann. With Lilli Palmer and Jean Sorel. (Franco-Austrian production known in Austria and Germany as *Julia, du Bist Zauberhaft.*)

29. *Stavisky* (1974). Directed by Alain Resnais. With Jean-Paul Belmondo and Anny Duperey.

AMERICAN FILMS

1. *The Magnificent Lie* (Paramount; 1931)
Directed by Berthold Viertel. Screenplay by Samson Raphaelson.
Ruth Chatterton, Ralph Bellamy, Stuart Erwin, Françoise Rosay, Charles Boyer, Tyler Brooke

2. *The Man from Yesterday* (Paramount; 1932)
   Directed by Berthold Viertel. Screenplay by Oliver H. P. Garrett, from a story by Nell Blackwell and Roland Edwards.
   Clive Brook, Claudette Colbert, Charles Boyer, Andy Devine, Alan Mowbray, Yola D'Avril

3. *Red-Headed Woman* (Metro-Goldwyn-Mayer; 1932)
   Directed by Jack Conway. Screenplay by Anita Loos, from the novel by Katherine Brush.
   Jean Harlow, Chester Morris, Lewis Stone, Leila Hyams, Una Merkel, May Robson, Charles Boyer, Harvey Clark, Henry Stephenson

4. *Caravan* (Fox; 1934)
   Directed by Erik Charell. Screenplay by Samson Raphaelson, from a play by Melchior Lengyel.
   Charles Boyer, Loretta Young, Jean Parker, Phillips Holmes, Louise Fazenda, C. Aubrey Smith, Eugene Pallette, Noah Beery, Charley Grapewin, Dudley Digges, Billy Bevan, Richard Carle, Lionel Belmore

5. *Private Worlds* (Walter Wanger/Paramount; 1935)
   Directed by Gregory La Cava. Screenplay by Lynn Starling, from the novel by Phyllis Bottome.
   Claudette Colbert, Charles Boyer, Joan Bennett, Joel McCrea, Helen Vinson, Samuel S. Hinds, Esther Dale, Guinn Williams

6. *Break of Hearts* (RKO Radio; 1935)
   Directed by Philip Moeller. Screenplay by Sarah Y. Mason and Victor Heerman, from a story by Lester Cohen.
   Katharine Hepburn, Charles Boyer, John Beal, Jean Hersholt, Sam Hardy, Inez Courtney, Jean Howard

7. *Shanghai* (Walter Wanger/Paramount; 1935)
   Directed by James Flood. Screenplay by Gene Towne, Graham Baker, and Lynn Starling.
   Charles Boyer, Loretta Young, Warner Oland, Alison Skipworth, Fred Keating, Charley Grapewin, Keye Luke, Walter Kingsford, Willie Fung

8. *The Garden of Allah* (David O. Selznick/United Artists; 1936)
   Directed by Richard Boleslawsky. Screenplay by Willis Goldbeck, W. P. Lipscomb, and Lynn Riggs, from the novel by Robert Hichens.
   Marlene Dietrich, Charles Boyer, Basil Rathbone, Joseph Schildkraut, Tilly Losch, John Carradine, C. Aubrey Smith, Lucile Watson, Henry Kleinbach, Frank Puglia

9. *History Is Made at Night* (Walter Wanger/United Artists; 1937)

Directed by Frank Borzage. Story and screenplay by Gene Towne and Graham Baker.

Charles Boyer, Jean Arthur, Colin Clive, Leo Carrillo, Ivan Lebedeff, George Meeker, Lucien Prival, Georges Renavent

10. *Conquest* (Metro-Goldwyn-Mayer; 1937)

Directed by Clarence Brown. Screenplay by Samuel Hoffenstein, Salka Viertel, and S. N. Behrman, from a biography of Marie Walewska by Waclaw Gasiorowsky as dramatized by Helen Jerome.

Greta Garbo, Charles Boyer, Reginald Owen, Alan Marshal, Henry Stephenson, Dame May Whitty, Leif Erikson, C. Henry Gordon, Vladimir Sokoloff

11. *Tovarich* (Warner Brothers; 1937)

Directed by Anatole Litvak. Screenplay by Casey Robinson, from a play by Jacques Deval as adapted by Robert E. Sherwood.

Claudette Colbert, Charles Boyer, Basil Rathbone, Anita Louise, Melville Cooper, Isabel Jeans, Morris Carnovsky, Heather Thatcher, Fritz Feld, Curt Bois, Victor Kilian

12. *Algiers* (Walter Wanger/United Artists; 1938)

Directed by John Cromwell. Screenplay by John Howard Lawson and James M. Cain, from a story by Detective Ashelbe.

Charles Boyer, Sigrid Gurie, Hedy Lamarr, Joseph Calleia, Alan Hale, Gene Lockhart, Johnny Downs, Stanley Fields, Nina Koshetz, Joan Woodbury, Walter Kingsford

13. *Love Affair* (RKO Radio; 1939)

Directed by Leo McCarey. Screenplay by Donald Ogden Stewart and Delmer Daves, from a story by Leo McCarey and Mildred Kram.

Irene Dunne, Charles Boyer, Maria Ouspenskaya, Lee Bowman, Astrid Allwyn, Maurice Moscovitch, Joan Leslie, Scotty Beckett

14. *When Tomorrow Comes* (Universal; 1939)

Directed by John M. Stahl. Screenplay by Dwight Taylor, from a story by James M. Cain.

Irene Dunne, Charles Boyer, Barbara O'Neil, Onslow Stevens, Nydia Westman, Fritz Feld, Nella Walker

15. *All This and Heaven Too* (Warner Brothers; 1940)

Directed by Anatole Litvak. Screenplay by Casey Robinson, from the novel by Rachel Field.

Bette Davis, Charles Boyer, Jeffrey Lynn, Barbara O'Neil, Virginia Weidler, Helen Westley, Walter Hampden, Henry Daniell, Harry Davenport, George Coulouris, Montagu Love, Janet Beecher, June Lockhart, Fritz Leiber, Ian Keith

16. *Back Street* (Universal; 1941)

Directed by Robert Stevenson. Screenplay by Bruce Manning and Felix Jackson, from the novel by Fannie Hurst.

Charles Boyer, Margaret Sullavan, Richard Carlson, Frank McHugh, Tim Holt, Esther Dale, Samuel S. Hinds, Peggy Stewart

17. *Hold Back the Dawn* (Paramount; 1941)

Directed by Mitchell Leisen. Screenplay by Charles Brackett and Billy Wilder, from a story by Ketti Frings.

Charles Boyer, Olivia deHavilland, Paulette Goddard, Victor Francen, Walter Abel, Rosemary DeCamp, Curt Bois, Mikhail Rasumny, Madeleine LeBeau, Micheline Cheirel

18. *Appointment for Love* (Universal; 1941)

Directed by William A. Seiter. Screenplay by Bruce Manning and Felix Jackson, from a play by Ladislaus Bus-Fekete.

Charles Boyer, Margaret Sullavan, Rita Johnson, Reginald Denny, Ruth Terry, Cecil Kellaway, Eugene Pallette

19. *Tales of Manhattan* (20th Century–Fox; 1942)

Directed by Julien Duvivier. Screenplay by Ben Hecht, Ferenc Molnar, Donald Ogden Stewart, Samuel Hoffenstein, Alan Campbell, Ladislas Fodor, Lamar Trotti, and Henry Blankfort.

Charles Boyer, Rita Hayworth, Charles Laughton, Ginger Rogers, Henry Fonda, Edward G. Robinson, Paul Robeson, Ethel Waters, Eddie Anderson, Thomas Mitchell, Cesar Romero, Eugene Pallette, Gail Patrick, Roland Young, George Sanders, Elsa Lanchester, Victor Francen, James Gleason, Harry Davenport, Mae Marsh, Sig Arno, Marion Martin, Hall Johnson Choir

20. *The Constant Nymph* (Warner Brothers; 1943)

Directed by Edmund Goulding. Screenplay by Kathryn Scola, from the novel by Margaret Kennedy.

Charles Boyer, Joan Fontaine, Alexis Smith, Charles Coburn, Brenda Marshall, Peter Lorre, Dame May Whitty, Jean Muir, Joyce Reynolds, Montagu Love, Eduardo Ciannelli, Marcel Dalio

21. *Flesh and Fantasy* (Universal; 1943)

Directed by Julien Duvivier. Screenplay by Ernest Pascal,

Samuel Hoffenstein, and Ellis St. Joseph, adapting works by
Oscar Wilde and Laslo Vadnay.

Charles Boyer, Barbara Stanwyck, Edward G. Robinson, Betty
Field, Robert Cummings, Thomas Mitchell, Robert Benchley,
Anna Lee, Edgar Barrier, C. Aubrey Smith, Dame May
Whitty, Charles Winninger, Clarence Muse, June Lang

22. *Gaslight* (Metro-Goldwyn-Mayer; 1944)
Directed by George Cukor. Screenplay by John Van Druten,
Walter Reisch, and John L. Balderston, from a play by Patrick
Hamilton.

Charles Boyer, Ingrid Bergman, Joseph Cotten, Dame May
Whitty, Angela Lansbury, Barbara Everest, Edmond Breon,
Halliwell Hobbes, Heather Thatcher, Emil Rameau

23. *Together Again* (Columbia; 1944)
Directed by Charles Vidor. Screenplay by Virginia Van Upp
and F. Hugh Herbert, from a story by Stanley Russell and
Herbert Biberman.

Irene Dunne, Charles Boyer, Charles Coburn, Mona Freeman,
Jerome Courtland, Elizabeth Patterson, Charles Dingle

24. *Confidential Agent* (Warner Brothers; Herman Shumlin)
Directed by Herman Shumlin. Screenplay by Robert Buckner,
from the novel by Graham Greene.

Charles Boyer, Lauren Bacall, Victor Francen, Wanda Hen-
drix, George Coulouris, Katina Paxinou, Peter Lorre, Miles
Mander, Ian Wolfe, George Zucco, Dan Seymour, John War-
burton

25. *Cluny Brown* (20th Century–Fox; 1946)
Directed by Ernst Lubitsch. Screenplay by Samuel Hoffenstein
and Elizabeth Reinhardt, from the novel by Margery Sharp.

Charles Boyer, Jennifer Jones, Peter Lawford, Helen Walker,
Reginald Gardiner, C. Aubrey Smith, Richard Haydn, Regi-
nald Owen, Sara Allgood, Una O'Connor, Florence Bates,
Ernest Cossart, Margaret Bannerman, Billy Bevan, Queenie
Leonard

26. *A Woman's Vengeance* (Universal; 1947)
Directed by Zoltan Korda. Screenplay by Aldous Huxley, from
his story "The Gioconda Smile."

Charles Boyer, Ann Blyth, Jessica Tandy, Sir Cedric Hardwicke, Mildred Natwick, Rachel Kempson, John Williams

27. *Arch of Triumph* (Enterprise/United Artists; 1948)

Directed by Lewis Milestone. Screenplay by Lewis Milestone and Harry Brown, from the novel by Erich Maria Remarque.

Ingrid Bergman, Charles Boyer, Charles Laughton, Louis Calhern, Ruth Warrick, Roman Bohnen, Stephen Bekassy, Ruth Nelson, Curt Bois, J. Edward Bromberg, Art Smith, John Lorenz, Hazel Brooks, Byron Foulger, Feodor Chaliapin

28. *The Thirteenth Letter* (20th Century–Fox; 1951)

Directed by Otto Preminger. Screenplay by Howard Koch, from a novel by Louis Chavanie.

Linda Darnell, Charles Boyer, Michael Rennie, Constance Moore, Françoise Rosay, Judith Evelyn, Guy Sorel

29. *The First Legion* (Sedif/United Artists; 1951)

Directed by Douglas Sirk. Screenplay by Emmet Lavery, from his play.

Charles Boyer, William Demarest, Lyle Bettger, Leo G. Carroll, Walter Hampden, Barbara Rush, Wesley Addy, Taylor Holmes, H. B. Warner, George Zucco

30. *The Happy Time* (Stanley Kramer/Columbia; 1952)

Directed by Richard Fleischer. Screenplay by Earl Felton, from Samuel Taylor's dramatization of a book by Robert Fontaine.

Charles Boyer, Louis Jourdan, Marsha Hunt, Kurt Kaszner, Linda Christian, Bobby Driscoll, Marcel Dalio, Jeanette Nolan, Richard Erdman

31. *Thunder in the East* (Paramount; 1953)

Directed by Charles Vidor. Screenplay by Jo Swerling, from a novel by Alan Moorehead.

Alan Ladd, Deborah Kerr, Charles Boyer, Corinne Calvet

32. *The Cobweb* (Metro-Goldwyn-Mayer; 1955)

Directed by Vincente Minnelli. Screenplay by John Paxton, from the novel by William Gibson.

Richard Widmark, Lauren Bacall, Charles Boyer, Gloria Grahame, Lillian Gish, John Kerr, Susan Strasberg, Oscar Levant, Tommy Rettig, Jarma Lewis, Paul Stewart, Fay Wray, Mabel Albertson

33. *Around the World in 80 Days* (Michael Todd/United Artists; 1956)

Directed by Michael Anderson. Screenplay by S. J. Perelman, James Poe, and John Farrow, from the novel by Jules Verne.

David Niven, Cantinflas, Robert Newton, Shirley MacLaine, and forty-four "cameo" players including Charles Boyer, Charles Coburn, Ronald Colman, Noël Coward, Marlene Dietrich, John Gielgud, Glynis Johns, Trevor Howard, Buster Keaton, Beatrice Lillie, Peter Lorre, John Mills, Robert Morley, Jack Oakie, George Raft, Frank Sinatra, Red Skelton

34. *The Buccaneer* (Cecil B. DeMille/Paramount; 1958)
Directed by Anthony Quinn. Screenplay by Jesse L. Lasky, Jr., and Berenice Mosk; from an earlier screenplay by Harold Lamb, Edwin Justus Mayer, and C. Gardner Sullivan; based in turn on Jeannie MacPherson's adaptation of a novel by Lyle Saxon.
Yul Brynner, Claire Bloom, Charlton Heston, Charles Boyer, Inger Stevens, Henry Hull, E. G. Marshall, Lorne Greene, Ted de Corsia, Douglas Dumbrille, Fran Jeffries

35. *Fanny* (Warner Brothers; 1961)
Directed by Joshua Logan. Screenplay by Julius J. Epstein, from three plays by Marcel Pagnol, as adapted for the Broadway stage by S. N. Behrman, Joshua Logan, and Harold Rome.
Leslie Caron, Maurice Chevalier, Charles Boyer, Horst Buchholz, Georgette Anys, Salvatore Baccaloni, Victor Francen, Lionel Jeffries, Raymond Bussières, Joel Flateau

36. *The Four Horsemen of the Apocalypse* (Metro-Goldwyn-Mayer; 1962)
Directed by Vincente Minnelli. Screenplay by Robert Ardrey and John Gay, from the novel by Vicente Blasco Ibáñez.
Glenn Ford, Ingrid Thulin, Charles Boyer, Lee J. Cobb, Paul Henreid, Paul Lukas, Yvette Mimieux, Karlheinz Böhm, George Dolenz, Kathryn Givney

37. *Love Is a Ball* (Martin Poll/United Artists; 1963)
Directed by David Swift. Screenplay by David Swift, Tom Waldman, and Frank Waldman, from a novel by Lindsay Hardy.
Glenn Ford, Hope Lange, Charles Boyer, Ricardo Montalban, Telly Savalas, Ulla Jacobson, Georgette Anys, John Wood

38. *A Very Special Favor* (Universal; 1965)
Directed by Michael Gordon. Story and screenplay by Stanley Shapiro and Nate Monaster.
Rock Hudson, Leslie Caron, Charles Boyer, Walter Slezak, Dick Shawn, Larry Storch, Nita Talbot, Norma Varden

39. *How to Steal a Million* (World Wide/20th Century–Fox; 1966)
Directed by William Wyler. Screenplay by Harry Kurnitz, from a story by George Bradshaw.

Audrey Hepburn, Peter O'Toole, Eli Wallach, Charles Boyer, Hugh Griffith, Fernand Gravet, Marcel Dalio, Jacques Marin

40. *Is Paris Burning?* (Transcontinental/Paramount; 1966)
Directed by René Clément. Screenplay by Gore Vidal and Francis Ford Coppola, from the book by Larry Collins and Dominique Lapierre.
Jean-Paul Belmondo, Charles Boyer, Leslie Caron, Alain Delon, Kirk Douglas, Glenn Ford, Gert Frobe, Yves Montand, Anthony Perkins, Simone Signoret, Robert Stack, Jean-Louis Trintignant, Orson Welles

41. *Casino Royale* (Charles K. Feldman/Columbia; 1967)
Directed by John Huston, Ken Hughes, Val Guest, Robert Parrish, and Joseph McGrath. Screenplay by Wolf Mankowitz, John Law, Michael Sayers, Billy Wilder, Ben Hecht, John Huston, Val Guest, Joseph Heller, and Terry Southern, suggested by a novel by Ian Fleming.
David Niven, Peter Sellers, Ursula Andress, Orson Welles, Joanna Pettet, Daliah Lavi, Terence Cooper; and Jean-Paul Belmondo, Charles Boyer, William Holden, Deborah Kerr, Peter O'Toole, George Raft, Woody Allen

42. *Barefoot in the Park* (Hal Wallis/Paramount; 1967)
Directed by Gene Saks. Screenplay by Neil Simon, from his play.
Robert Redford, Jane Fonda, Charles Boyer, Mildred Natwick, Herbert Edelman, James Stone, Mabel Albertson, Fritz Feld

43. *The April Fools* (Cinema Center/National General; 1969)
Directed by Stuart Rosenberg. Screenplay by Hal Dresner.
Jack Lemmon, Catherine Deneuve, Myrna Loy, Charles Boyer, Peter Lawford, Jack Weston, Harvey Korman, Sally Kellerman

44. *The Madwoman of Chaillot* (Warner Brothers–Seven Arts; 1969)
Directed by Bryan Forbes. Screenplay by Edward Anhalt, from the play by Jean Giraudoux.
Katharine Hepburn, Danny Kaye, Yul Brynner, Charles Boyer, Richard Chamberlain, Edith Evans, Margaret Leighton, Giulietta Masina, John Gavin, Paul Henreid, Claude Dauphin, Nanette Newman, Oscar Homolka, Donald Pleasence

45. *The Day the Hot Line Got Hot* (American International; 1969)
Directed by Étienne Perier. Screenplay by Paul Jarrico, from a story by Gordon Trueblood and Dominique Fabre.

Charles Boyer, Robert Taylor, George Chakiris, Marie Dubois, Marta Grau, Irene D'Astrea, Josefina Tapias, Gerard Tichy

46. *Lost Horizon* (Ross Hunter/Columbia; 1973)

Directed by Charles Jarrott. Screenplay by Larry Kramer, from the novel by James Hilton.

Peter Finch, Liv Ullmann, Sally Kellerman, Bobby Van, Michael York, George Kennedy, Charles Boyer, John Gielgud, Olivia Hussey, James Shigeta

47. *A Matter of Time* (American International; 1976)

Directed by Vincente Minnelli. Screenplay by John Gay.

Ingrid Bergman, Liza Minnelli, Charles Boyer, Fernando Rey, Spiros Andros, Tina Aumont

INDEX

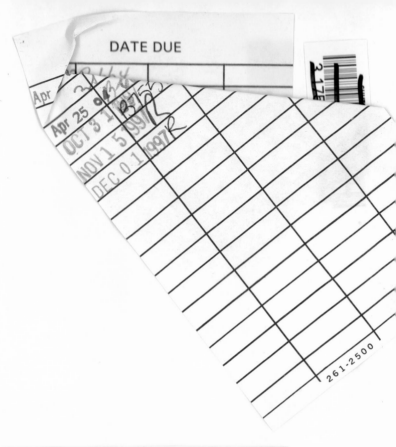